EXPLORING POSTMODERNISM

UTRECHT PUBLICATIONS IN GENERAL AND COMPARATIVE LITERATURE

Utrecht Publications in General and Comparative Literature publishes studies in English which fall into three main groups:
a) studies which approach the history and structure of literature from a supra-national point of view;
b) theoretical studies, especially studies devoted to larger issues such as genre, periodisation, symbolic mode, and manner of presentation (narrative, drama and lyric);
c) methodological studies, including studies devoted to the history of poetics and literary scholarship.

Inquiries and submissions should be addressed to:

The Secretary, Utrecht Publications in General and Comparative Literature
Instituut voor Algemene Literatuurwetenschap
Muntstraat 4, 3512 EV UTRECHT, The Netherlands

Volume 23

Matei Calinescu and Douwe Fokkema (eds.)

EXPLORING POSTMODERNISM

EXPLORING POSTMODERNISM

Selected papers presented at a Workshop on Postmodernism
at the XIth International Comparative Literature Congress,
Paris, 20-24 August 1985

edited by

Matei Calinescu and Douwe Fokkema

JOHN BENJAMINS PUBLISHING COMPANY
AMSTERDAM/PHILADELPHIA

1987

Library of Congress Cataloging in Publication Data

Exploring Postmodernism: selected papers presented at a workshop on Postmodernism at the XIth International Comparative Literature Congress, Paris, 20-24 August 1985 / edited by Matei Calinescu and Douwe Fokkema.
     p.   cm. -- (Utrecht publications in general and comparative literature, ISSN 0167-8175; v. 23)
Bibliography: p.
Includes index.
1. Postmodernism -- Congresses. 2. Literature, Modern -- 20th century -- History and criticism -- Congresses. 3. Criticism -- History -- 20th century -- Congresses. I. Calinescu, Matei. II. Fokkema, Douwe Wessel, 1931-   . III. International Comparative Literature Association. Congress (11th: 1985: Paris, France). IV. Series.
PN98.P67E97   1987   87-30008
809'.04 -- dc 19   CIP
ISBN 90 272 2199 5 (alk. paper)

Preface

If the deferral of definite meaning is one of the characteristics of Postmodernism, it would seem appropriate to see work on Postmodernist literature as an ongoing process. Indeed, the history of Postmodernism will never reach a final and definite stage, but this has less to do with the features of Postmodernist writing than with the nature of historiography.

The present volume is the second one in a series of studies on Postmodernism. In 1986 *Approaching Postmodernism* (edited by Douwe Fokkema and Hans Bertens) appeared, containing contributions to a workshop held in Utrecht in September 1984. *Exploring Postmodernism* holds the proceedings of a workshop which took place in Paris on August 21 and 22, 1985, as part of the XIth Congress of the International Comparative Literature Association (ICLA). In spite of the nature of Postmodernism and of historiography, we do not plan an extensive series of similar publications. The research, of which the results are offered here, may be an ongoing affair, but — at the request of the Coordinating Committee of the *Comparative History of Literature in European Languages* — we will attempt to come to a provisional conclusion soon. Three years ago the Research Center on Postmodernism — whose mailing address is that of the Instituut voor Vergelijkende Literatuurwetenschap, University of Utrecht, Utrecht, The Netherlands — was charged with the preparation of a volume Postmodernism in the ICLA sponsored *Comparative History*, scheduled to appear in 1989 or 1990. After the publication of the two volumes, *Approaching Postmodernism* and *Exploring Postmodernism*, the next step will have all appearances of being more "definite" and will certainly be more comprehensive and cohesive.

Most contributors to the workshop are represented here with their papers. Other participants — contributors and discussants — were: Christopher Butler (Oxford), Amy Colin (Seattle), August Fry (Amsterdam), Sally Hassan (Milwaukee), Ingeborg Hoesterey (Bloomington, Indiana), Gerhard Hoffmann (Würzburg), Elrud Ibsch (Amsterdam), Bruce King (Florence, Alabama), Olga Scherer (Paris), Lies Wesseling (Utrecht), and others who attended the ICLA Congress and for a change dropped in to enjoy the always lively debate. The two editors wish to thank the contributors for keeping their promises and respecting the deadlines, and the discussants for their valuable and spirited interventions which in some cases led the authors to change their texts and in many other instances opened up new vistas for future research.

The interest of the Coordinating Committee in the Postmodernism project led to the decision to assist the editors of this volume with a grant which they wish to acknowledge here with gratitude. We are much obliged to the graduate students John Arnold, Ed van Eeden, and Aleid Fokkema who checked bibliographical and other details.

Thanks are due also to the organizer of the XIth Congress of the ICLA in Paris, Professor Daniel Pageaux, who provided the workshop with a cool and spacious room in the Sorbonne and who also in other respects has been most helpful.

February 1987   Matei Calinescu (Indiana University, Bloomington, Ind.)
                  Douwe Fokkema (University of Utrecht)

Contents

General Problems

Introductory Remarks: Postmodernism, the Mimetic and Theatrical Fallacies

Matei Calinescu

I should like to offer, as opening remarks to our workshop, a few general, perhaps overly general, reflections on the concept of postmodernism in recent usage. My background theme is the larger issue of periodization and the status of period terms in the various discourses that deal with questions of historical understanding. My foreground theme is the ways in which the users of the term "postmodernism" are liable to two fallacies, which will be called the mimetic or "jigsaw puzzle fallacy" and the "theatrical fallacy."

The great diversity of contexts in which the term postmodernism is currently encountered marks the remarkable success of a verbal coinage that has been in circulation for only about forty years. The inventor of the term was the historian-prophet Arnold J. Toynbee, whose notion of a "Post-Modern Age" of Western history appealed to the apocalyptic sensibilities of the Black Mountain poets (Charles Olson in particular) and then became assimilated — with different meanings, narrow or broad, positive or negative — into the idiom of critics writing about contemporary literature, and, more specifically about that part of contemporary literature which is visibly or invisibly — i.e. ambiguously, ironically — committed to innovation. Among the early users of "postmodernism" are critics with such diverse and not seldom conflicting backgrounds as Irving Howe, Harry Levin, Ihab Hassan, or that *enfant terrible* of American criticism, Leslie Fiedler. Over the last fifteen years or so the term postmodernism has been employed — in acceptations ranging from the celebratory to the intensely polemical — by sociologists (Daniel Bell), philosophers (Jean-François Lyotard, Jürgen Habermas, Richard Rorty, Gianni Vattimo), philosophers of science (Stephen Toulmin), art critics (Douglas Davies, Rosalind Krauss, and recently Guy Scarpetta in his important book *L'Impureté*), and architecture critics and historians (Charles Jencks).

In all of these instances, postmodernism designates at once a historical category and a systematic or ideal concept. A user may choose to focus on one or the other of these two semantic dimensions, depending on what he wants to do with the term. But the apparent absence of one of the two axes of meaning does not entail the cancellation of its function: the hidden element continues to play its role in defining the "field of tension" within which the term reorders, shapes, and structures the semantic materials to which it is applied. However, when either one of the parts of the duality is suppressed, postmodernism loses its ability to discriminate among historical nuances, on the one hand, or to create transhistorical structures of recurrence, on the other. In today's theoretical discourse, the more likely object of attack is the historical dimension. Thus, those still under the powerful if diffuse influence of structuralist antihistoricism (one of the legacies of the 1960s and 1970s) will attempt to delete the historical component of postmodernism. But success in this instance would only transform the term into a huge and empty abstraction.

While they ostensibly reject the historical sense of postmodernism, serious poststructuralist thinkers will almost instinctively preserve, even at the price of self-contradiction, the possibilities it offers. A good example is provided by Umberto Eco's *Postscript to The Name of the Rose*. "I believe," Eco writes, "that postmodernism is not a trend to be chronologically defined, but, rather, an ideal category — or, better still, a *Kunstwollen*, a mode of operating." And he goes on to refer to Nietzsche's *Thoughts Out of Season* in order to stress the "harm done by historical studies," and to complain that "the past conditions us, harries us, blackmails us" (Eco 1984:66). But, as soon as he tries to define postmodernism, history creeps back into his discourse. Diachronic reference (unaffected by occasional denials) is easy to identify and, even more strikingly, the examples Eco gives to illustrate his conceptual opposition between the avant-garde and postmodernism come without exception from the history of twentieth century culture. No hint is made with regard to either the transhistorical use of the postmodernism/avant-garde distinction, or to the kinds of insights this might lead to. Eco writes: "The historic avant-garde (but here I would also consider avant-garde a metahistorical category) tries to settle scores with the past. ... The avant-garde destroys, defaces the past: *Les Demoiselles d'Avignon* is a typical avant-garde act. Then the avant-garde goes further, destroys the figure, cancels it, arrives at the abstract, the informal, the white canvas, the slashed canvas, the charred canvas" (1984:66). Further on Eco notes that "the moment comes when the avant-garde (the modern) can go no further. ... The postmodern reply to the modern consists of recognizing that the past, since it cannot be really destroyed, because its destruction leads to silence, must be revisited: but with irony, not innocently" (1984:67). One has no trouble noticing that the metahistorical concepts proposed by Eco are elaborations of a limited (modern) historical material. Throughout his charming essay, Eco never seriously tries to test, intuitively or otherwise, the validity of his transhistorical claims. His ideal types, after being emphatically asserted, are left dangling.

The unsuccessful exorcism of the historical dimension of postmodernism is also apparent in the fact that Eco's definition does not contain anything that would make it usable in other than historically-oriented approaches. The same is true of Jean-François Lyotard's general epistemological definition of the postmodern in *La Condition postmoderne* (1979), as well as of his more recent discussion of aesthetic postmodernism (1983a).

Modernity, Lyotard claims, legitimated knowledge by resorting to great narrative scenarios or "grands récits" (the French Revolution's grand story of enlightenment and emancipation, the Hegelian dialectic of the self-realization of *Geist*, the classical political economy's narrative of the wealth of nations, the Marxist vision of the proletariat bringing about a classless or "transparent" society). In our time no one believes in such philosophical "grands récits" and postmodernity gives legitimacy to knowledge only by means of small, local, paradoxical, paralogical "récits." But if such an epochal shift has indeed occurred, one wonders why Lyotard has insisted that one should not interpret his "postmodern condition" as a periodizing category. (He specifically wrote: "Postmodern is probably a very bad term, because it suggests the idea of 'periodization' and to 'periodize' is still a 'classical' or 'modern' idea" — trans. from 1983b:69). May he have meant that his view of postmodernity has nothing to do with a nineteenth-century kind of stage theory of historical evolution, in which the succession of stages is completely determined and therefore predictable? Or may he have tried to reaffirm the profound antihistoricism of his metaphysics, rooted in a bizarre Manicheism? (Calinescu: 1979)

Actually, Lyotard's opposition between modernity and postmodernity, seen within the corpus of his philosophical work, is just another way of personifying the eternal conflict between Ahriman (domination, capital, the acquisitive drive, the will to infinity, mastery, control, richness) and Ormazd (the desire for opacity, paralogy, non-communication, autonomy, the "figural" and "deconstructive" search for "incommensurabilities"). Modernity would then be a synonym for Lyotard's strangely timeless notion of capitalism, while postmodernism would be a personification of an equally timeless desire for freedom and justice. Be that as it may, many literary critics have understood — or happily misunderstood — Lyotard's postmodernism as an essentially historical construct, ignoring its recondite, tortuous, and ultimately absurd mythical-philosophical underpinnings. This was possible because the directly historical insights permitted by Lyotard's concept appeared interesting and refreshing when taken independently from their complicated and finally confusing Manichean framework.

Thus, at a 1984 conference on postmodernism (Fokkema and Bertens 1986), Lyotard was quoted almost exclusively for purposes of cultural-historical reference. Although Lyotard did not perhaps think of it, his concept turned out to be a subtle historical "ideogram." What does this demonstrate? Simply that, when one tries to deal intelligently with temporal categories, history cannot be shunned. When the historical perspective is truly abandoned, the price to be paid is high: vacuous generality. To this, internal contradiction is clearly preferable. Concealed or not, it is the historical dimension that gives postmodernism versatility and precision when the term is used transhistorically (as Lyotard himself uses it when he speaks of Montaigne or Rabelais as postmoderns). Conversely, one could say that the synchronic vocation of the term enables it, when used historically, to discriminate, to capture significant similarities or differences, and to reveal recurrencies and surprising continuities in the historical flow.

There is no need for me to deal here with the history of the word. This has been done several times over the last decade by, among others, Ihab Hassan (1982), Michael Köhler (1977), and myself (1977). The wide current appeal of postmodernism (including of course those who love to hate it) explains why the neologism has become so loose and fuzzy, all the way from the chatty language of cultural journalism to philosophical discourse. In popular parlance, it evokes to its fans styles that are surprising, amusingly kinky, fancily eclectic, pleasantly eccentric. To its opponents, postmodernism is synonymous with bad taste, blustering kitsch and the atrocious encroachment of camp. By itself, this is neither good nor bad. Earlier terms comparable to postmodernism in scope and trendiness also became catchwords in their day, even in a commercial sense. Thus, when decadence was in vogue in late nineteenth century Paris, chic restaurants put on their menu a strange new meal called "salade à la décadente." A few decades later, one could come across newspaper ads for "avant-garde" furniture and even kitchen appliances.

Like *fin de siècle* decadence (with which it shares a number of other significant features), postmodernism claims to be the self-consciousness of the cultural present. Even its more sophisticated proponents tend to see it as nothing less than a new "épistémè" in Foucault's sense, a new Kuhnian paradigm for a radically new "informational" age, or a joyous rebirth of diversity after the austere negativity of modernism. To its enemies, postmodernism is an ominous triumph of the indifferentiation of mass culture, a (nauseatingly sweet) totalitarianism of kitsch, an imminent collapse of all values.

But neither the current antithetical character of postmodernism nor its use as a misty mythological catchall, however irritating they may be, should prompt us to discard the term from our historical-critical lexicon. In regard to my larger background theme (the desirable status of period terms in cultural-historical discourse) a reminder is in order: period terms function best when they are used heuristically, as strategic constructs or means by which we inventively articulate the continuum of history for purposes of focused analysis and understanding. Strategic is the key word here. (For another "strategic" approach to literary terminology see McHale 1986.) It suggests goal-directed action, permanent readiness to weigh possible scenarios against each other, and ingenuity in the selection of those scenarios that are at the same time most promising and unpredictable. (The right degree of unexpectedness is a major strategic value.) All this is of course easier said than done. In practice, period concepts — as I shall illustrate by the example of postmodernism — are liable to as many pitfalls, infelicities, and distortions as historical understanding itself. Of these, I shall refer only in passing to the mimetic fallacy or — borrowing the apt phrase of Michael Oakeshott — the fallacy of the "jigsaw puzzle." I will give more attention to the intellectually more hazardous fallacy which was first identified by Francis Bacon, under the rubric of his *idola theatri*.

Historical inquiry is often misconceived, in the words of Michael Oakeshott, as "the resolution of a jigsaw puzzle, what is on the table being made to correspond to the picture on the lid of the box." But this box has never existed, except in the mind of historians who (more often than not unreflectively) espouse a correspondence theory of truth. History, as Oakeshott convincingly argues, is not reconstruction (there is nothing to reconstruct): it is exclusively and rigorously construction. Whenever the genuine historian, working under complex constraints, puts together a configuration of change and "gives it a name (usually not his own and reluctantly appropriated), by calling it 'the Carolingian Empire,' the 'Protestant Reformation,' or ... 'European Liberalism,' we must understand him to be begging us not to place too much weight on these identifications, and above all not to confuse his tentative, multiform identities with the stark, monolithic products of practical and mythological understanding which these expressions may also identify" (Oakeshott 1983:117). In other words, a properly historically understood past is to be found "nowhere else than in history books."

This approach can be profitably transposed to cultural history. Postmodernism, then, will be nothing but a provisional construction against which our more specific definitions of the cultural present are to be tested and evaluated. In this process, the concept of postmodernism itself is not fixed and can undergo any number of changes. There certainly are constraints (one of them being an undogmatic readiness to correct, amend, and adjust its meaning), but our constructions will never be under the obligation to correspond to any "facts," or groupings of "facts," or relationships among "facts" given once and for all. This is so simply because facts are never given but rather, as the etymology *facta* suggests, fabrications (albeit never arbitrary), functions of our choices or beliefs or hypotheses. Under such circumstances, it is clear why the plausibility of the concept of postmodernism — as a tentative frame for a more sophisticated model to be assembled — cannot be guaranteed beforehand. Each particular use of the term will have to create its own validity.

As to the mimetic fallacy, there are few if any writings about postmodernism that are entirely free from it. On the other hand, I do not know of any significant study of postmodernism that sees its object as a "reality" that is out there, to be discovered and mapped. What may appear as a result of the mimetic illusion is almost always a mere *façon de parler*, which is based on certain mimetic metaphors (the mind as a mirror, the mirror of nature, etc.) built into our language. The more serious effects of the jigsaw puzzle concept have been limited, among others, due to a widespread philosophical tendency, particularly in the last half century, toward perspectivism or epistemological relativism. Since the late 1950s, the influence of structuralism and systems theory on literary studies has also played a role: systems or structures are not established by way of one-to-one correspondences with reality.

"Theatricality" can lead to confusions by far more serious than the jigsaw puzzle fallacy may be held responsible for. Structuralist or systems approaches, while checking the intrusion of naive mimesis into the constructive critical discourse, are not immune to the temptation (spurred by ideological convictions) to ground themselves in a "reality" that will proclaim itself at once deeper and more revealing than the reality of positivist-factualist thought. Theatricality has a way of dramatizing the old philosophical distinction between appearance and essence, between surface phenomena and profound — "really real" — processes. A quasi-narrative principle of conflict is thus introduced in the realm of theory: to get to the truth one must unmask or demystify the deceptions of naive realism, one must tear up the veil of illusory appearances and courageously identify the hidden actual causes of what one perceives. Reflection becomes an attempt to unravel a complex con game or, more somberly, a wicked conspiracy. A paranoid strain is always present in this style of thinking. Since the notion of theatricality comes from Francis Bacon, let me briefly recall what he wrote on the "idols of the theatre" in his *Novum Organum*. They "have crept into men's minds from the various dogmas of peculiar systems of philosophy, and also from the perverted rules of demonstration, and these we denominate idols of the theatre: for we regard all the systems of philosophy hitherto received or imagined, as so many plays brought out and performed, creating fictitious and theatrical worlds. Nor do we speak only of the present systems, ... since numerous other plays of a similar nature can still be composed and made to agree with each other, the causes of most opposite errors being generally the same" (Book I, XLIV [Bacon 1904:391]).

Today of course we cannot share Bacon's confidence in empirical data or in induction, which he saw as the great correctives of our theoretical assumptions, unchecked demonstrations, and tendentious projections. Karl Popper has convincingly argued that induction itself is an entirely fantastic concept. A more adequate model of knowledge is the trial-and-error procedure in which we face not "facts" but problems, and in which we dogmatically assert hypotheses, spelling out what could disconfirm them (according to the criterion of falsifiability), and subsequently submitting them to intense criticism for the purpose of error elimination. In this sequence, the "dogmatic moment" is a necessary first mental step, an attempt to solve a given problem in accordance with initial expectations of what the best solution might be. As a young man, Popper remembers in his *Autobiography*, "I was ... much concerned with the problem of *dogmatic thinking and its relation to critical thinking*. What especially interested me was the idea that the dogmatic thinking, which I regarded as prescientific, was a stage that was needed if critical thinking was to be possible." And, a few pages later, he adds: "The critical phase consists in giving up the dogmatic theory ... and in trying out other dogmas. [But] sometimes the dogma was so strongly entrenched that no disappointment could shake it" (Popper 1974: 31, 35). Except in such cases of entrenched dogmatism, trials or expectations or dogmas will be dropped as soon as they become untenable in the light of a successful refutation or of criticism that proves them to be weak, loose, poor in content, trivial.

But even in the new theoretical context, Bacon's remark about theatrical worlds remains, I think, metaphorically valid and suggestive. *Mutatis mutandis*, theatricality would be, in a Popperian trial-and-error process of thought, the attempt to do away with the critical stage and to generalize the dogmatic moment by making it self-contained, invulnerable to testability, in a word, infallible. In consequence, the more theatrical a theory is, the higher its degree of infallibility will be. Good theory, on the contrary, not only recognizes the possibility that it be mistaken, but openly and precisely describes the conditions under which it would no longer hold itself tenable and would give up its claims to truth.

Returning to the discussion of what I have called the theatrical fallacy in the use of postmodernism, the example that comes almost naturally to mind is the (neo)Marxist treatment of postmodernity. (It may be worthwhile to recall that Karl Popper saw Marxism as one of the two great irrefutable theories of our time, the other one being psychoanalysis.) As one might well have expected from a theory that claimed to have discovered the scientific laws of history, Marxism has articulated and staunchly defended a doctrine of socio-economic and cultural development known as historical materialism. Due to the strong, quasi-religious or prophetic component of original Marxism, many of its adherents (beginning with Marx and Engels themselves) believed in their blueprint as if it had been real, indeed incalculably more so than the historical record itself. Thus, mere hypothetical schemes and abstract constructions were theatricalized, in an almost literal sense: world history assumed the shape of a huge allegorical masque illustrating the career of the original sin of production through the climax of demonic capitalism — with its frightening *Walpurgisnacht* of commodities and its myriad perverse enchantments, alienations, and fetishisms — to the final redemption by Revolution.

This broad script leaves room for a certain amount of improvisation and also for differences in interpretation. For the purpose of these remarks it suffices to note the great interpretive split between "Western Marxism" and the official Marxisms in communist countries. The Western Marxists have postponed the advent of the true revolution as they strive to define a less than paradisiacal "feasible socialism" that should avoid the monstrous mistakes of "real socialism" (real in this phrase meaning failed). Post-revolutionary Eastern Marxists say the only feasible socialism (not yet perfect but on the way to becoming so) is theirs, and look ahead to achieving the final goal of historical evolution: posthistoric scientific communism. From their perspective, postmodernism could only be a new phase in the inevitable dissolution of capitalism, in its anxious advance toward ineluctable death. The partisan study of this phase may be useful, but only to the extent that it underscores once again the necessity of socialism as the only path to collective salvation. It goes without saying that one should always be on one's ideological guard against the noxious influences that the culture of postmodernism is bound to exert. What I have outlined here is an ideal case and we must keep in mind that in officially Marxist societies the degree to which conformity is required can and does vary a great deal. No wonder then that, in certain communist countries (particularly in Eastern Europe), postmodernist texts can occasionally be published by state-run presses and sympathetic discussions of postmodernism be printed in state-sponsored cultural journals.

Western Marxists are caught in a much more complex and fluid ideological situation than their counterparts in the East. Their attitude toward postmodernism will therefore be troubled by ambivalences and strained by inner tensions. On the one hand, postmodernism is attractive to them because it is intellectually fashionable and thus offers them an opportunity to address a significant segment of the Western intelligentsia. This attractiveness is further increased by the fact that many of the members of the trend-setting postmodern minority have had a radical political orientation, at least as regards the politics of culture. Thus, the postmodernists appear to the more enlightened Western Marxists as potential "fellow-travellers." On the other hand, though, Western Marxists cannot ignore that the idea of revolution, with its implications of "totality" (a revolution is by definition an all-or-nothing proposition) has lost in postmodernism the prestige it enjoyed in left-wing as well as in right-wing modernist culture. The monistic and reductionist tendencies of modernist thought (often combined with a relentless polemicism) appear to be on the wane as postmodernism rediscovers plurality and favors a more dialogic, self-consciously intertextual, polyphonic and ironic concept of both the cultural tradition and innovation. (For a more extensive treatment of this topic, see Calinescu 1983). Also, postmodernism is less programmatically unpopular than modernism was, and seems to have abandoned the elitism of the avant-garde in both its aesthetic and political versions.

The Western Marxist ambivalence in regard to postmodernism is illustrated in a recent piece by Fredric Jameson, "Postmodernism and Consumer Society," included in Hal Foster's anthology *The Anti-Aesthetic* (1983). One of Jameson's main contentions is that postmodernism is much less subversive (aesthetically and above all politically) than the styles of high modernism were in their time. This loss of subversiveness — of a value that to Jameson is so essential as to be unquestionable — transforms postmodernism into nothing more than a kind of domesticated (anti)modernism, confined to a strange circular "textualism," and self-condemned, wittingly or not, to play the role of a reinforcer of the detested "logic of consumer capitalism." The postindustrial (and culturally postmodern) society in which we live, Jameson writes, has brought about "new types of consumption; planned obsolescence; the penetration of advertising, television and the media to a hitherto unparalleled degree throughout society; ... the growth of the great net of superhighways and the arrival of automobile culture" (Jameson 1983:124-125). Postmodernism, in this broad scenario, is essentially the cultural aspect of "the emergence of this new moment of late, consumer or multinational capitalism. [Postmodernism's] formal features in many ways express the deeper logic of this particular system" (1983:125).

It is not hard to see that this scenario is largely consistent with the standard (vulgar) Marxist scenario of declining capitalism's efforts to arrest social development and postpone the coming of the revolution. Ideologically (read: theatrically), postmodernism in this instance is nothing but the projection — the performance — of the last but one act from the great Marxist masque. Jameson's production of the play reconfirms that external historical and cultural events are easy to fit into a mythological script, and also that such events can serve, in the circular logic of intellectual mythology, as verifications of the fundamental premises.

This, however, accounts for only one side of Jameson's attitude. The other side reveals the critic's appreciation for some of the styles invented or practiced by artists whom he regards as postmodern — in music, John Cage and the "popular modes" utilized by composers like Philip Glass and Terry Riley; in poetry, John Ashbery and the recent "Language Poets"; in fiction Thomas Pynchon, William Burroughs, and the now rather old French *nouveau roman*. In discussing a piece by the talk poet Bob Perelman ("China"), Jameson comments favorably on the self-conscious, self-reflexive textuality of the poem and, what is undoubtedly more important to the critic, on its correct political orientation (China points toward a "third way," a way that exhilaratingly avoids the impasses in which the two superpowers are hopelessly deadlocked). Clearly, what Jameson says about Perelman is in contradiction with his general thesis that postmodernism plays into the hands of multinational capitalism.

The critic's ambivalence becomes even more explicit in the concluding part of his essay, when he asks himself whether postmodernism is indeed devoid of all subversiveness or social-critical value. The dilemma is stated unequivocally: "We have seen that there is a way in which postmodernism replicates or reproduces — reinforces — the logic of consumer capitalism; the more significant question is whether there is also a way in which it resists that logic. But this is a question we must leave open" (Jameson 1983:125). But why? — one feels tempted to ask in turn. If the question about the critical value of postmodernism is so important, what could have prevented the author from addressing it? An explanation, however brief, would have been in order. My own explanation is that the Marxist theatrical scheme (the tidy equation of postmodernism with the culture of late capitalism) would have been greatly watered down if the answer to the question had been other than strongly negative. The author must have realized that the doctrinal framework of his argument (as opposed to the examples he adduces in its support) would have become extremely fragile and that his essay might have appeared as a self-consuming ideological artifact, not a good recommendation for a serious Marxist.

As I see it, a certain degree of theatricalism is unavoidable in any critical-theoretical undertaking. To resist it would be futile if not counterproductive. Why not instead welcome it, in the hope that it might suggest new articulations for our ideas, new insights, new ways of exploring the infinite intertextual maze in which, as critics, we are caught? A low degree of theatricality may also prove, on the level of literary detail, heuristically fruitful. That is to say that critics inspired by ideas coming from Marxism, or from other contemporary schools of thought (psychoanalysis, phenomenology, various structuralisms or poststructuralisms) can and do produce exciting critical work as long as they manage to keep large ideological fictions at bay.

A high degree of theatricalism is an entirely different matter: in treating literature as a mere illustration or even verification of doctrinal fictions, it robs the delicate literary systems and subsystems of their life; its results are too predictable, too general, too rigid, in a word, too boring. Even more boring are the kinds of questions that a high degree of theatricality will ask from culture — questions that are answerable only in the most abstract and fatuous terms. Is artistic modernism mainly characterized by its subversiveness? Or is it, on the contrary, as more orthodox Eastern Marxists (a Georg Lukács, for instance) propose, an irredeemably decadent movement, irrationalist, pathological, and completely intoxicated by *Angst* and a sense of *Geworfenheit*? Is postmodernism nothing but a tame extension of subversive modernism? Or — if Lukács' views are to be updated — is postmodernism an even more deliquescent form of the cultural sickness called modernism? Remarkably, whether such questions are answered positively or negatively, the possibilities for discussion and argument they open up are equally meager, intellectually unexciting, and predictably banal.

To conclude, I would like to suggest that a theatrically moderate and self-skeptical treatment of postmodernism, a treatment that should be as sensitive to plurality and richness as it should be suspicious of doctrinaire rigidities, might be a proper way of exploring postmodernism. A pluralistic methodology, beyond its obvious merits in dealing with a plural phenomenon such as literature, could also turn out to be the best defense against the ghost of totality which haunts all great theatrical-ideological schemes. Literary terminology, which has been the concern of these remarks, also can be energized by inventive pluralization. As Malcolm Bradbury has argued in his thoughtful essay, "Modernisms/Postmodernisms," there are many modernisms, many postmodernisms, and "in the end the study of Modernism can only be a study of Modernisms," the same being true of postmodernism (1983:327). Such a direction of critical inquiry — such a movement from the One to the Many, from monologue to dialogue, from sameness to discrimination — points to one of the most pervasive themes of postmodernism. Of course such a movement cannot even be imagined by an ideologist, whose goal is to establish the truth of his ideology: he will try, occasionally with a display of great intelligence, to dissolve apparent multiplicity into essential unity. Moderate (and self-conscious) theatricality is in principle open to the project of pluralization and discrimination, which is an integral part of the extended postmodernist project.

REFERENCES

Bacon, Francis. 1904. *The Physical and Metaphysical Works*, ed. John Devey. London: George Bell and Sons.

Bradbury, Malcolm. 1983. "Modernisms/Postmodernisms," in Hassan and Hassan 1983:311-328.

Calinescu, Matei. 1977. *Faces of Modernity: Avant-Garde, Decadence, Kitsch*. Bloomington: Indiana University Press.

-----. 1979. "Marxism as a Work of Art: Poststructuralist Readings of Marx," *Stanford French Review* 3, 1: 123-135.

-----. 1983. "From the One to the Many: Pluralism in Today's Thought," in Hassan and Hassan 1983: 263-288.

Eco, Umberto. 1984. *Postscript to The Name of the Rose*. New York: Harcourt Brace Jovanovich.

Fokkema, Douwe W. and Hans Bertens, eds. 1986. *Approaching Postmodernism*. Amsterdam and Philadelphia: Benjamins.

Foster, Hal, ed. 1983. *The Anti-Aesthetic: Essays on Postmodern Culture*. Port Townsend, Wash.: Bay Press.

Hassan, Ihab. 1982. *The Dismemberment of Orpheus*, 2nd ed. Madison: University of Wisconsin Press.

Hassan, Ihab and Sally Hassan, eds. 1983. *Innovation/Renovation: New Perspectives on the Humanities*. Madison: University of Wisconsin Press.

Jameson, Fredric. 1983. "Postmodernism and Consumer Society," in Foster 1983:111-125.

Köhler, Michael. 1977. "'Postmodernismus': Ein begriffshistorischer Überblick," *Amerikastudien* 22, 1: 8-17.

Lyotard, Jean-François. 1979. *La Condition postmoderne: Rapport sur le savoir*. Paris: Minuit. For an English translation see Lyotard 1984.

-----. 1983a. "Answering the Question: What Is Postmodernism?" in Hassan and Hassan 1983:329-341.

-----. 1983b. "Règles et Paradoxes et Appendice Svelte," *Babylone* 1: 67-80.

-----. 1984. *The Postmodern Condition: A Report on Knowledge*, trans. Geoff Bennington and Brian Massumi. Minneapolis: University of Minnesota Press. Translation of Lyotard 1979.

McHale, Brian. 1986. "Change of Dominant from Modernist to Postmodernist Writing," in Fokkema and Bertens 1986:53-79.

Oakeshott, Michael. 1983. *On History and Other Essays*. Oxford: Oxford University Press.

Popper, Karl. 1974. "Autobiography," in Schilpp 1974:3-181.

Scarpetta, Guy. 1985. *L'Impureté*. Paris: Grasset.

Schilpp, Paul Arthur, ed. 1974. *The Philosophy of Karl Popper*, Book One. La Salle, Illinois: Open Court.

2

Pluralism in Postmodern Perspective*

Ihab Hassan

Postmodernism once more — that breach has begun to yawn! I return to it by way of pluralism, which itself has become the irritable condition of postmodern discourse, consuming many pages of both critical and uncritical inquiry. Why? Why pluralism now? This question recalls another that Kant raised two centuries ago: "*Was heisst Aufklärung?*", meaning: "Who are we now?" The answer was a signal meditation on historical presence, as Michel Foucault saw.[1] But to meditate on that topic today — and this is my central claim — is really to inquire: "*Was heisst Postmodernismus?*"

Pluralism in our time finds (if not founds) itself in the social, aesthetic, and intellectual assumptions of postmodernism — finds its ordeal, its rightness, there. I submit, further, that the critical intentions of diverse American pluralists — Meyer Abrams, Wayne Booth, Kenneth Burke, Matei Calinescu, Ronald Crane, Nelson Goodman, Richard McKeon, Stephen Pepper, not to mention countless other artists and thinkers of our moment — engage that overweening query, "What is postmodernism?", engage and even answer it tacitly. In short, like a latter-day M. Jourdain, they have been speaking postmodernism all their lives without knowing it.

But what *is* postmodernism? I can propose no rigorous definition of it, any more than I could define modernism itself. For the term has become a current signal of tendencies in theater, dance, music, art, and architecture; in literature and criticism; in philosophy, theology, psychoanalysis, and historiography; in cybernetic technologies and even in the sciences. Indeed, postmodernism has now received the bureaucratic accolade of the National Endowment for the Humanities, in the form of a Summer Seminar for Col-

* Reprinted from *Critical Inquiry* 12, no. 3 (March 1986).

lege Teachers; and beyond that, it has penetrated the abstractions of "late" Marxist critics who, only a decade ago, dismissed postmodernism as another instance of the dreck, fads, and folderol of a consumer society. Clearly, then, the time has come to theorize the term, if not define it, before it fades from awkward neologism to derelict cliché without ever attaining to the dignity of a cultural concept.

To theorize postmodernism though, is to change its character in the making no less than to acknowledge its errancies, vexations. These bear on problems of cultural modeling, literary periodization, cultural change — the problems of critical discourse itself in an antinomian phase.[2] Still, the exhaustions of modernism, or at least its self-revisions, have prompted incongruous thinkers to moot its supervention. Thus, for instance, Daniel Bell, a "conservative" sociologist, testifies to "the end of the creative impulse and ideological sway of modernism, which, as a cultural move-ment, has dominated all the arts, and shaped our symbolic expressions, for the past 125 years (Bell 1976: 7). And thus, too, a "radical" philosopher, Jürgen Habermas, tries to distinguish — vainly, as I see it — between the "premodernism of old conservatives," the "antimodernism of the young conservatives," and the "postmodernism of the neoconservatives" (Haber-mas 1981: 13).

This is not the time, however, nor the place, to theorize postmodern-ism in depth. Instead, I want to offer a catena of postmodern features, a paratactical list, staking out a cultural field. My examples will be selective; my traits may overlap, conflict, antecede, or supersede themselves. Still, together, they limn a region of postmodern "indetermanences" (indetermi-nacy lodged in immanence) in which critical pluralism takes shape.[3]

II

Here, then, is my catena:

1. *Indeterminacy*, or rather, indeterminacies. These include all manner of ambiguities, ruptures, displacements, affecting knowledge and society. We may think of Heisenberg's principle of uncertainty, Gödel's proof of incompleteness, Kuhn's paradigms and Feyerabend's dadaism of science. Or we may think of Harold Rosenberg's anxious art objects, de-defined. And in literary theory? From Bakhtin's dialogic imagination, Barthes' *textes scriptibles*, Iser's literary *Unbestimmtheiten*, Bloom's misprisions, de Man's allegorical readings, Fish's affective stylistics, Holland's transactive analysis, and Bleich's subjective criticism, to the last fashionable *aporia* of

unrecorded time, we undecide, relativize. Indeterminacies pervade our actions, ideas, interpretations; they constitute our world.

2. *Fragmentation*. Indeterminacy often follows from fragmentation. The postmodernist only disconnects; fragments are all he pretends to trust. His ultimate opprobrium is "totalization," any synthesis whatever, social, epistemic, even poetic. Hence his preference for montage, collage, the found or cut-up literary object, for paratactical over hypotactical forms, metonymy over metaphor, schizophrenia over paranoia. Hence, too, his recourse to paradox, paralogy, parabasis, paracriticism, the openness of brokenness, unjustified margins. Thus Lyotard (1983: 341) exhorts: "Let us wage war on totality; let us be witnesses to the unpresentable; let us activate the differences and save the honor of the name."[4] The age demands differences, shifting signifiers, and even atoms dissolve into elusive sub-particles, a mere mathematical whisper.

3. *Decanonization*. In the largest sense, this applies to all canons, all conventions of authority. We are witnessing, Lyotard (1979) argues again, a massive "delegitimation" of the master-codes in society, a desuetude of the metanarratives, favoring instead *"les petites histoires,"* which preserve the heterogeneity of language games.[5] Thus, from the "death of god" to the "death of the author" and "death of the father," from the derision of authority to revision of the curriculum, we decanonize culture, demystify knowledge, deconstruct the languages of power, desire, deceit. Derision and revision are versions of subversion, of which the most baleful example is the rampant terrorism of our time. But "subversion" may take other, more benevolent, forms: minority movements or the feminization of culture, which also require decanonization.

4. *Self-less-ness, Depth-less-ness*. Postmodernism vacates the traditional self, simulating self-effacement — a fake flatness, without inside/outside — or its opposite, self-multiplication, self-reflection. Critics have noted the "loss of self" in modern literature (Sypher 1962); but it was originally Nietzsche who in *Der Wille zur Macht* declared the "subject" "only a fiction": "the ego of which one speaks when one censures egoism does not exist at all"[6] (Nietzsche 1967: 199). This determinates the "deep" romantic ego, which postmodernism suppresses or disperses, and sometimes tries to recover, though it remains under dire suspicion in poststructuralist circles as a "totalizing principle." Losing itself in the play of language, in the differences from which reality is plurally made, the self impersonates its absence, even as death stalks its games. It diffuses itself in depth-less styles, refusing,

eluding, interpretation.[7]

5. *The Unpresentable, Unrepresentable*. Like its predecessor, post-modern art is irrealist, aniconic. Even its "magic realism" dissolves in ethereal states; its hard, flat surfaces repel mimesis. Postmodern literature, particularly, often seeks its limits, entertains its "exhaustion," subverts itself in forms of articulate "silence." It becomes liminary, contesting the modes of its own representation. Like the Kantian Sublime, which thrives on the formlessness, the emptiness, of the Absolute — "Thou shalt not make graven images" — "the postmodern would be," in Lyotard's (1983: 340) audacious analogue, "that which, in the modern, puts forward the unpresentable in presentation itself...."[8] But the challenge to representation may also lead a writer to other liminal states: the Abject, for instance, rather than the sublime, or Death itself — more precisely, "the exchange between signs and death," as Julia Kristeva put it. "What is unrepresenta-bility?" Kristeva (1980: 141) asks. "That which, through language, is part of no particular language.... That which, through meaning, is intolerable, unthinkable: the horrible, the abject."[9]

Here, I think, we reach a peripety of negations. For with my next defi-niens, irony, we begin to move from the deconstructive to the reconstruc-tive tendency of postmodernism, though both tendencies, of course, coexist.

6. *Irony*. This could also be called, after Kenneth Burke, perspec-tivism. In absence of a cardinal principle or paradigm, we turn to play, interplay, dialogue, polylogue, allegory, self-reflection, in short, to irony. This irony assumes indeterminacy, multivalence, aspires to clarity, the clar-ity of demystification, the pure light of absence. We meet variants of it in Bakhtin, Burke, de Man, Jacques Derrida and Hayden White. And in Alan Wilde (1981: 10) we see an effort to discriminate its modes: "mediate irony", "disjunctive irony," and "postmodern" or "suspensive irony", "with its yet more radical vision of multiplicity, randomness, contingency, and even absurdity...."[10] Irony, perspectivism, reflexiveness: these express the ineluctable recreations of mind in search of a truth that continually eludes it, leaving it only with an ironic access or excess of self-consciousness.

7. *Hybridization*, or the mutant replication of genres, including parody, travesty, pastiche. The "de-definition," deformation, of cultural genres engenders equivocal modes: "paracriticism", "fictual discourse," the "new journalism," the "nonfiction novel," a promiscuous category of "para-literature" or "threshold literature," at once young and very old.[11]

Cliché and plagiarism ("playgiarism," Raymond Federman punned), parody and pastiche, pop and kitsch, enrich re-presentation. In this view, image or replica may be as valid as its model (the *Quixote* of Borges' Pierre Menard), may even bring an "*augment d'être.*" This makes for a different concept of tradition, one in which continuity and discontinuity, high and low culture, mingle not to imitate but to expand the past in the present. In that plural present, all styles are dialectically available in an interplay between the Now and the Not Now, the Same and the Other. Thus, in post-modernism, Heidegger's concept of "equitemporality" becomes really a dialectic of equitemporality, a new relation between historical elements, without any suppression of the past in favor of the present — a point that Fredric Jameson (1983) misses when he criticizes postmodern literature, film, and architecture for their ahistorical character, their "presentifica-tions."[12]

8. *Carnivalization.* The term, of course, is Bakhtin's, and it riotously embraces indeterminacy, fragmentation, decanonization, self-less-ness, irony, hybridization, all of which I have already adduced. But the term also conveys the comic or absurdist ethos of postmodernism, anticipated in the "heteroglossia" of Rabelais and Sterne, jocose pre-postmodernists. Car-nivalization further means "polyphony," the centrifugal power of language, the "gay relativity" of things, perspectivism and performance, participation in the wild disorder of life, the immanence of laughter (Bakhtin 1968 and 1981).[13] Indeed, what Bakhtin calls novel or carnival — that is, anti-system — might stand for postmodernism itself, or at least for its ludic and subver-sive elements, which promise renewal. For in carnival, "the true feast of time, the feast of becoming, change, and renewal," human beings, then as now, discover "the peculiar logic of the 'inside out' (*à l'envers*), of the 'turn-about,' ... of numerous parodies and travesties, humiliations, profana-tions, comic crownings and uncrownings. A second life...." (Bakhtin 1968: 10-11).

9. *Performance, Participation.* Indeterminacy elicits participation; those gaps must be filled. The postmodern text, verbal or nonverbal, invites performance: it wants to be written, revised, answered, acted out. Indeed, so much of postmodern art calls itself performance, transgressing genres. As performance, art — or theory for that matter — declares its vulnerabil-ity to time, to death, to audience, to the Other.[14] "Theatre" becomes — to the edge of terrorism — the active principle of a paratactical society, decanonized if not really carnivalized. At its best, as Poirier (1971: xv, xiii)

contends, the performing self expresses "an energy in motion, an energy with its own shape"; yet in its "self-discovering, self-watching, finally self-pleasuring response to ... pressures and difficulties," that self may also veer toward solipsism, lapse into narcissism.[15]

10. *Constructionism.* Since postmodernism is radically tropic, figurative, irrealist — "what can be thought of must certainly be a fiction," Nietzsche (1967: 291) thought — it constructs reality in post-Kantian, indeed post-Nietzschean, "fictions."[16] Scientists seem now more at ease with heuristic fictions than many humanists, last realists of the West. (Some literary critics even kick language, thinking thus to stub their toes on a stone.) Such effective fictions suggest the growing intervention of mind in nature and culture, an aspect of what I have called the "new gnosticism," evident in science and art, in social relations and high technologies (Hassan 1975: 121-150; Hassan 1980a: 139-172).[17] But constructionism appears also in Burke's "dramatistic criticism," Pepper's "world hypothesis," Goodman's "ways of worldmaking," White's "prefigurative moves," not to mention current hermeneutic or poststructuralist theory. Thus postmodernism sustains the movement "from unique truth and a world fixed and found," as Goodman (1978: x) remarked, "to a diversity of right and even conflicting versions or worlds in the making."

11. *Immanence.* This refers, without religious echo, to the growing capacity of mind to generalize itself through symbols. Everywhere now, we witness problematic diffusions, dispersals, dissemination; we experience the extension of our senses, as McLuhan crankily presaged, through new media and technologies. Languages, apt or mendacious, reconstitute the universe — from quasars to quarks, and back, from the lettered unconscious to black holes in space — reconstitute it into signs of their own making, turning nature into culture, and culture into an immanent semiotic system. The language animal has emerged, his/her measure the intertextuality of all life. A patina of thought, of signifiers, of "connexions" now lies on everything the mind touches in its gnostic (noö)sphere, which physicists, biologists, and semioticians, no less than mystic theologians like Teilhard de Chardin, explore. The pervasive irony of their explorations is also the reflexive irony of mind meeting itself at every dark turn.[18] Yet in a consuming society, such immanences can become more vacuous than fatidic. They become, as Jean Baudrillard (1983b: 43) says, pervasively "ob-scene": "a collective vertigo of neutralization, a forward escape into the obscenity of pure and empty form...."

These eleven "definientia" add up to a surd, perhaps absurd. I should be much surprised if they amounted to a definition of postmodernism, which remains, at best, an equivocal concept, disjunctive category, doubly modified by the impetus of the phenomenon itself as by the shifting perceptions of its critics. (At worst, postmodernism appears to be a mysterious, if ubiquitous, ingredient, like raspberry vinegar which instantly turns any recipe into *nouvelle cuisine*.)

Nor do I believe that my eleven "definientia" serve to distinguish postmodernism from modernism; for the latter itself abides as a fierce evasion in our literary histories (cf. de Man 1971: 142-165, and Paz 1974). But I do suggest that the foregoing points — elliptic, cryptic, partial, provisional — argue twin conclusions: (a) *critical pluralism is deeply implicated in the cultural field of postmodernism*; and (b) *a limited critical pluralism is in some measure a reaction against the radical relativism, the ironic indetermanences, of the postmodern condition, an attempt to contain them*.

III

So far, my argument has been prelusive. I must now attend to those efforts which seek to limit — quite rightly, I believe — the potential anarchy of our postmodern condition with cognitive, political, or affective constraints. That is, I must briefly consider criticism as genre, power, and desire — as Kenneth Burke did, long ago, in his vast synoptics of motives.

Is criticism a genre? Critical pluralists often suppose that it may be so.[19] Yet even that most understanding of pluralists, Wayne Booth, is forced finally to admit that a full "methodological pluralism," which must aspire to a perspective on perspectives, only "duplicates the problem with which we began"; and so he concludes: "I cannot promise a finally satisfactory encounter with these staggering questions, produced by any simple effort to be a good citizen in the republic of criticism (Booth 1979: 33-34)." The conclusion is modest but also alert. He knows that the epistemic foundations of critical pluralism themselves rest on moral, if not spiritual, grounds. "Methodological perspectivism" — as he sometimes calls his version of pluralism — depends on "shared tenancies" which in turn depend on a constitutive act of rational, just, and vitally sympathetic understanding. In the end, Booth stands on a kind of Kantian — or is it Christian? — categorical imperative of criticism, with all that it must ethically and metaphysically imply.

Could it have been otherwise? Throughout history, critics have disagreed, pretending to make systems out of their discord, and out of their beliefs, epistemic structures. The "shared tenancies" of literary theory may make for hermeneutic communities of provisional trust, enclaves of genial critical authority. But can any of these define criticism both as a historical and cognitive genre? That may depend on what we intend by genre. Traditionally, genre assumed recognizable features within a context of both persistence and change; it was a useful assumption of identity upon which critics (somewhat like Stanley and Livingston) often presumed. But that assumption, in our heteroclitic age, seems ever harder to maintain. Even genre theorists invite us, nowadays, to go beyond genre: "the finest generic classifications of our time," Paul Hernadi (1972: 184) says, "make us look beyond their immediatè concern and focus on the *order of literature*, not on *borders between literary genres.*"[20] Yet the "order of literature" itself has become intensely moot.

In boundary genres particularly — and certain kinds of criticism may have become precisely that — the ambiguities attain new heights of febrile intensity. For as Morson (1981: 49) notes, "it is not meanings but appropriate procedures for discovering meaning" that become disputable — "not particular readings, but how to read." Since genres find their definition, *when* they find any, not only in their formal features but also in labile interpretive conventions, they seldom offer a stable, epistemic norm. This makes for certain paradoxes in the "law of genre," as Derrida lays it, a "mad law," though even madness fails to define it. As one might expect from the magus of our deconstructions, Derrida insists on undoing genre, undoing its gender, nature, and potency, in exposing the enigma of its "exemplarity." The mad "law of genre" yields only to the "law of the law of genre": "a principle of contamination, a law of impurity, a parasitical economy" (Derrida 1980: 206).

One is inclined to believe that even without the de-creations of certain kinds of writing, like my own paracriticism, the configurations we call Literature, Literary Theory, Criticism, have now become "essentially contested concepts" — quite like postmodernism itself —, horizons of eristic discourse.[21] Thus, for instance, the latest disconfirmation of critical theory, the latest "revisionary madness": Knapp and Michaels' statement against theory.[22] Drawing on the pragmatism of Richard Rorty and the stylistics of Stanley Fish, the authors brilliantly, berserkly, contend that "true belief" and "knowledge" are epistemologically identical, that critical theory has no methodological consequences whatever. "If our arguments are true, they can have only one consequence...; theory should stop," the authors conclude (Knapp and Michaels 1983: 800). In fact, it is their own conclusion that will have little consequence, as Knapp and Michaels themselves admit. So much, then, for the case of the self-consuming theorist.

My own conclusion about the theory and practice of criticism is securely unoriginal: like all discourse, criticism obeys human imperatives, which continually redefine it. It is a function of language, power, and desire, of history and accident, or purpose and interest, of value and, above all, of *belief*, which reason articulates and consensus, or authority, both enables and constrains.[23] (This statement itself expresses a reasoned belief.) If, then, as Thomas Kuhn (1970: 163) claims, "competing schools, *each of which constantly questions the very foundations of the others*," reign in the humanities; if, as Victor Turner (1974: 14) thinks, the "culture of any society at any moment is more like the debris, or 'fall out' of past ideological systems, rather than itself a system"; if also, as Jonathan Culler (1981: 30) contends, "'interpretive conventions' ... should be seen as part of ... [a] boundless context"; again, if as Jeffrey Stout (1982: 5) maintains, "theoretical terms should serve interests and purposes, not the other way around"; and if, as I submit, the principles of literary criticism are historical (that is, at once arbitrary, pragmatic, conventional, and contextual, in any case not axiomatic, apodictic, apophantic), then how can a generic conception of criticism limit critical pluralism or govern the endless deferrals of language, particularly in our indetermanent, our postmodern period?[24]

IV.

To exchange a largely cognitive view of our discipline for another that admits more freely politics, desires, beliefs, is not necessarily to plunge into chaos. It is, I think, an act of partial lucidity, applied to our ideological, our human needs. The act, I stress, remains partial, as I hope will become eventually clear. For the moment, though, I must approach power as a constraint on postmodern relativism, and thus a factor in delimiting critical pluralism.

No doubt, the perception that power profoundly engages knowledge reverts to Plato and Aristotle, if not to the *I Ching* and the Egyptian *Book of the Dead*. In the last century, Marx theorized the relation of culture to class, and his terms persist in a variety of movements, from totemic Marxism to Marxism with a deconstructionist mask or receptionist face. But it is Michel Foucault, of course, who now gives us the most cunning speculations on the topic.[25] The whole burden of his work, since *Folie et déraison* (1961), has been to expose the power of discourse and the discourse of power, to discover the politics of knowledge. More recently, though, his ideology had become antic to the chagrin of his orthodox critics.

Foucault (1977: 200) still maintained that discursive practices "are embodied in technical processes, in institutions, in patterns for general behavior, in forms of transmission and diffusion...." But he also accepted the Nietzschean premise that a selfish interest precedes all power and knowledge, shaping them to its own volition, pleasure, excess. Increasingly, Foucault saw power itself as an elusive relation, an immanence of discourse, a conundrum of desire: "It may be that Marx and Freud cannot satisfy our desire for understanding this enigmatic thing which we call power, which is at once visible and invisible, present and hidden, ubiquitous" (Foucault 1977: 213). That is why, in his late essay on "The Subject and Power," Foucault seemed more concerned with promoting "new kinds of subjectivity" (based on a refusal of those individual identities which states force upon their citizens) than with censuring traditional modes of exploitation (Dreyfus and Rabinow 1982: 216-220).

In a Foucauldian perspective, then, criticism appears as much a discourse of desire as of power, a discourse, anyway, both conative and affective in its personal origins. A neo-Marxist like Fredric Jameson, however, would found criticism on collective reality. He would distinguish and "spell out the priority, within the Marxist tradition, of a 'positive hermeneutic' based on social class from those ['negative hermeneutics'] still limited by anarchist categories of the individual subject and individual experience" (Jameson 1981: 286). Again, a leftist critic like Edward Said (1983: 5) would insist that the "realities of power and authority ... are the realities that make texts possible, that deliver them to their readers, that solicit the attention of critics."

Other critics, less partisan and less strenuously political, might concur. Indeed, the "institutional view" of both literature and criticism now prevails among critics as incongruous in their ideologies as David Bleich, Wayne Booth, Donald Davie, Stanley Fish, E.D. Hirsch, Frank Kermode, Richard Ohmann.... Here, bravely, is Bleich (1983: 411):

> Literary theory should contribute to the changing of social and professional institutions such as the public lecture, the convention presentation,

the classroom, and the processes of tenure and promotion. Theoretical work ought to show how and why no one class of scholars, and no one subject (including theory) is self-justifying, self-explanatory, and self-sustaining (Bleich 1983: 411; cf. also Hernadi 1978: 49-112).

The ideological concern declares itself everywhere. A bristling issue of *Critical Inquiry* (9, no. 1 [September 1982]) explores the "politics of interpretation"; and the facile correlation of ideology to criticism drives a critic even so disputatious as Gerald Graff (1983) to protest the "pseudo-politics of interpretation" in a subsequent number. At the same time, a critic as exquisitely reticent as Geoffrey Hartman acknowledges the intrusions of politics in his recent work (Hartman 1983). The activities of GRIP (acronym for the Group for Research on the Institutionalization and Professionalization of Literary Study) seem as ubiquitous as those of the KGB or the CIA, though far more benign. And the number of conferences on "Marxism and Criticism", "Feminism and Criticism", "Ethnicity and Criticism", "Technology and Criticism", "Mass Culture and Criticism," keeps American airports snarled and air carriers in the black.

All these, of course, refract the shifts in our "myths of concern" (Frye) since the Fifties. But they reflect, too, the changes in our idea of criticism itself, from a Kantian to a Nietzschean, Freudian, or Marxist conception (to name but three) from an ontological to a historical apprehension, from a synchronous or generic discourse to a diachronic or conative activity. The recession of the neo-Kantian idea, which extends through Ernst Cassirer, Susanne Langer, and the old New Critics, ambiguously to Murray Krieger, implies another loss: that of the imagination as an autochthonous, autotelic, possibly redemptive power of mind. It is also the loss, or at least dilapidation, of the "Imaginary Library": a total order of art, analogous to Malraux's *musée imaginaire*, which triumphs over time and brute destiny.[26] That ideal has now vanished; the Library itself may end in rubble. Yet in our eagerness to appropriate art to our own circumstances and exercise our will on texts, we risk to deny those capacities — not only literary — which have most richly fulfilled our historical existence.

I confess to some distaste for ideological rage (the worst are now full of passionate intensity *and* lack all conviction) and for the hectoring of both religious and secular dogmatists.[27] I admit to a certain ambivalence toward politics, which can overcrowd our responses to both art and life. For what is politics? Simply, the right action when ripeness calls. But what is politics again? An excuse to bully or shout in public, vengeance vindicating itself as justice and might pretending to be right, a passion for self-avoidance, immanent mendacity, the rule of habit, the place where history rehearses its nightmares; the *dur désir de durer*, a deadly banality of being. Yet we must all heed politics because it structures our theoretical consents, literary evasions, critical recusancies — shapes our ideas of pluralism even as I write here, now.

V

Politics, we know, becomes tyrannical. It can dominate other modes of discourse, reduce all facts of the human universe — error and epiphany, chance, boredom, pain, dream — to its own terms. Hence the need, as Julia Kristeva (1982b: 78) says, for a "psychoanalytic intervention ... a counterweight, an antidote, to political discourse which, without it, is free to become our modern religion: the final explanation."[28] Yet the psychoanalytic explanation can also become as reductive as any other, unless desire itself qualifies its knowledge, its words.

I mean desire in the largest sense — personal and collective, biological and ontological — a force that writers from Hesiod and Homer to Nietzsche, William James, and Freud have reckoned with. This includes the Eros of the Universe, which Whitehead (1955: 276) conceived as "the active entertainment of all ideals, with the urge to their finite realization, each in its due season." But I mean desire also in its more particular sense, which Valéry understood when he wryly confessed that every theory is a fragment of an autobiography. (Lately, the fragments have grown larger, as anyone who follows the oedipal *psychomachia* of critics must agree.) And I mean desire, too, as an aspect of the pleasure principle, that principle so freely invoked and seldom evident in criticism.

Here, Roland Barthes comes elegantly to mind. For him, the pleasure of the text is perverse, polymorph, created by intermittences of the body even more than of the heart. Rupture, tear, suture, scission enhance that pleasure; so does erotic displacement. "The text is a fetish object, and *this fetish desires me*," he confides (Barthes 1975: 27). Such a text eludes judgment by anterior or exterior norms. In its presence, we can only cry: "that's it for me", the Dionysiac cry *par excellence* — Dionysiac, that is, in that peculiarly Gallic timbre. Thus, for Barthes, the pleasure of the text derives both from the body's freedom to "pursue its own ideas" and from "value shifted to the sumptuous rank of the signifier" (1975: 17, 65).

We need not debate here the celebrated, if dubious, distinctions

Barthes makes in that talismanic text; we need only note that pleasure becomes a constitutive critical principle in his later work. Thus in *Leçon*, his inaugural lecture at the Collège de France, Barthes insists on the "truth of desire," which discovers itself in the multiplicity of discourse: "*autant de langages qu'il y a de désirs*" (1978: 25). The highest role of the professor is to make himself "fantasmic," to renew his body so that it becomes contemporaneous with his students, unlearn (*désapprendre*). Perhaps then he can realize true *sapientia*: "*nul pouvoir, un peu de savoir, un peu de sagesse, et le plus de saveur possible*" (1978: 46).

Fragments d'un discours amoureux shows a darker side of desire; for pain and solitude here attend the subject more than delight. Simulating discretely a lover's speech, rendering it in broken figures, such as a modern dancer may perform, Barthes presents us with an encyclopedia of affective culture, ordered by no principle other than the alphabet of desire. Yet the spirit of the Erinyes pervades the work's pages; and the text to which it always returns, without ever leaving, is that incontinent book of love, death, and madness, *Die Leiden des jungen Werthers*, which so many in Europe read and, reading, learned to sigh and die. Thus both love and suicide become textual mimesis; in the book of Barthes, language and desire meet continually at the limits of their mutual destruction. There is no possibility of explication, of hermeneutics, in this forlorn, imaginary confession which strokes language in erotic foreplay: "*Je frotte mon langage contre l'autre. C'est comme j'avais des mots en guise de doigts...*" (Barthes 1977: 87).[29]

Other versions of this critical suasion come easily to mind.[30] But my point is not only that critical theory is a function of our desires; nor simply that criticism often takes pleasure or desire as its concern, its theme. My point is rather more fundamental: much current criticism conceives language and literature themselves as organs of desire, to which criticism tries to adhere erotically ("*se coller*," Barthes says), stylistically, even epistemically. "Desire and the desire to know are not strangers to each other...," Kristeva notes; and "interpretation is infinite because Meaning is made infinite by desire..." (Kristeva 1982b: 82, 86). Happily, this last remark leads into my inconclusion.

Let me recover, though, the stark lineaments of my arguments. Critical pluralism finds itself implicated in our postmodern condition, in its relativisms and indetermanences, which it attempts to restrain. But cognitive, political, and affective restraints remain only partial. They all finally

fail to delimit critical pluralism, to create consensual theory or practice. —
Is there anything, in our era, that *can* found a wide consensus of discourse?

VI

Clearly, the imagination of postmodern criticism is a disestablished imagination. Yet clearly, too, it is an intellectual imagination of enormous vi-
brancy and scope. I share in its excitement, my own excitement mixed with
unease. That unease touches more than our critical theories; it engages the
nature of authority and belief in the world. It is the old Nietzschean cry of
nihilism: "the desert grows!" God, King, Father, Reason, History,
Humanism have all come and gone their way, though their power may still
flare up in some circles of faith. We have killed our gods — in spite or lucidity, I hardly know — yet we remain ourselves creatures of will, desire,
hope, belief. And now we have nothing — nothing that is not partial, provisional, self-created — upon which to found our discourse.

Sometimes I imagine a new Kant, come out of Königsberg, spirited
through the Iron Curtain. In his hand he holds the "fourth critique," which
he calls *The Critique of Practical Judgment*. It is a masterwork, resolving all
the contradictions of theory and praxis, ethics and aesthetics, metaphysical
reason and historical life. I reach for the sublime treatise; the illustrious
ghost disappears. Sadly, I turn to my bookshelf and pick out William
James' *The Will to Believe*.

Here, it seems, is friendly lucidity, and an imagination that keeps
reason on the stretch. James speaks crucially to our condition in a "pluralistic universe." I let him speak:

> He who takes for his hypothesis the notion that it [pluralism] is the perma-
> nent form of the world is what I call a radical empiricist. For him the crud-
> ity of experience remains an eternal element thereof. There is no possible
> point of view from which the world can appear an absolutely single fact
> (1956: ix).

This leaves the field open to "willing nature." James again:

> When I say "willing nature," I do not mean only such deliberate volitions
> as may have set up habits of belief that we cannot now escape from, — I
> mean all such factors of belief as fear and hope, prejudice and passion,
> imitation and partisanship, the circumpressure of our caste and set. As a
> matter of fact we find ourselves believing, we hardly know how or why
> (1956: 9).

This was written nearly a century ago and remains — so I *believe* — impeccable, unimpugnable. It proposes a different kind of "authority" (lower case), pragmatic, empirical, permitting pluralist beliefs. Between these beliefs, there can only be continual negotiations of reason and interest, mediations of desire, transactions of power or hope. But all these still rest on, rest in, beliefs, which James knew to be the most interesting, most valuable, part of man. In the end, our "passional nature," he says, decides *an option between propositions, whenever it is a genuine option that cannot by its nature be decided on intellectual grounds ...*" (James 1956: 11). James even suggests that, biologically considered, "our minds are as ready to grind out falsehood as veracity, and he who says, 'Better go without belief forever than believe a lie!' merely shows his own preponderant private horror of becoming a dupe" (1956: 18).

Contemporary pragmatists, like Rorty, Fish, or Michaels, may not follow James so far. Certainly they would balk, as do most of us now, when James' language turns spiritual:

> Is it not sheer dogmatic folly to say that our inner interests can have no real connection with the forces that the hidden world may contain? ... And if needs of ours outrun the visible universe, why *may* not that be a sign that an invisible universe is there? ... God himself, in short, may draw vital strength and increase of very being from our fidelity (James 1956: 55, 56, 61).

I do not quote this passage to press the claims of metaphysics or religion. I do so only to hint that the *ultimate* issues of critical pluralism, in our postmodern epoch, point that way. And why, particularly, in our postmodern epoch? Precisely because of its countervailing forces, its indetermanences. Everywhere now we observe societies riven by the double and coeval process of planetization and retribalization, totalitarianism and terror, fanatic faith and radical disbelief. Everywhere we meet, in mutant or displaced forms, that conjunctive/disjunctive technological rage which affects postmodern discourse.

It may be that some rough beast will slouch again toward Bethlehem, its haunches bloody, its name echoing in our ears with the din of history. It may be that some natural cataclysm, world calamity, or extraterrestrial intelligence will shock the earth into some sane planetary awareness of its destiny. It may be that we shall simply bungle through, muddle through, wandering in the "desert" from oasis to oasis, as we have done for decades, perhaps centuries. I have no prophecy in me, only some slight foreboding, which I express now to remind myself that all the evasions of our knowledge and actions thrive on the absence of consensual beliefs, an absence that also energizes our tempers, our wills. This is our postmodern condition.

As to things nearer at hand, I openly admit: I do not know how to prevent critical pluralism from slipping into monism or relativism, except to call for pragmatic constituencies of knowledge, sharing values, traditions, expectancies, goals. I do not know how to make our "desert" a little greener, except to invoke enclaves of genial authority, where the central task is to restore civil commitments, tolerant beliefs, critical sympathies.[31] I do not know how to give literature or theory or criticism a new hold on the world, except to remythify the imagination, at least locally, and bring back the reign of wonder into our lives. In this, my own elective affinities remain with Emerson: "Orpheus is no fable: you have only to sing, and the rocks will crystallize; sing, and the plant will organize; sing, and the animal will be born" (Emerson 1912: 79).

But who nowadays believes it?

NOTES

1.   "Maybe the most certain of all philosophical problems is the problem of the present time, of what we are, in this very moment," writes Michel Foucault in "The Subject and Power," reprinted as "Afterword" in Dreyfus and Rabinow 1982: 210. The essay also appeared in *Critical Inquiry* 8 (1982): 777-796.

2.   I have discussed some of these problems in Hassan 1982: 262-268. See also Claus Uhlig, "Toward a Chronology of Change," Dominick LaCapra, "Intellectual History and Defining the Present as 'Postmodern'," and Matei Calinescu, "From the One to the Many: Pluralism in Today's Thought," in Hassan and Hassan 1983.

3.   For an elaboration of "indetermanence," see Hassan 1980a: 89-124.

4.   See also Hayden White on the paratactical style in art and society: "The Culture of Criticism," in Hassan 1971b: 66-69; and see William James on the affinities between parataxis and pluralism: "It may be that some parts of the world are connected so loosely with some other parts as to be strung along by nothing but the copula *and*.... This pluralistic view, of a world of *additive* constitution, is one that pragmatism is unable to rule out from serious consideration" (James 1955: 112).

5.   For other views of decanonization, see Fiedler and Baker 1979, and *Critical Inquiry* 10, no. 1 (September 1983).

6.   See also the discussion of the postmodern self in Caramello 1983.

7.   The refusal of depth is, in the widest sense, a refusal of hermeneutics, the "penetration" of nature or culture. It manifests itself in the white philosophies of poststructuralism as

well as in various contemporary arts. See, for instance, Robbe-Grillet (1965: 49-76), and Sontag (1966: 3-14).

8. See also Hayden White's perceptive discussion of the politics of the sublime (White 1982).

9. See also Kristeva 1982a, and her most recent discussion of "the unnameable" in Kristeva 1982b: 84-85, 91.

10. Wayne Booth (1983) makes a larger claim for the currency of irony in postmodern times, a "cosmic irony," deflating the claims of man's centrality, and evincing a striking parallel with traditional religious languages.

11. The last term is Gary Saul Morson's, who provides an excellent discussion of threshold literature, parody, and hybridization (Morson 1981: 48-50, 107-108, 142-143).

12. For a counter-statement, see Portoghesi (1982: 11) and Calinescu (1983: 286).

13. See also the issue on Bakhtin of *Critical Inquiry* 10, no. 2 (December 1983).

14. See Régis Durand's (1983) defense, against Michael Fried, of the performing principle in postmodern art. See also Richard Schechner (1983).

15. See also Lasch 1978.

16. William James (1955: 166) understood this when he said: "You can't weed out the human contribution ... altho the stubborn fact remains that there *is* a sensible flux, what is *true of it* seems from first to last to be largely a matter of our creation."

17. It was José Ortega y Gasset (1968: 184), however, who made this prescient, gnostic statement in 1925: "Man humanizes the world, injects it, impregnates it with his own ideal substance and is finally entitled to imagine that one day or another, in the far depths of time, this terrible outer world will become so saturated with man that our descendants will be able to travel through it as today we mentally travel through our own inmost selves — he finally imagines that the world, without ceasing to be the world, will one day be changed into something like a materialized soul, and, as in Shakespeare's *Tempest*, the winds will blow at the bidding of Ariel, the spirit of ideas." And before Ortega, William James (1955: 105): "The world is One just so far as its parts hang together by any definite connexion. It is many just so far as any definite connexion fails to obtain. And finally it is growing more and more unified by those systems of connexion at least which human energy keeps framing as time goes on." But see also Jean Baudrillard's version of a senseless immanence (1983a).

18. Active, creative, self-reflexive patterns seem also essential to advanced theories of artificial intelligence. See the article on Douglas R. Hofstadter's latest work by James Gleick (1983).

19. See, for instance, the persuasive article of Ralph Cohen (1975). Cohen also sees literary change itself as a genre. See Cohen 1983 and the responses of Hayden White and Michael Riffaterre to it in *Critical Exchange* 13 (Spring 1983): 18-26 and 27-38.

20. See, further, the two issues on convention and genre, of *New Literary History* 13, no. 1 (Autumn 1981) and 14, no. 2 (Winter 1983).

21. The term "essentially contested concept" is developed by W.B. Gallie (1968). See also Booth's lucid discussion of it (1979: 211-215, 366).

22. See Knapp and Michaels 1982, and the subsequent responses in *Critical Inquiry* 9, no. 4 (June 1983). "Revisionary Madness" is the title of Daniel T. O'Hara's response (726-742).

23. The relevance of belief to knowledge in general, conventions in particular, is acknowledged by thinkers of different persuasions, even when they disagree on the nature of truth, realism, and genre. Thus, for instance, both Nelson Goodman (1983: 270) and Menachem Brinker (1983: 273) agree that belief is "an accepted version" of the world; and E.D. Hirsch (1983: 396-397) concurs with both.

24. I am aware that other thinkers distinguish between "variety" and "subjectivity" of understanding in an effort to limit radical perspectivism; see, for instance, Pepper 1942, Toulmin 1972, and Bealer 1982. But I wonder why their arguments have failed to eliminate, or at least reduce, their differences with relativists; or why, again, Richard Rorty and E.D. Hirsch find it possible to disagree about the "question of objectivity," which became the theme of a conference at the University of Virginia in April, 1984.

25. Habermas (1968 and 1971) also offers vigorous neo-Marxist critiques of knowledge and society. Burke (1945) preceded both Foucault and Habermas in this large political and logological enterprise.

26. "If social circumstances ... contradict too powerfully the [Romantic] world view of literature, then the Imaginary Library, first its enabling beliefs and eventually its institutional manifestations, can no longer exist," remarks Alvin B. Kernan (1982: 166).

27. Though "everything is ideological," as we nowadays like to say, we need still to distinguish between ideologies — fascism, feminism, monetarism, vegetarianism, etc. — between their overt claims, their hidden exactions. Even postmodernism, as a political ideology, requires discriminations. Lyotard, for instance, believes that "the postmodern condition is a stranger to disenchantment as to the blind positivity of delegitimation" (trans. from Lyotard 1979: 8); while Hal Foster claims a "postmodernism of resistance," a "counter-practice not only to the official culture of modernism but also to the 'false normativity' of a reactionary postmodernism" (1983: xii). Interestingly enough, French thinkers of the Left — Foucault, Lyotard, Deleuze, Baudrillard — seem more subtle in their ideas of "resistance" than their American counterparts. This is curious, perhaps paradoxical, since the procedures of "mass", "consumer," or "postindustrial" society are more advanced in America than in France. But see also, as a counterstatement, Edward Said's critique of Foucault (Said 1982).

28. In our therapeutic culture, the language of politics and the discourse of desire constantly seek one another, as if the utopian marriage of Marx and Freud could find consummation, at last, in our words. Hence the political use of such erotic or analytic concepts as "libidinal economy" (Lyotard 1974), "seduction" (Baudrillard 1979), "delirium" or "abjection" (Kristeva 1982a), "anti-Oedipus" (Deleuze and Guattari 1977), and "the political unconscious" (Jameson 1981). See also Hassan 1983.

29. A few sentences in the paragraph which this sentence concludes have appeared in Hassan 1980b.

30. In America, the work of Leo Bersani has addressed such questions as: "Can a psychology of fragmentary and *dis*continuous desires be reinstated? What are the strategies by which the self might be once again theatricalized? How might desire recover its original capacity for projecting nonstructurable *scenes*?" And it answers them by suggesting that *the* "desir-

ing self might even disappear as we learn to multiply our discontinuous and partial desir-
ing selves" in language (Bersani 1976: 6-7).

31. William James (1956: 30) once more: "No one of us ought to issue vetoes to the other,
nor should we bandy words of abuse. We ought, on the contrary, delicately and profoundly to respect one another's mental freedom: then only shall we bring about the intellectual republic; then only shall we have that spirit of inner tolerance without which all
our outer tolerance is soulless, and which is empiricism's glory; then only shall we live and
let live, in speculative as well as in practical things." How far, beyond this, does any postmodern pluralist go?

REFERENCES

Bakhtin, M.M. 1968. *Rabelais and His World*, trans. Helena Iswolsky.
Cambridge, Ma.: MIT Press.
-----. 1981. *The Dialogic Imagination*, ed. Michael Holquist, trans. Caryl
Emerson and Michael Holquist. University of Texas Press Slavic Series,
no. 1. Austin: University of Texas Press.
Barthes, Roland. 1975. *The Pleasure of the Text*, trans. Richard Miller.
New York: Hill and Wang. Translation of *Le Plaisir du texte*, 1973.
-----. 1977. *Fragments d'un discours amoureux*. Collection Tel Quel. Paris:
Seuil.
-----. 1978. *Leçon*. Paris: Seuil.
Baudrillard, Jean. 1979. *De la séduction*. Paris: Galilée.
-----. 1983a. "The Ecstacy of Communication," in Foster 1983: 126-134.
-----. 1983b. "What Are You Doing After the Orgy?" *Artforum* (October):
42-46.
Bealer, George. 1982. *Quality and Concept*. Oxford: Clarendon Press.
Bell, Daniel. 1976. *The Cultural Contradictions of Capitalism*. New York:
Basic Books.
Bersani, Leo. 1976. *A Future for Astyanax: Character and Desire in Litera-
ture*. Boston: Little, Brown and Co.
Bleich, David. 1983. "Literary Theory in the University: A Survey," *New
Literary History* 14: 411-413.
Booth, Wayne C. 1979. *Critical Understanding: The Powers and Limits of
Pluralism*. Chicago: University of Chicago Press.
-----. 1983. "The Empire of Irony," *Georgia Review* 37: 719-737.
Brinker, Menachem. 1983. "On Realism's Relativism: A Reply to Nelson
Goodman," *New Literary History* 14: 273-276.
Burke, Kenneth. 1945. *A Grammar of Motives*. New York: Prentice Hall.

Calinescu, Matei. 1983. "From the One to the Many: Pluralism in Today's Thought," in Hassan and Hassan 1983: 263-288.

Caramello, Charles. 1983. *Silverless Mirrors: Book, Self and Post-Modern American Fiction.* Tallahassee: University Presses of Florida.

Cohen, Ralph. 1975. "Literary Theory as Genre," *Centrum* 3, no. 1: 45-64.

-----. 1983. "A Propaedeutic for Literary Change," *Critical Exchange* 13: 1-17.

Culler, Jonathan. 1981. "Convention and Meaning: Derrida and Austin," *New Literary History* 13: 15-30.

Deleuze, Gilles and Félix Guattari. 1977. *The Anti-Oedipus: Capitalism and Schizophrenia.* New York: Viking Press. Translation of *L'Anti-Oedipe,* 1972.

De Man, Paul. 1971. *Blindness and Insight: Essays in the Rhetoric of Contemporary Criticism.* New York: Oxford University Press.

Derrida, Jacques. 1980. "La Loi du genre / The Law of Genre," *Glyph* 7: 176-201/202-232.

Dreyfus, Hubert L. and Paul Rabinow, eds. 1982. *Michel Foucault: Beyond Structuralism and Hermeneutics.* With an Afterword and an Interview with Michel Foucault. Chicago: University of Chicago Press.

Durand, Régis. 1983. "Theatre / SIGNS / Performance," in Hassan and Hassan 1983: 211-224.

Emerson, Ralph Waldo. 1912. *Journals, 1803-1882,* eds. Edward Waldo Emerson and Waldo Emerson Forbes, vol. VIII: 1849-1855. Boston and New York: Houghton Mifflin.

Fiedler, Leslie and Houston A. Baker, Jr., eds. 1979. *English Literature: Opening Up the Canon.* Selected Papers from the English Institute, n.s. 4. Baltimore: Johns Hopkins University Press, 1981.

Foster, Hal, ed. 1983. *The Anti-Aesthetic: Essays on Postmodern Culture.* Port Townsend, Wash.: Bay Press.

Foucault, Michel. 1977. *Language, Counter-Memory, Practice: Selected Essays and Interviews,* ed. Donald F. Bouchard, trans. Donald F. Bouchard and Sherry Simon. Ithaca, N.Y.: Cornell University Press.

Gallie, W.B. 1968. *Philosophy and the Historical Understanding.* New York: Schocken Books.

Garvin, Harry R., ed. 1980. *Bucknell Review: Romanticism, Modernism, Postmodernism.* Lewisbury, Pa.: Bucknell University Press.

Gleick, James. 1983. "Exploring the Labyrinth of the Mind," *The New York Times Magazine,* August 21: 23-100.

Goodman, Nelson. 1978. *Ways of Worldmaking*. Harvester Studies in Philosophy 5. Hassocks: Harvester Press.

-----. 1983. "Realism, Relativism, and Reality," *New Literary History* 14: 269-272.

Graff, Gerald. 1983. "The Pseudo-Politics of Interpretation," *Critical Inquiry* 9: 597-610.

Habermas, Jürgen. 1968. *Technik und Wissenschaft als "Ideologie."* Frankfurt: Suhrkamp.

-----. 1971. *Knowledge and Human Interests*, trans. Jeremy J. Shapiro. Boston: Beacon Press.

-----. 1981. "Modernity versus Postmodernity," *New German Critique* 22: 3-14. Reprinted in Foster 1983: 3-15.

Hartman, Geoffrey. 1983. "The New Wilderness: Critics as Connoisseurs of Chaos," in Hassan and Hassan 1983: 87-110.

Hassan, Ihab, ed. 1971b. *New Essays on the Humanities in Revolution*. Middletown, Conn.: Wesleyan University Press.

-----. 1975. *Paracriticisms: Seven Speculations of the Times*. Urbana: University of Illinois Press.

-----. 1980a. *The Right Promethean Fire: Imagination, Science, and Cultural Change*. Urbana: University of Illinois Press.

-----. 1980b. "Parabiography: The Varieties of Critical Experience," *Georgia Review* 34: 593-612.

-----. 1982. *The Dismemberment of Orpheus: Toward a Postmodern Literature*. 2nd ed. Madison: University of Wisconsin Press. First ed. 1971.

-----. 1983. "Desire and Dissent in the Postmodern Age," *Kenyon Review*, n.s. 5, no. 1: 1-18.

Hassan, Ihab and Sally Hassan, eds. 1983. *Innovation/Renovation: New Perspectives on the Humanities*. Madison: University of Wisconsin Press.

Hernadi, Paul. 1972. *Beyond Genre: New Directions in Literary Classification*. Ithaca, N.Y.: Cornell University Press.

-----. 1978. *What is Literature?* Bloomington: Indiana University Press.

Hirsch, E.D. 1983. "Beyond Convention?" *New Literary History* 14: 389-397.

James, William. 1955. *Pragmatism... together with Four Related Essays Selected from The Meaning of Truth*. New York: Longmans.

-----. 1956. *The Will to Believe and Other Essays in Popular Philosophy*. New York: Dover Publications.

Jameson, Fredric. 1981. *The Political Unconscious: Narrative as a Socially*

Symbolic Act. London: Methuen.

-----. 1983. "Postmodernism and Consumer Society," in Foster 1983: 111-126.

Kernan, Alvin B. 1982. *The Imaginary Library: An Essay on Literature and Society*. Princeton, N.J.: Princeton University Press.

Knapp, Steven and Walter Benn Michaels. 1982. "Against Theory," *Critical Inquiry* 8: 723-742.

-----. 1983. "A Reply to our Critics," *Critical Inquiry* 9: 790-800.

Kristeva, Julia. 1980. "Postmodernism?" in Garvin 1980: 136-141.

-----. 1982a. *Powers of Horror: An Essay on Abjection*. New York: Columbia University Press.

-----. 1982b. "Psychoanalysis and the Polis," trans. by Margaret Waller, *Critical Inquiry* 9: 77-92.

Kuhn, Thomas S. 1970. *The Structure of Scientific Revolutions*. 2nd ed. Chicago: University of Chicago Press.

Lasch, Christopher. 1978. *The Culture of Narcissism: American Life in an Age of Diminishing Expectations*. New York: Norton.

Lyotard, Jean-François. 1974. *Economie libidinale*. Paris: Minuit.

-----. 1979. *La Condition postmoderne: Rapport sur le savoir*. Paris: Minuit.

-----. 1983. "Answering the Question: What Is Postmodernism?" in Hassan and Hassan 1983: 329-341.

Morson, Gary Saul. 1981. *The Boundaries of Genre: Dostoyevsky's "Diary of a Writer" and the Traditions of Literary Utopia*. Austin: University of Texas Press.

Nietzsche, Friedrich. 1967. *The Will to Power*, ed. Walter Kaufmann, trans. Walter Kaufmann and R.J. Hollingdale. London: Weidenfeld and Nicolson.

Ortega y Gasset, José. 1968. *The Dehumanization of Art and Other Essays on Art, Culture, and Literature*, trans. Helene Weyl. Princeton, N.J.: Princeton University Press.

Paz, Octavio. 1974. *Children of the Mire: Modern Poetry from Romanticism to the Avantgarde*. Cambridge: Harvard University Press.

Pepper, Stephen C. 1942. *World Hypotheses: A Study in Evidence*. Berkeley and Los Angeles: University of California Press.

Poirier, Richard. 1971. *The Performing Self: Compositions and Decompositions in the Languages of Contemporary Life*. London: Oxford University Press.

Portoghesi, Paolo. 1982. *After Modern Architecture*, trans. Meg Shore.

New York: Rizzoli.

Robbe-Grillet, Alain. 1965. *For a New Novel*, trans. Richard Howard. New York: Grove Press. Translation of *Pour un nouveau roman* (1963).

Said, Edward W. 1982. "Travelling Theory," *Raritan* 1: 41-67.

-----. 1983. *The World, the Text, and the Critic*. Cambridge: Harvard University Press.

Schechner, Richard. 1983. "News, Sex, and Performance Theory," in Hassan and Hassan 1983: 189-210.

Sontag, Susan. 1966. *Against Interpretation and Other Essays*. New York: Delta.

Stout, Jeffrey. 1982. "What Is the Meaning of a Text?" *New Literary History* 14: 1-12.

Sypher, Wylie. 1962. *Loss of Self in Modern Literature and Art*. New York: Random House.

Toulmin, Stephen Edelton. 1972. *Human Understanding*, I: *The Collective Use and Evolution of Concepts*. Princeton, N.J.: Princeton University Press.

Turner, Victor. 1974. *Dramas, Fields, and Metaphors: Symbolic Action in Human Society*. Ithaca, N.Y.: Cornell University Press.

White, Hayden. 1982. "The Politics of Historical Interpretation: Discipline and De-Sublimation," *Critical Inquiry* 9: 124-128.

Whitehead, Alfred North. 1955. *Adventures of Ideas*. New York: Free Press.

Wilde, Alan. 1981. *Horizons of Assent: Modernism, Postmodernism, and the Ironic Imagination*. Baltimore and London: Johns Hopkins University Press.

3

Teleology in Postmodern Fiction

1. The definition of Postmodernism

Some definitions of Postmodernism seem to echo the thesis of *Der 18. Brumaire des Louis Bonaparte*, that history repeats itself as farce. The innovations of the early twentieth century, the argument goes, are employed tongue in cheek by certain contemporary writers. Their strategies imply distancing, demystification, eclecticism — the death not only of individual styles, but also of local traditions and of a sense of history — as well as a cult of pastiche, miming, deconstructive montage, grafting, superimposing one text on the other, self-reflexive or self-referential metafiction, and parody.

In many cases a sociological or ideological interpretation is attached to this description. It is assumed that the social context of Modernism was a bourgeoisie whose solid values were inimical to the anarchistic message of the avant-garde, while Postmodernism is faced with a huge mass society which "presents nothing approximating the stubborn resistance to cultural innovation" (Graff 1984: 60). Far from being elitist, postmodern culture is popular (Fiedler 1975: 157, 161), it "is closely related to the emergence of this new moment of late, consumer or multinational capitalism" (Fredric Jameson, in Foster 1985: 125), and it represents the "dissolution of art into the prevailing forms of commodity production" (Eagleton 1985: 60).

What I want to suggest is that such definitions are more problematic than they seem to be. First of all, the term "postmodern" has a clear and accepted meaning only in a few countries. If we wish to extend its use to the whole Western world, we cannot bypass a terminological problem. Postmodernism is always defined in opposition or at least in relation to something else, but it never is quite clear what that other pole exactly is. The obvious candidate would be Modernism, but it is far from self-evident what Modernism denotes. It is not too much of an exaggeration to say that unlike "the terms Gothic, Renaissance, Baroque, Mannerist, Romantic or Neo-Classical, it designates no describable object in its own right at all," because it is "a portmanteau concept" whose referent is a wide variety of very diverse aesthetic practices (Anderson 1985: 112-113). In some languages the term Modernism is hardly used at all, and in English it is either coterminous with "avant-garde," or not clearly distinguished from it.

My intention in this paper is to suggest that if Postmodernism is to be accepted as a period term in the history of Western culture, its continuity with some phenomena of the early twentieth century should be taken more seriously. It is almost impossible to draw the line between this trend and its antecedents, because Postmodernism does not seem to imply more than a reorganization — in terms of priority — of older strategies. Such characteristics of Postmodernism signalled as the aesthetic and epistemological break with the past or the crisis of cultural authority should not be overemphasized. For one thing, it cannot be denied that the weakening of historicity and the collapse of the semi-autonomy of the cultural sphere began much earlier, with the eclecticism of the later nineteenth century and with Art Nouveau; further, it is by no means true that all the innovations of the early twentieth century have become commercialized or even assimilated by our age. Some works which are called postmodern are continuations of avant-garde experimentation and provoke resistance. It is not surprising that once a literary critic tries to put his hand on a specific structural device which supposedly characterizes Postmodernism, such as the discontinuity and fragmentation of character — the denial of an essentialist view of human nature —, he must go back to *Finnegans Wake* and *Between the Acts* (Caramello 1983: 36; Wilde 1981: 48, 87). Or, to take another important criterion given by some critics, I cannot accept the thesis that pastiche — and not parody — is characteristic of postmodern cultural production (Jameson 1984: 64), because it depends not only on the artist's intention but also on the consumer's attitude whether an imitation is ironic or not. "Le comique, la puissance du rire est dans le rieur et nullement dans l'objet du rire" (Baudelaire 1971: I, 308). It would not be easy to prove that Stravinsky's *Pulcinella* (1919) is closer to parody than some of the stories of Barthelme or the treatment of Sadean conventions in *Virginie, Her Two Lives* (1982) by John Hawkes.

The cult of pastiche has been certainly anticipated by the Neoclassicism of the years following World War I, while the extension of the concept of art is a characteristically avant-garde ambition. Paradoxically, those who emphasize the strangeness of postmodern objects reiterate an assertion made about the avant-garde at the beginning of the twentieth century, and disregard the postmodern artists' awareness that "Everything that can be said has been said many times" (Barthelme 1970: 99).

Even more objections can be raised against the notion of a break between Postmodernism and earlier artistic trends if the internal development of individual authors is brought into focus. The career of Beckett indicates that Postmodernism may be seen as having gradually evolved from the forms of the earlier twentieth century. Even more conspicuous is the organicity in Nabokov's evolution. The imitative character of *Pale Fire* (1962) owes much to native traditions of Russian narrative literature, and ironic eclecticism has been a dominant feature of Nabokov's writing from the very beginning: *Podlets* (1927) — later published in English as *An Affair of Honor* (1966) — is almost a rewritten version of Čechov's *Single Combat* (1891). It seems certain that Nabokov's influence on American writers started in the late 1950s, at a time when his earlier work — being not available in English — was virtually unknown. His inclusion in the postmodern canon suggests that some of the organic connections with an earlier period may have escaped critics who coined the term.

2.   *Causality and teleology*

To show that the existing definitions of Postmodernism are less convincing than they are assumed to be, I shall focus on one of the most widely held assumptions, the thesis that "causality is lost" in postmodern culture (Foster 1985: XIV). I shall confine my analysis to narrative fiction, which suggests that the law of causality is bound up with a sense of teleology. Or, as Nietzsche (1980: 424) said: "Der Glaube an causae fällt mit dem Glauben an τέλη."

Causality and teleology are regulating principles: "we construct these from the text and then read the text as formed by them" (Harshaw 1984: 229). As such, they seem to be essential in narrative structures. Story development, implying continuity, is almost inconceivable without these interdependent fictional constructs, they determine the perspective from which events are evaluated. Causality depends on purpose, which, in turn, implies the preservation of an individual, a community, an institution, a faith, or a culture (Nietzsche 1980: 186). In consequence, a loss of causality would mean a loss of a belief in such end-values. The thesis of the death of Christianity comes close to such a scepticism, but it seems probable that the interpretive habits of most people in the Western world are still under the influence of some more or less laicized form of that two-thousand-year-old tradition.

It is easy to assert that before the twentieth century the structure of most works of narrative fiction was based on some kind of teleology, whereas from the early decades of this century onwards post-Nietzschean doubt began to undermine belief in linear succession, and that this reaction transformed the textual composition of the works. The random ordering of bits of plot became especially strong in recent years, changing our reading habits and generic expectations. The truth may be far more complex. Suffice it to point out two of the reasons why the above description is not only simplistic but also a-historical. Postmodernism has had its great precursors, and Sukenick may be right to assert that "the new tradition coexisted with the old tradition from the beginning, not as the exception that proves the rule but as an alternative rule" (Sukenick 1981: 37). There may be different models of teleology, and with respect to some of these *Tristram Shandy* or *Jacques le fataliste* may be more subversive than Sukenick's *98.6* (1975).

The other factor complicating matters is the teleology of reading. I have the impression that literary scholars have not paid enough attention to the question how far the reader is responsible for interpreting a piece of narrative as a goal-directed process. Lucien Goldmann's interpretation of *La Jalousie* (1957) has been written off by Robbe-Grillet, and with good reason, for to read that novel as an illustration of reification (Ricardou and van Rossum-Guyon 1972: I, 179) is to jump to a grossly simplifying conclusion. Important as it may be to refute such reductionist distortions, it would be even more important to answer the question whether readers brought up in a Western culture with a heritage marked by Christianity and historicism can resist the temptation of reading some kind of teleology into narrative texts. If literature is an exchange, the recuperation of sense is irresistible. The point to make is not so much that postmodern art is derivative, it is rather that its consumers cannot help viewing it in relation to the past.

A good example is the history of the reception of *Naked Lunch* (1959), which some writers believe to be the work that "marks the beginning of the Postmodern era" (Federman 1984: 5). Twenty-five years ago it seemed to be chaotic to many readers. Their impression may have been influenced by the narrator's own words: "There is only one thing a writer can write about: *what is in front of his senses at the moment of writing....* I am a recording instrument.... I do not presume to impose 'story', 'plot', 'continuity'" (Burroughs 1959: 221). Today this book may seem to be far more teleological; it can be read as a confession, a spiritual autobiography, a negative parable about the destruction of the soul, an attack upon addiction, the loss of personal integrity, and brainwash.

Some people argue that any metaphysical interpretation of a postmodern text is invalid, because Postmodernism would be bound up with a total disbelief in ultimate goals. For Proust or Joyce, God had been replaced by art, whereas for Beckett even art lost its supreme value. Undoubtedly, numerous postmodern novels published in the United States deny any form of transcendence, from Barthelme's *The Dead Father* (1975) to Elkin's *The Living End* (1980), and a similar refusal of Christianity characterizes the *nouveau roman*, but once again I should like to caution against sweeping generalizations. The work of William H. Gass embodies a devotion to cultural traditions in general and to art in particular which is as religious as that of James had been, and the first section of Pynchon's *Gravity's Rainbow* (1973) has an inscription from Wernher von Braun about his firm "belief in the continuity of our spiritual existence after death."

The assumption that postmodern literature is conspicuously against religion becomes even more questionable if we turn to the literatures of Central Europe. *Iskola a határon* (1959) — translated into English as *School at the Frontier* (1966) — is a novel by Géza Ottlik which has exerted a decisive influence on Hungarian works written in a style strongly reminiscent of American Postmodernism. It is an ambiguous commentary upon a controversial verse of Saint Paul's *Epistle to the Romans*: "Non est volentis, neque currentis, sed miserentis Dei," an elliptic sentence which Luther interpreted as a proof of man's free will, while Calvin considered it an explicit reference to predestination. What is more, Péter Esterházy, whose eight books present a combination of narrative and stylistic features which can be regarded as characteristically postmodern, is a Roman Catholic writer, even if his God may be more hidden than that of earlier religious novelists. His *A szív segédigéi* (*The Auxiliaries of the Heart*, 1984) — the latest volume of *Bevezetés a szépirodalomba* (*An Introduction to Literature*) , a series of works exploring new possibilities of narrative — is written in the form of a prayer (for a German translation see Esterházy 1985).

With all these reservations made, it is probably easier to understand why I am rather unwilling to abide the assumption that the loss of teleology is a distinguishing feature of postmodern fiction. Instead of subscribing such a sweeping generalization, my aim is rather a modest analysis of the strategies used by postmodern writers to undermine traditional forms of teleology and to suspend meaning by frustrating our reading habits and assumptions about intelligibility, thus blocking our regular interpretive moves. To be sure, it is a truism that the postmodern strategies of disrupting narrative make it difficult to piece together a story, to decide what "actually" happens and what is memory, dream, hallucination, or simply part of the narrative act, but it is probably less often realized that all these strategies are successful only if they both activate and disrupt the reader's sense of teleology.

Far from pretending to give a full classification, my intention is to focus on three types of narrative strategy: circularity, the open ending, and aleatory arrangement.

3. *Circularity*

The first seems to be the simplest, but also the most radical of these methods. Some believe that *Finnegans Wake* has still not been surpassed in certain respects by later experimentation, and this claim is supported by the fact that Joyce aimed to invalidate one of the most universal laws, the teleology of reading. A less well-known precursor is *Le Chiendent* (1933), the first novel of Queneau. Without exaggeration, it could be safely maintained that this book is a *nouveau roman avant la lettre*. *Le père Taupe*, an extremely poor dealer in second-hand goods is unwilling to sell a door. Madame Cloche, *la sage-femme*, has the idea that *le père Taupe* is an avaricious millionaire whose treasure is hidden behind the door. She makes a young and pretty waitress marry the old beggar to get hold of his money. Several people are told about the secret and they all want to have the treasure. A war starts. After the death of *le père* it becomes evident that nothing is hidden behind the door, but the war lasts several decades. One of the very few survivors suggests that everybody should go home and start his life again, but another person reminds him that this would be impossible, because the survivors are no more than characters in a novel which is almost finished. The last two sentences correspond to the beginning of the book.

An analogy with a novel like *Dans le labyrinthe* (1959), written some twenty-five years later, seems to be quite obvious. In Robbe-Grillet's work the soldier has a box which seems to have some hidden meaning, in the same way as the door of *le père Taupe* takes on an almost mysterious significance in the war fought by the characters in *Le Chiendent*. The meaning — the goal towards which the whole sequence of events seems to be directed — becomes invalidated at the end of both novels.

There is no progress, only repetition. Accordingly, narrative is not teleological, but circular. Works suggesting such a conception are numerous in the last three decades — from Nabokov's *Pnin* (1957), at the end of which a character begins to tell a story related in the first chapter, to *L'Immortelle* (1963), a *ciné-roman* by Robbe-Grillet, ending with the smiling face of the woman whose death seemed to give a tragic turn to the story, or to "Menelaiad," a story by Barth included in *Lost in the Funhouse* (1968), consisting of fourteen sections half of which are variations upon the other half (and these rewritten versions are printed in reverse order).

In many postmodern works circularity is based on repetition, which is also a favorite regulating principle in recent music. As in the works of Steve Reich and others, in stories by Coover or Barth repetition makes dialectical development impossible. What we have here is not a brand-new discovery, but rather a greater emphasis on a way of organizing the material which has been somewhat neglected in the last two or three centuries. Once it has been pushed into the foreground, more and more antecedents can be discovered. Like earlier movements, Postmodernism has reinterpreted the past. Flann O'Brien's *The Third Policeman*, written in 1940, is about a circular and interminably repetitive private hell, Nabokov's *Zaščita Lužina* (1930) — later published as *The Defense* — has a hero for whom everything seems to have happened before; and one could go even further back than to Gertrude Stein, Raymond Roussel, and Borges, and point out circularity and repetitious structures in Proust. The question is not so much whether Nietzsche's idea of eternal recurrence had any influence on writers; it is more important to observe that by the end of the twentieth century there may exist readers who do not look for teleology and try to interpret works of the past in the light of certain contemporary texts. Postmodernism is also a matter of reading habits and of a conception of time, although it depends on certain structural elements whether a "postmodern reading" is possible or not.

4. *Open ending*

The teleology of narrative can be conspicuously manifest in the ending of a text; and thus an open ending seems to be an effective way of undermining teleology. Barbara Herrnstein Smith (1968) distinguishes two basic types of closure, formal and thematic, and I would suggest that a similar distinction can be made between anti-closures. Formal anti-closure is exemplified by texts which break off in the middle of a sentence, such as "Title" in Barth (1968), "Sentence" in Barthelme (1970), or "An Encounter" in Coover (1983). One could also cite Barthelme's "Views of My Father Weeping" (1970), but this is a slightly different case: the last word is "Etc.", suggesting the impossibility not only of a formal but also of a thematic closure.

Before going on to the second type, I wish to underline the limitations of formal endings. Syntactic fragmentation in itself does not necessarily indicate the absence of teleology in the world constructed by the work. Especially not if the text is of some length. Several sections, including the *finale*, break off in the middle of a sentence in *Gravity's Rainbow*, but this surface fragmentation merely conceals, and does not contradict the antisocial message formulated by Enzian near the end of the novel.

At any rate, we must be very cautious to speak of anti-closures, because to a great extent it is the reader who decides whether the last words or pages of a novel mark the end or the beginning of a process. To mention but one example, Robbe-Grillet's *L'Année dernière à Marienbad* (1961) can be interpreted in two different ways: as a story about two lovers who escape from the labyrinthine castle of M (*mari/maître?*), or as an endless repetition of the same scene, depending upon the elements you wish to underline in the closure.

There are, of course, more obvious cases. The text may end just before a climax is reached or an enigma solved. The point of Pynchon's *The Crying of Lot 49* (1966) seems to be an auction the title refers to, but the last words do not fulfill that expectation: "The auctioneer cleared his throat. Oedipa settled back, to await the crying of lot 49."

A more ambiguous case seems to be *Egy családregény vége* (*The End of a Genealogical Novel*, 1977) by Péter Nádas. The ready-made pattern of a well-known subgenre is invoked. There are two main types of the genealogical novel, and the author's choice in itself is telling: instead of the more teleological form of Mann's *Buddenbrooks, Verfall einer Familie*, the repetitive, mythic structure of Faulkner's *Absalom, Absalom!* is recalled. The hero is called Péter Simon, a name which not only refers to a disciple of Jesus but is also identical with the name of one of the hero's ancestors. How far will the fate of a young man living in Hungary, in the second half of the twentieth century, conform to the prophecy of his ancestor? That is the question raised by the novel. The ending may admit of different interpretations. The life of the earlier generations seems to have confirmed the relevance of tradition, and there are signs indicating that the hero may be one of the elect. In the last chapter, however, Péter Simon enters a chaotic world full of uncertainty. He may have lost his belief in the values inherited from the past, and this may lead to an alienation from tradition. If this is so, the novel will be read as an anti-parable suggesting the impossibility of continuing to write genealogical novels. I would even risk a more general hypothesis and assume that the reader allegorizes a tale when reading some teleology into it; thus the parable may be the archetype of narrative teleology.

Besides open closures, variant endings may also undermine teleology. An obvious example would be Fowles' *The French Lieutenant's Woman* (1969), but the overall structure of this novel is too conventional to make it more than symptomatic of the dependence of the teleology of action on the paradigmatic expectations of the reading public — symptomatic also of the aversion of the present age for Victorian endings, the "distribution at the last of prizes, pensions, husbands, wives, babies, millions, appended paragraphs, and cheerful remarks," as James scornfully wrote more than a century ago (James 1963: 52-53). Much more radical is Robbe-Grillet's *La Maison de rendez-vous* (1965), which relates thirteen versions of a murder. In this case the reader's expectations are frustrated, because the novel gives no clues as to the identity of the murderer and the victim and neither discloses what instrument has been used in the killing.

An ending can be called open if it does not gratify the reader's desire. *Kairos,* "a point in time filled with significance, charged with meaning derived from its relation to the end," as opposed to *chronos*, "passing" or "waiting time" (Kermode 1967: 46), is also a matter of convention. Gombrowicz has become a model for postmodern writers, in Central Europe at least, partly because he reversed the accepted order of *chronos* and *kairos*: in the middle of his early novel *Ferdydurke* (1937) there are two prefaces, and the book ends with the hero's marriage with a girl he does not want to have for a wife. The conventional value attached to *kairos* has been lost, as in Queneau's *Zazie dans le métro* (1959), where the heroine's lack of fulfillment is emphasized in the last words:

- Alors tu t'es bien amusée?
- Comme ça.
- T'as vu le métro?

- Non.
- Alors, qu'est-ce que t'as fait?
- J'ai vieilli. (Queneau 1959: 189)

Many of the more recent postmodern novels belong to either of these two types. Perhaps the conclusion is not too far-fetched that for postmodern writers both anticipations and closures have lost their distinctive features. "It is important to begin when everything is over," because "in eternity, beginning is consummating," as Coover writes in his metafictional story significantly called "Beginnings" (Coover 1983: 40, 51).

5. *Aleatory arrangement*

Beyond doubt, open endings mark a departure from the rules of Aristotelian poetics. An open ending resembles an anticipation, an *Auftakt*. In other words, teleology may be related to proportion and to the order of structural elements. An unexpected order may weaken teleology. Thus, teleology has questionable relevance if the narrative space is composed of parallel planes, so that different parts of the text may be read in a different order. Readers of Nabokov's *Pale Fire* can either read the verse novel first and the commentary next, or they can turn to the latter whenever they wish to consult it. Similar alternatives are proposed in *Termelési-regény* (*A Novel of Production*, 1979), Esterházy's longest book to date. This work was published with two bookmarks, one red and the other black, to encourage the reader to read the first part, a parody of a genre of Socialist Realism, simultaneously with the second part, a spiritual biography of the author. A superficial reading will disclose no connection whatsoever between the main text and the footnotes. On closer consideration, however, the latter create an alternative teleology which contradicts that of the generic parody.

Esterházy is certainly one of the major writers of Postmodernism in Central Europe and his works show the ambivalent attitude the representatives of this trend have toward teleology. He has a double allegiance, taking a passionate interest both in writing practices for their own sakes and in the achieved forms. A careful reader of his books cannot help arriving at the conclusion that form and teleology are inextricably linked. On the one hand, he shows a preference for the open, intertextual work of art, which implies an abolition of the romantic distinctions between artists and non-artists, art and life, fiction and nonfiction, novel and autobiography, and a dismissal of the teleological view of artistic creation. In the United States readers may encounter a similar attitude in the works of Raymond Federman. Some of Esterházy's works suggest that he is not keen on asking himself why he writes and how valuable the product of his activity can be for others, or whether he is moving in some direction, "developing" as an artist. The logical consequence of such premises would be that art is on one level with life in being non-intentional. On the other hand, Esterházy is also attracted by value-judgments, which — as John Cage argues — "are destructive to ... curiosity and awareness" (Kostelanetz 1970: 27).

My reference to the American composer is fully intentional, for it seems that Cage's idea of aggregates has inspired the Hungarian writer to juxtapose apparently disparate linguistic utterances and let unexpected relationships of incompatible texts emerge. The aesthetic implications of this strategy are far-reaching. Esterházy seems to endorse Cage's ideal of open form, which implies a refusal of hierarchy — possibly the basis of all teleology. Thus Cage maintains that he is "interested in any part not as a closed-in thing by itself but as a going-out one to interpenetrate with all other things, even if they are arts, too. All of these things, each one of them seen as of first importance; no one of them as more important than another" (Kostelanetz 1970: 115).

Such an artistic attitude, this awareness of the eternal present as a complexity in which man lives, is not, however, quite compatible with Esterházy's care for linearity in the history of Hungarian prose, which is a product of the evolutionary mode of thinking inherited from the eighteenth and nineteenth centuries. The ideal of the "open work," which plays a crucial role in the partly autobiographical, partly metafictional second half of *A Novel of Production*, seems to be at variance with Esterházy's concern for loyalty to what he regards as the great tradition of Hungarian prose-writing and his craving for craftsmanship, for a total control over the material, for the finely wrought work, the well-made form of the finished product. The first of these two attitudes implies a rejection of the hold of any elite, whereas the second is the manifestation of a highly elitist view of art: the writer works for a relatively small circle of connoisseurs who can identify the texts he quotes from and will understand what is written between the lines.

In *A Novel of Production* both tendencies can be felt. The names of the printers working on the book are inserted in the second part, which clearly indicates the author's belief in the role of indeterminacy and even chance in creation. Besides, this second part is also an attempt to abolish the distinction between life and art. Yet some of the metalinguistic passages are outspokenly historical, even academic: the underlying hypothesis is that Hungarian fiction has too long been submissive to the restrictions of nineteenth-century Realism, and this argument is put forward with the aim of asserting the necessity of writing fiction which is consistent with what the author regards as contemporary values.

These two tendencies are even more apparent in Esterházy's more recent work. The idea of *An Introduction to Literature* is at variance with any possible interpretation of teleology. The five volumes published so far have very little in common; they are not governed by comparable regularities. The incessant flow of words characterizing *Függő* (*Dependent*, 1981) does not seem to be related to the extremely economical, decidedly artificial syntax of *Fuharosok* (*Carters*, 1983), and even the two parts of *Ki szavatol a lady biztonságáért?* (*Who Will Guarantee the Lady's Security?*, 1982) are poles apart: the metafictional strategies used in "Ágnes" (Esterházy 1982) are prosaic if compared to the visionary, Surrealist style of "Daisy." *Kis magyar pornográfia* (*A Handbook of Hungarian Pornography*, 1984) comes very close to exclusively representing the anarchistic side of his art, being a collection of fragments, some of them dirty or political jokes, whereas *The Auxiliaries of the Heart* is a deeply religious and even sublime testimony to the memory of the author's mother. In sum, ontologically different possible worlds are joined together with the apparent aim of making the reader responsible for discovering links between apparently disjointed parts. To make the recuperation of sense difficult, the hermeneutic code — another of the preconditions of teleology — is neglected. The narrative strategies are employed rather to reveal a state of affairs than to answer questions. A sign of the relative absence of the hermeneutic code is the almost total absence of narrative suspense. Esterházy is not fascinated by the technique of detective stories, and does not count upon the reader's ignorance of a given move. Pushing psychological motivation into the background, he generates a polysemy which admits of a wide range of interpretations. In order to change reading habits, he rejects a number of conventions of narrative prose, among them that of the narrator as a generalizing observer — which is another means of creating the impression of teleology (Szegedy-Maszák 1984).

In short, the often quoted observation that "the old analogy between Author and God, novel and world, can no longer be employed unless deliberately as a false analogy" (Barth 1968: 125) is especially true of Esterházy's work. In general, his activity shows many important analogies with that of other Postmodern writers. The title of *Dependent*, for example, referring to both a grammatical category and the uncertainty of man's position in the world, implies a treatment of relatedness which Barthes detected in the novels of Sollers: "Les 'routes' suivies par le discours ne sont ... ni celle de la chronologie (*avant/après*), ni celle de la logique narrative (implication d'un événement par un autre): le seul régime est ici celui de la constellation" (Barthes 1979: 40). Like *Paradis* (1981), a novel published in the same year as the first volume of *An Introduction to Literature, Dependent* has neither paragraphs nor periods; it seems to be an endless flow without a real beginning or end, lacking points of expectation and fulfillment. The discontinuous and a-causal structuring of the narrative prevents any closure of the text or resolution of the plot.

The same idea of aggregates, underlying *An Introduction to Literature*, may be the structuring principle of works which sometimes are called shuffle novels. Once more, I wish to emphasize how relative the originality of postmodern innovations is in a historical perspective. Some of these works follow the pattern of the picaresque, in which certain episodes are interchangeable. A characteristic example is Federman's *Take It or Leave It* (1976), an unpaged autobiographical novel about someone born in France who escaped from a train transporting Jews to a concentration camp and later settled down in the United States. Even *The Unfortunates* (1969), a seemingly randomly assembled "novel in a box" by the ill-fated British novelist Bryan Stanley Johnson, probably the most imaginative work in the genre, does not surpass the limits of controlled aleatory. This *Ich-Erzählung* relates the story of a football reporter sent to a city where he remembers a close friend who had studied there and had become a scientist of genius but died as a young man, pointlessly, horribly, of cancer. It consists of twenty-seven sections, "Temporarily held together by a removable wrapper." Memory is a-chronological; therefore, most of the sections can be read in any order. Still, there are two exceptions: the first and the last sections are marked as such, indicating that even this highly original writer, whose ambition was to strip narrative almost completely of the traditional means of story development, could not accept uncontrolled aleatory, although he considered any form of teleology arbitrary, arguing that "one should act on one's own interests AS IF it were all chaos — that is, one will come to less harm, suffer less disappointment, if nothing is to be EXPECTED from such a chaotic state" (Johnson 1970).

Like circularity and open ending, the shuffle novel must also be seen as a product of historical evolution. In this case montage is the obvious ante-cedent, and *Collages* (1964) by Anaïs Nin marks the transition between ear-lier types of discontinuity and postmodern assemblage. Since the unnum-bered sections of this novel do not constitute a plot, they suggest alternative orders of reading, reminding us that the arrangement of shuffle novels is based upon the old idea that the reader cannot be forced to read the differ-ent parts of a text in the order in which they have been printed. As always, the present reinterprets the past; postmodern works may encourage us to change our reading habits.

6.   *Negative teleology and the discontinuity of narrative structures*

Besides circular forms, open endings, and the aleatory arrangement of the different parts, there are certainly other ways of undermining narrative teleology. Let it suffice to mention but three other possibilities. The first is the false teleology of ironic works. This type is so obviously related to the concept of anti-closure that sometimes the difference is only that the ironic narrator signals at an early stage of the action that the reader's desire will not be gratified at the end. *Der Mann ohne Eigenschaften* may be regarded as the most influential of the early manifestations of such a negative teleol-ogy. The first part ends with a letter addressed to Ulrich by his father which informs the hero of the decision made in Vienna "das ganze Jahr 1918 zu einem Jubiläumsjahr unseres Friedenskaisers auszugestalten" (Musil 1972: 79). The reader knows the futility of this decision, and so the *Kaiser*'s jubilee becomes a symbol of aimlessness. Negative or ironic teleology occurs very frequently in postmodern fiction, from Bohumil Hrabal's col-lection *Kluby poezie* (1981), in which the hero's job is to destroy the books he respects, to *The Command* (1981) by Péter Hajnóczy, a novella about a soldier waiting for a command that will never be given. I cannot help observing how characteristic this type seems to be of literatures in Central Europe. A historical explanation for this preference may be that in the twentieth century political life has been more discontinuous in this region than in most other parts of the world, and that the unexpected turns have created an atmosphere of unfulfilled promise. An outstanding artistic expression of this sense of history is *Eleslövészet* (*Shooting with Live Ammunition*, 1981), the first novel of Lajos Grendel, a writer whose ethnic background is partly German, partly Slovak and Hungarian, so that he is exceptionally well qualified to judge the fate of Cental Europe. History has a double face in this novel: on the one hand it is a series of changeless states and abrupt, violent, and inorganic ruptures, on the other hand it is marked by eternal recurrence: the roles and the basic situation, "the scenes of suffering, murder, persecution, and people reporting each other to the authorities are the same..., only the place of churches on fire may vary" (Grendel 1981: 55).

Grendel's second novel, *Galeri* (*Gallery*, 1982) shows how closely linked two other anti-teleological devices are: discontinuity of character and of point of view. Once more, it is worth remembering that these structural principles are not a postmodern invention. The literary double, or *Doppelgänger*, is a favorite device of Romanticism and even of Jacobean drama. Complexity of voice and focalization makes teleology at least ambiguous in, for instance, *Wuthering Heights*, and the indeterminate identity of character creates the impression that the present is no more than a repetition of the past in Gyula Krúdy's *Napraforgó* (*Sunflower*, 1918), in Faulkner's *Absalom, Absalom!*, or in *Master i Margarita*, the posthumously published novel of Michail Bulgakov.

Postmodern writers, however, have stretched the experiment. The eleven-year-old heroine of Hawkes' *Virginie* has two lives. In 1740 she is a servant; in 1945 the sister of a Parisian taxi driver. The story is told in a journal, and the eighteenth-century entries alternate with the twentieth-century ones, emphasizing their close resemblance. Thus we have two versions of a young girl's initiation to love, organized by a man. More interesting is the relation of the duke d'Auge to Cidrolin in Queneau's *Les Fleurs bleues* (1965). Historical anecdotes alternate with sections about the present age. First the duke lives in 1264, then in 1439, in 1614, and in 1789, until in 1964 he meets Cidrolin. Until their final encounter each chapter ends with either of the heroes falling asleep, but the closure makes it impossible for the reader to decide whether it is the duke who has had dreams about Cidrolin or vice versa.

Like *La Maison de rendez-vous* or Robbe-Grillet's film *La belle Captive* (1983), this novel clearly shows that the notion of the integrity of character is related to a teleological ordering of narrative time. In any case, the discontinuity of time, space, speech act, point of view, and character, which creates the impression that the narrative leads nowhere, is not only a dominant feature of the fiction of Borges, Queneau, Beckett, Robbe-Grillet, Claude Ollier, and Robert Pinget, but also a strategy with a long ancestry.

Our brief analysis of structural principles in narrative seems to verify our hypothesis that the subversion of teleology is not a distinguishing feature of postmodern fiction. It cannot be doubted, however, that postmodern fiction tends to relegate teleology to a lower rank than most literary trends of the past. A final question remains to be asked about the cause of this tendency.

I can think of two main reasons. One is the revaluation of personality and psyche, leading to a reinterpretation of human motives and of causality in general. No less fundamental seems to be the reaction against evolutionism started by Nietzsche. Theoreticians of Postmodernism often refer to *Der Wille zur Macht* as the most important work which foreshadows the antihistorical attitude underlying the activity of the representatives of this movement, and with good reason.

Weltgeschichte is but theodicy disguised; so the loss of religious faith may imply a loss of belief in progress. Still, it remains to be seen how far man can do without teleology. That seems to be the fundamental dilemma of writers of postmodern fiction.

REFERENCE

Anderson, Perry. 1985. "Capitalism, Modernism and Postmodernism," *New Left Review* 152: 60-73.

Barth, John. 1968. *Lost in the Funhouse*. New York: Bantam Books, 1969.

Barthelme, Donald. 1970. *City Life*. New York: Farrar, Straus and Giroux.

Barthes, Roland. 1979. *Sollers écrivain*. Paris: Seuil.

Baudelaire, Charles. 1971. *Ecrits sur l'art*. Paris: Livre de poche.

Burroughs, William S. 1959. *Naked Lunch*. New York: Grove Press, 1982.

Caramello, Charles. 1983. *Silverless Mirrors: Book, Self and Postmodern American Fiction*. Tallahassee: University Presses of Florida.

Coover, Robert. 1983. *In Bed One Night and Other Brief Encounters*. Providence, R.I.: Burning Deck.

Eagleton, Terry. 1985. "Capitalism, Modernism and Postmodernism," *New Left Review* 144: 96-113.

Esterházy, Péter. 1982. *Agnes*. Berlin: Literarisches Colloquium.

-----. 1985. *Die Hilfsverben des Herzens*. Salzburg: Residenz Verlag.

Federman, Raymond, ed. 1981. *Surfiction: Fiction Now... and Tomorrow*. 2nd. ed. Chicago: Swallow Press. First edition 1975.

-----. 1984. "Fiction in America Today or The Unreality of Reality," *Indian*

Journal of American Studies 14: 5-16.

Fiedler, Leslie A. 1975. "Cross the Border — Close that Gap: Post-Modernism," in Pütz and Freese 1984: 151-166.

Foster, Hal, ed. 1985. *Postmodern Culture*. London and Sydney: Pluto.

Graff, Gerald. 1984. "Babbitt at the Abyss: The Social Context of Postmodern Fiction," in Pütz and Freese 1984: 58-82.

Grendel, Lajos. 1981. *Eleslövészet: Nem/zetiségi/antiregény*. Bratislava: Madách.

Harshaw [Hrushovski], Benjamin. 1984. "Fictionality and Fields of Reference: Remarks on a Theoretical Framework," *Poetics Today* 5: 227-251.

James, Henry. 1963. *Selected Literary Criticism*. London: Heinemann.

Jameson, Fredric. 1984. "Postmodernism, or the Cultural Logic of Late Capitalism," *New Left Review* 146: 53-92.

Johnson, B.S. 1970. Letter to the author, 2 February 1970 (unpublished).

Kermode, Frank. 1967. *The Sense of an Ending: Studies in the Theory of Fiction*. New York: Oxford University Press.

Kostelanetz, Richard. 1970. *John Cage*. New York and Washington: Praeger.

Musil, Robert. 1972. *Der Mann ohne Eigenschaften*. Reinbek bei Hamburg: Rowohlt.

Nietzsche, Friedrich. 1980. *Der Wille zur Macht: Versuch einer Umwertung aller Werte*. Stuttgart: Alfred Kröner.

Ottlik, Géza. 1966. *School at the Frontier*. New York: Harcourt, Brace and World.

Pütz, Manfred and Peter Freese, ed. 1984. *Postmodernism in American Literature*. Darmstadt: Thesen.

Queneau, Raymond. 1959. *Zazie dans le métro*. Paris: Gallimard.

Ricardou, Jean and Françoise van Rossum-Guyon, eds. 1972. *Nouveau roman: hier, aujourd'hui*. 2 vols. Paris: Union Générale d'Éditions.

Smith, Barbara Herrnstein. 1968. *Poetic Closure: A Study of How Poems End*. Chicago and London: University of Chicago Press.

Sukenick, Ronald. 1981. "The New Tradition in Fiction," in Federman 1981: 34-45.

Szegedy-Maszák, Mihály. 1984. "Postmodernism in Hungarian Literature," *Zeitschrift für Kulturaustausch* 34: 150-156.

Wilde, Alan. 1981. *Horizons of Assent: Modernism, Postmodernism and the Ironic Imagination*. Baltimore and London: Johns Hopkins University Press.

4

Allegory, Hermeneutics, and Postmodernism

Mihai Spariosu

Preliminary Historical and Theoretical Considerations

This paper will examine the relationship between allegory and hermeneutics and its metamorphosis in postmodernism. According to Webster's *New World Dictionary*, "allegory" is (1) "a story in which people, things, and happenings have another meaning, as in a fable or parable: allegories are used for teaching and explaining; (2) the presenting of ideas by means of such stories; symbolical narration or description." A historical examination of the term, however, would show that it goes beyond these narrow literary boundaries. "Allegory" comes from the Greek *allegoria*, which meant the "description of one thing under the image of another," but came, originally, from *allos*, other, and *agourein*, to speak in the *agora*, the assembly or market place. In ancient Greece, allegory was clearly related to the birth of the science of interpretation or hermeneutics, which was in turn based upon the old science of divination, arising in the wake of the invention of writing and the birth of the text. In the text, as opposed to speech, the speaker was no longer there to clarify or stand by his meaning. The written words became ambiguous, pointing to an authority or a "signified" outside the text. The notions of truth and falsehood also gained a new usage in connection with the presence or absence of the speaking authority. The Greek word *aletheia* means unhiddenness or unveiledness, i.e., that which one arrives at through a process of interpretation. Allegory, then, came into being as the discourse of the absent authority or the other, for which it substituted. At first it was specifically used by Homer's apologists to preserve his cultural authority in the Greek *polis*: Homer had come under the attack of certain philosophers and theologians for telling "lies" or "myths" about the gods, so the allegorists claimed that his "true" meaning was hidden and had to be revealed or disclosed; in other words, that it had to be interpreted. Gradually, allegory also came to be employed by religious or mystical sects (from the Greek *mustikos*, secret, hidden), secret brotherhoods, etc., who encoded their meaning so that it would become inaccessible to those who did not have the key to it. In Antiquity, then, allegory functioned both as a rhetorical figure and as an exegetic instrument. In the Middle Ages and the Renaissance allegory preserved both its rhetorical and hermeneutical functions, being employed in reading the Bible, and then, as we can see, e.g., in Dante's famous letter to Can Grande, in reading literature. In English literature, Spenser's *Fairie Queene* is the most familiar example of Renaissance allegorical poetry, and allegory as a rhetorical figure or an interpretive device remained in common use until the end of the Neoclassical period. With the advent of Romanticism, allegory lost its cultural prestige and was replaced by symbol, a related term which was now turned into allegory's symmetrical opposite.[1] The devaluation of allegory was the direct consequence of the loss of the traditional sense of community and convention, on which both allegory and hermeneutics depend, and the establishment of such Romantic notions as individuality, originality, creative freedom, and genius. Allegory regained some of its prestige in the modernist period, when artists turned again to the traditional values of Antiquity and Classicism, even though now these values could often be expressed only in an ironic or *parodic* mode (e.g. in the works of T.S. Eliot, James Joyce, Thomas Mann). Allegory also regained its hermeneutical function in connection with the rise of semiotics, for which all literature and, by extension, all language is "allegorical," being an infinite network of deferments, displacements, and substitutions that point to and stand in for an absent, perhaps imaginary, referent or origin.[2]

The history of the use of the term shows that allegorical discourse may appear, as a rule, under two interrelated circumstances: when the wealth of experience is felt to be so overwhelming that it can only be dealt with on several levels or a multiplicity of dimensions, and this we may term the *pluralistic* use of allegory; and when what is felt as truth is, for some reason, unreachable, inaccessible or elusive. Because of its double structure of openness and closure, which necessarily implies ambiguity, allegory may also be put to what may be termed a *totalitarian* use, especially in political discourse. In the latter case, the science of interpretation or hermeneutics, which is the allegorical discourse *par excellence*, ultimately becomes "doublespeak" to borrow Orwell's phrase from *Nineteen Eighty-Four*. In a totalitarian context, then, allegory returns to its concrete etymological meaning of the discourse of the other, or what is not or cannot be spoken of in the agora or out in the open.

Allegory, Hermeneutics, and Postmodernist Literature

The main thesis of this paper is that postmodernist literature attempts to deal with a world in which all discourse has become allegorical. Postmodernist literary texts will take an anti-allegorical stand, either by building and then destroying allegorical structures within their own fictional framework, or by postulating a world of simulacra without depth, center, or meaning, where events are governed not by necessity or causation, but by pure chance. At the same time, these texts turn against interpretation, denying either its possibility or its legitimacy.[3] By pointing to the arbitrary and authoritarian nature of interpretation and truth, postmodernist literature also points to the functional or performative character of these categories, revealing their origin in an archaic, power-oriented, pre-allegorical mentality which had, at one time, been naked and unashamed. In what follows I shall explore this thesis in connection with *Under the Volcano*, *Pale Fire*, and *Nineteen Eighty-Four* — three literary works that debate what I consider postmodernist issues.

Lowry's *Under the Volcano* has been seen by critics as a book packed with allegory and symbolism and its first readers have compared it (unfavorably) with the work of James Joyce and T.S. Eliot. Lowry himself encouraged this kind of reading, as his Letter to Jonathan Cape shows (Lowry 1965). One certainly cannot deny the existence of an intricate allegorical framework in the novel, but the question to be asked is whether Lowry writes another version of *The Waste Land* or *Ulysses*, or puts his allegorical framework to uses that are significantly different from those of Eliot or Joyce. And, if the latter is the case, what does the novelty of his approach to allegory consist in? We may find an answer to both questions, if we examine the way Lowry handles his main character (and *alter ego*), the Consul.

In his well-known essay, "*Coriolanus* — Or the Delights of Faction," Kenneth Burke shows how the events and the personae in Shakespeare's play, including the protagonist, are constructed in such a way that they not only conspire to bring about Coriolanus' victimization but also make this victimization acceptable and even aesthetically pleasurable. The same thing can be said about *Under the Volcano* — there are several key references in the book to *Coriolanus* and to other Elizabethan plays — but with a crucial difference: in *Coriolanus*, as in many Greek and Elizabethan tragedies, the victim or the scapegoat does not deliberately promote his own sacrifice, whereas in Lowry's novel he brings about his own victimization. In this respect, the tragic pattern in *Under the Volcano* is Christian rather than Greek, if we see the Passion as a tragedy in which Christ promotes his own crucifixion. The Consul is not only the protagonist but also, in more than one sense, the "maker" of his own tragedy.

The Consul sees himself not only as Christ but also as Adam, Faust, William Blackstone, and the black magician of the Cabala. From his letter of Chapter I we learn that he was at one time writing a book on the Cabala which he never finished. In Chapter IV, Hugh and Yvonne also refer to this unfinished project:

> "Geoffrey said something this morning about going on with his book — for the life of me I don't know whether he's still writing one or not, he's never done any work on it since I have known him, and he's never let me see scarcely any of it, still, he keeps all those reference books with him —"
> "Yes," Hugh said, "how much does he really know about all this alchemy and Cabala business? How much does it mean to him?"
> "That's just what I was going to ask you. I've never been able to find out —" (Lowry 1947:118).

The thought suggests itself that the Consul has stopped writing his book and has started enacting it instead. If we accept this premise, then the Cabalistic themes in the *Volcano* assume an important function: they are a convenient framework within which the Consul may act out his tragedy. He fictionalizes his entire life through the Cabala; he casts himself in the role of a white magician who, through the abuse of his powers, has turned into a black one, and then proceeds to construe in this light all the events that will subsequently lead to his death. The Cabalistic correspondences provide the Consul with a unifying *poetic* principle which ties together the threads of his plot. An elaborate system of correspondences such as the Cabala satisfies not only man's mystical but also his aesthetic impulse, as Lowry himself points out in his Letter to Jonathan Cape. It has, moreover, the advantage of being able to accommodate within itself all the other fictional material with which the Consul builds his tragedy: Adam's fall, the damnation of Faust, and the Passion itself.

If the Consul enacts his book, he leaves the task of writing it to someone else. In his Letter to Cape, Lowry suggests that his novel can be read, beginning with Chapter II, as Laruelle's film script. After he points out the multiple functions of the Ferris wheel at the end of Chapter I, and at the beginning of the tragedy, he adds: "or superficially it [the wheel] can be seen simply in an obvious movie sense, as the wheel of time whirling back-wards until we have reached the year before and Chapter II and in this sense, if we like, we can look at the rest of the book through Laruelle's eyes, as if it were his creation" (Lowry 1965:71). Laruelle can be seen, apart from his role as Judas, as a sort of evangelist, an eyewitness of the Passion, whose mission is to record the event for posterity. In more than one sense the Consul writes his "tragedy" through him. On the Day of the Dead Laruelle seems possessed by the spirit of the Consul whom he sees everywhere. He has not only the Consul's English manner and way of dres-sing, but also his habit of moving through a "forest of symbols." In Chapter I the film director and producer is even tempted to start re-enacting the Consul's tragedy, or at least its first step, by ordering tequila. However, he overcomes this temptation, burns the Consul's compelling Cabalistic letter, and thus he can start writing the story. But Laruelle, if he is indeed the "au-thor," has designed the reading process itself in such a way that it invites eternal return. At the "end" of the narrative the reader is compelled to go back to the first chapter which starts "making sense" to him only after hav-ing read the rest of the book; and thus he is caught in the reading process again.

By providing an epilogue, "Laruelle" presumably seeks not only to break off this infernal, circular reading pattern, but also to separate himself from the Consul. Thus Lowry himself becomes twice removed from his fic-tional *alter ego*: in this context it is rather ironical that critics should gener-ally have seen the Consul as a glorified, romantic version of his creator, and the symbolic frameworks of the narrative as belonging to Lowry, rather than to his fictional doubles. Even as he devises a complicated symbol-mak-ing machine in the *Volcano*, Lowry frustrates the symbol-happy critic by handing it over to his characters. So, it is the Consul, and not Lowry, who is a poor master of his craft, not unlike Goethe's apprentice-sorcerer, unable to control this formidable *moulin-à-symboles* gone mad. Just before his death, at the height of his delirium, the Consul literally sputters out the dismantled pieces of his "tragedy" which had, for him, lost all sense and coherence:

> The Consul didn't know what he was saying: "Only the poor, only through
> God, only the people you wipe your feet on, the poor in spirit, old men
> carrying their fathers and philosophers weeping in the dust, America
> perhaps, Don Quijote —" he was still brandishing the sword. . . . "if you'd
> only stop interfering, stop walking in your sleep, stop sleeping with my
> wife, only the beggars and the accursed"   (Lowry 1947:372).

The Consul's "tragedy" can make sense only *outside* the fictional frame of
the story, hence the epilogue which functions as a sort of regenerator of
meaning, in contrast to the Consul's de-allegorized, delirious world:

LE GUSTA ESTE JARDIN

QUE ES SUYO ?

EVITE QUE SUS HIJOS LO DESTRUYAN!

(Do you enjoy this garden which is yours?

Don't let your children destroy it!)

The garden here may again be read allegorically as the garden of Eden
or as a symbol of human constructive effort. But, assuming that Laruelle is
the "author" of this epilogue, its message remains highly inconclusive, if
not ironical: he is about to leave the desolate, delapidated garden — the
scene of the Consul's tragedy — for an even more troubled paradise,
Europe of 1939, poised on the brink of World War II. And as Laruelle himself observes in Chapter I, no matter what the outcome of this war would
be, "one's own battle would go on," in other words, nothing will change.
For Lowry, then, allegory in the sense of a story "used for teaching and
explaining" seems no longer possible.

Although like Joyce and other modernist writers, Lowry playfully
creates elaborate allegorical systems, unlike these writers, he hands them
over to his characters who destroy them even as they destroy themselves; in
other words, in Lowry's literary universe these allegorical systems become
"self-consuming artifacts," not unlike García Márquez's world of Macondo.
One may add that for Lowry himself, just as for the Consul, the hermeneutic circle will become a vicious one, with all meaning lost and turned against
itself, its only logic, that of suicide.

Another example of a playful allegorical work which consumes itself is
Nabokov's *Pale Fire*. As in the case of *Under the Volcano*, the novel's fictional world is handed over to the main character, this time not an
alcoholic, guilt-ridden, British Consul, but an eccentric, if not insane,
exiled king-scholar who edits and annotates a long poem, entitled "Pale
Fire." This poem is the unfinished labor of an American academic poet who

has inadvertently fallen victim to a murder plot designed to kill none other than his royal admirer and would be editor.

At the most obvious level, Nabokov's book is a higly sophisticated and hilarious parody of a respectable, age-old hermeneutical practice, the scholarly commentary on a literary text. Charles Xavier Kinbote, the exiled Zemblan king, befriends John Shade, his famous neighbor, hoping that the latter would transpose in verse the story of his reign over and escape from Zembla, a fabulous Northern land, not to be confused with Nova Zembla (an English corruption of Novaia Zemlya), mentioned in one of Pope's poems, as the commentator himself learnedly points out. If Kinbote had had his way, John Shade would have written the usual allegorical poem (say, a modern version of the *Fairie Queene*). Shade would have dressed in allegorical garb the king's adventures and misadventures, thus immortalizing him after the fashion of the bards of yore, without, however, betraying his disguise. Instead, the poet chooses to present a biographical event that lies much closer to his heart than the Zemblan monarch's fate: the tragic suicide of his sensitive but unattractive teenage daughter in the wake of a fruitless blind date. Faced with bitter disappointment in the aftermath of Shade's death, Kinbote decides to publish the latter's poem anyway, at the same time telling his own story in the critical footnotes. Thereby he does precisely what he says, in a note, that he has no desire of doing: "twist and batter an unambiguous *apparatus criticus* into the monstrous semblance of a novel" (Nabokov 1962:71). Although at first sight preposterous, his attitude toward the poem does not differ essentially from that of many less whimsical, but equally self-aggrandizing scholars. His foreword to the poem makes up in honesty for what it lacks in subtlety:

> To this poem we must now turn. My Foreword has been, I trust, not too skimpy. Other notes, arranged in a running commentary, will certainly satisfy the most voracious reader. Although those notes, in conformity with custom, come after the poem, the reader is advised to consult them first and then study the poem with their help, rereading them of course as he goes through its text, and perhaps, after having done with the poem, consulting them a third time so as to complete the picture. I find it wise in such cases as this to eliminate the bother of back-and-forth leafings by either cutting out and clipping together the pages with the text of the thing, or, ever more simply, purchasing two copies of the same work which can then be placed in adjacent position on a comfortable table. . . . Let me state that without my notes Shade's text has no human reality at all since the human reality of such a poem as his (being too skittish and reticent for an autobiographical work), with the omission of many pithy lines

carelessly rejected by him, has to depend entirely on the reality of its author and his surroundings, attachments and so forth, a reality that only my notes can provide. To this statement my dear poet would probably not have subscribed, but, for better or worse, it is the commentator who has the last word   (Nabokov 1962:25).

Through his parody, Nabokov exposes not only the vanity of scholars but also, more importantly, the arbitrary nature of any interpretative act. Although apparently unconnected to the poem's subject-matter, Kinbote's commentary creates an intricate "web of sense" around it. He sets up an elaborate framework of correspondences between the poem and his own life which then becomes fatefully intertwined with that of the poet. The poem, which may be described as an Augustan meditation on mortality and immortality in the manner of Pope's *Essay on Man*, gains a fresh perspective in the light of Shade's death at the hands of his own "blind date," Gradus, the regicide manqué. What starts out as sheer chance turns out to be, in Kinbote's interpretation, an intricate pattern woven by divine providence. Thus the poem can be read as a poetic allegory. Kinbote himself points to this fact, when he aptly, if rather pompously, paraphrases Shade's sybilline line, "Man's life as a commentary to an abstruse, unfinished poem" (57) by "human life is but a series of footnotes to a vast, obscure unfinished masterpiece" (214).

If life is a series of obscure, unrelated events governed by chance, the act of interpretation is an act of will through which man creates a "web of sense" or a world of illusion to interpose between himself and the abyss. Kinbote reveals a great deal of method in his madness when he muses about the interplay of chance and necessity which led to the selection of the inept Gradus as the would-be assassin of the king, and then observes: "I have staggered the notes referring to him [Gradus] in such a fashion that the first (see note to line 17 where some of his other activities are adumbrated) is the vaguest while those that follow become gradually clear as gradual Gradus approaches in space and time" (123). Kinbote, comically, if unintentionally, refers again to his own method of composition when he criticizes Shade's synchronous arrangement of themes in the poem: "the whole thing [the juxtaposition of the television series in Shade's parlor and the tragic consequences of the blind date] strikes me as too labored and long, especially since the synchronization device has been already worked to death by Flaubert and Joyce" (156). Kinbote also works this device to death, that is, the death of Shade. Throughout his commentary he does precisely what the poet wants his poem to do. When Shade finds out that his quest of eternal life was based on a misprint (mountain-fountain), he remarks:

> But all at once it dawned on me that *this*
> Was the real point, the contrapuntal theme;
> Just this: not texts, but texture; not the dream
> But topsy-turvical coincidence,
> Not flimsy nonsense, but a web of sense.
> Yes! It sufficed that I in life could find
> Some kind of link-and-bobolink, some kind
> Of correlated pattern in the game,
> Plexed artistry, and something of the same
> Pleasure in it that they who played it found (53).

"They who played [the game]" and whom the poet wants to imitate remain indefinite and presumably are the gods or our creators. Shade sees them as divine players who play a "game of worlds," and the image of the world as a divine game is old as the hills, being present in all ancient cultures, from Mesopotamia to India, to China, and to ancient Greece:

> It did not matter who they were. No sound
> No further light came from this involute
> Abode, but there they were, aloof and mute,
> Playing a game of worlds, promoting pawns
> To ivory unicorns and ebon fauns;
> Kindling a long life here, extinguishing
> A short one there; killing a Balkan king . . .
>   Coordinating these
> Events and subjects with remote events
> And vanished objects. Making ornaments
> Of accidents and possibilities (53).

Like Shade, his double, Kinbote plays a game of worlds through his commentary, weaving "some kind of correlated pattern" on the analogy of divine play. Leibniz's famous dictum, *Cum deus calculat, fit mundus*, which Heidegger translates appropriately as "Während Gott spielt, wird Welt" (Heidegger 1958:170) receives poetic expression at the end of Shade's poem:

> I feel I understand
> Existence, or at least a minute part
> Of my existence, only through my art,
> In terms of combinational delight;
> And if my private universe scans right,

So does the verse of galaxies divine
Which I suspect is an iambic line.
I'm reasonably sure that we survive
And that my darling somewhere is alive,
As I am reasonably sure that I
Shall wake at six tomorrow, on July
The twenty-second, nineteen fifty-nine,
And that the day will probably be fine;
So this alarm clock let me set myself,
Yawn, and put back Shade's 'Poems' on their shelf (54).

One may, however, point out that this eighteenth-century view of the universe as God's rational and predictable mechanical game is ironically belied by Shade's own blind date with death (he does not wake up the following morning, indeed he will never wake up again in this world). The blind, irrational and unpredictable game of chance ultimately prevails both in Shade's poem, left unfinished, and in Kinbote's commentary, which remains equally inconclusive. The game of interpretation is a game of making sense out of nonsense and in *Pale Fire* its nature is one of semblance, illusion or simulacrum. As Kinbote himself points out, Zembla is not a corruption of "Zemlya," but of "Semblerland, a land of reflections, of 'resemblers'" (208). Interpretation is a result of the arbitrary play of identity and difference. When challenged by the Oxford visitor to deny, if he can, the "astounding similarity of features" between King Charles and Kinbote, John Shade counters: "I have seen the King in newsreels, and there is no resemblance. Resemblances are shadows of differences. Different people see different similarities and similar differences" (ibid.). One may further argue, as Kinbote does, that he himself and not Gradus is the true regicide. In Zemblan "Kinbote" means a "king's destroyer": A king who "seeks his identity in the mirror of exile" cannot be called anything other than his own murderer.

The arbitrary juxtaposition of Shade's poem and Kinbote's commentary creates a vast interplay of mirroring reflections, in which any allegorical framework or system of interpretation gets hopelessly lost. What remains is the eternal play of simulacra, the eternal game of creation and destruction which the world plays with itself, without telos or meaning, for the sheer sake of the game.

In *Pale Fire*, the eternal game of the world is seen mostly in its nonviolent, aesthetic or artistic aspect. Whereas its violent aspect is by no means absent, it is largely pushed into the background and turned into farce. By

contrast, in Orwell's *Nineteen Eighty-Four* the "game of worlds" unambigu-
ously reveals itself to be the pure play of power, in both its rational and pre-
rational form.

One does not usually think of *Nineteen Eighty-Four* as being a playful
book, perhaps because the original, archaic link between power, violence,
and play becomes obscured in a rational or literate mentality. As I show
elsewhere, play had a central role in an oral, pre-rational or aristocratic
mentality, such as that present in archaic Greece, being the primary way in
which power conceptualized itself. With the advent of a literate mentality
play became separated from power, which began to present itself as reason,
knowledge, morality, and truth. Consequently, play lost its centrality in culture, being tamed and repressed alongside all the other archaic values.[4] A
"return" to these values — and my assumption is that what we call "postmodernism" is precisely such a return — also presupposes a revaluation of
play by reestablishing its connection to power. The modern thinker who
initiates the return to a pre-rational aristocratic mentality is Nietzsche and,
in this sense, his thought is crucial in understanding the modern period. In
Nietzsche play again becomes the exuberant, violent impulse, beyond good
and evil, also called *der Wille zur Macht*, which tirelessly engenders and
destroys innumerable worlds. Nietzsche, moreover, is one of the initiators
of the "aesthetic" turn in modern thought, whereby art and play again
become the main ways of conceptualizing experience. Orwell's novel can
also be understood as an imaginary construction of a world based on a
naked, unashamed and playful will to power, and a comparison between
Nietzsche and Orwell would yield some interesting insights not only into
the latter's work, but also into the governing assumptions of postmodernism in general. Here I can only touch upon some of the main points that
such a comparison would entail, concentrating on what interests me most in
the present context: the notion of interpretation and its corollary, the
notion of allegory.[5]

In *Nineteen Eighty-Four*, Orwell has his main character, Winston
Smith, an ordinary intellectual with traditional, middle-class values, move
in a Nietzschean world of "sovereign" men or overmen, who have
organized themselves according to the principles of "oligarchical collectivism," reminiscent of a Leninist-Stalinist brand of communism. Smith
engages in a game of passive and then active resistance against the
authorities, a game in which he has as many chances of winning as a mouse
has against a cat. Once in the hands of the thought police, O'Brien, his tor-

turer-teacher, plays with him an elaborate power game which results in Smith's understanding and full emotional acceptance of the principle that "might is right." He not only renounces any thought of resistance against Big Brother but comes to love him, by identifying with what he perceives to be the latter's unbeatable strength.

In the eternally bright cells of the thought police, Smith's rational, commonsensical view of reality receives blow after blow from O'Brien's sophisticated, perspectivist view of the world as a manifestation of the Will to Power. O'Brien is Nietzsche's "philosophical man of power" or "artist-tyrant" as Nietzsche describes him in one of his notes in *The Will to Power* (504):

> . . . the possibility has been established for the production of international racial unions whose task will be to rear a master race, the future "masters of the earth"; — a new tremendous aristocracy, based on the severest self-legislation, in which the will of philosophical men of power and artist-ty-rants will be made to endure for millenia — a higer kind of men, who, thanks to their superiority in will, knowledge, riches, and influence, employ democratic Europe as their most pliant and supple instrument for getting hold of the destinies of the earth, so as to work as artists upon "man" himself. . . .

Like Nietzsche's artist-tyrant, O'Brien works upon Smith the way a sculptor works upon clay or stone, molding him according to his own will. In order to achieve his purpose, O'Brien sets out to prove to his victim that there is no reality outside the reality of power which is, as in Nietzsche, nothing but a feeling of power. In order to achieve this feeling of power one has to merge one's individuality with the collective consciousness, the equivalent of the Nietzschean ecstatic Dionysian experience (hence the two-minute hate periods in *Nineteen Eighty-Four* during which the individual merges into and identifies with the collective frenzy typical of any scapegoat ritual). Only this collective feeling of power creates "reality," the rest is an illusion. As O'Brien puts it:

> Only the disciplined mind can see reality, Winston. You believe that real-ity is something objective, external, existing in its own right. You also believe that the nature of reality is self-evident. When you delude yourself into thinking that you see something, you assume that everyone else sees the same thing as you. But I tell you, Winston, that reality is not external. Reality exists in the human mind, and nowhere else. Not in the individual mind, which can make mistakes, and in any case soon perishes: only in the mind of the Party, which is collective and immortal. Whatever the Party

holds to be the truth, is truth. It is impossible to see reality except by looking through the eyes of the Party. That is the fact that you have got to
relearn, Winston. It needs an act of self-destruction, an effort of the will.
You must humble yourself before you can become sane (Orwell
1949:214).

Here, then, reality is a matter of interpretation, but for O'Brien, as for
Nietzsche, interpretation is no longer the process of cognition through
which the agent discovers the world as it is already constituted: on the contrary, it is the process through which he creates the world as he goes along.
In this respect, O'Brien is an anti-positivist, and Nietzsche's criticism of the
positivist assumption of the existence of "facts" independent of interpretation is also O'Brien's criticism of Smith's commonsensical notion of reality.
In *The Will to Power*, Nietzsche writes:

> Against positivism which halts at phenomena — "There are only facts" —
> I would say: No, facts is precisely what there is not, only interpretations...
>
>   In so far as the word "knowledge" has any meaning, the world is
> knowable; but it is *interpretable* otherwise, it has no meaning behind it, but
> countless meanings. — "Perspectivism."
>
>   It is our needs that interpret the world; our drives and their For and
> Against. Every drive is a kind of lust to rule; each one has its perspective
> that it would like to compel all the other drives to accept as a norm   (267).

In other words, it is the Will to Power that "interprets":

> . . . it [the Will to Power] defines limits, determines degrees, variations of
> power. Mere variations of power could not feel themselves to be such:
> there must be present something that wants to grow and interprets the
> value of whatever else wants to grow. Equal *in that* — In fact interpreta-
> tion is itself a means of becoming master of something. (The organic pro-
> cess constantly presupposes interpretations.)   (342)

Nietzsche's perspectivism, then, just like the party's notion of "double
think" can be understood as a multiplicity of "interpretations" where truth
and fiction, taken in their traditional epistemological and ethical sense, are
relative and interchangeable. This "perspectivism" or "doublethink" is far
from meaning something like our contemporary "pluralism" or benign
acceptance of the other's point of view; nor does it lead to axiological or
epistemological relativism; on the contrary, its context is strictly agonistic
or competitive. Again, to quote Nietzsche:

> Perspectivism is only a complex form of specificity. My idea is that every
> specific body strives to become master over all space and to extend its

force (its will to power) and to thrust back all that resists its extension. But it continually encounters similar efforts on the part of other bodies and ends by coming to an arrangement ("union") with those of them that are sufficiently related to it: thus they then conspire together for power. And the process goes on   (339).

This, translated in political terms, is the principle of oligarchic collectivism expounded by O'Brien. Just like Nietzsche's, O'Brien's view of truth and fiction goes beyond a purely epistemological or ethical perspective. As in oral or pre-rational mentality, truth and lie are not moral categories, but have a *performative* value, and may be used indifferently as long as they further the goals of power. Epistemologically speaking, truth is not something to be found or discovered in the nature of things, but rather "something that must be created and that gives a name to a process." It is a "*processus in infinitum*, an active determining — not a becoming-conscious of something that is in itself firm and determined." Truth, then, is also an agonistic notion, indeed it is a "word for the will to power," and its criterion "resides in the enhancement of the feeling of power"   (290).

We can now readily see why allegory is not possible in a world where truth is created, rather than discovered: allegory depends on a notion of truth that is hidden and needs to be brought out in the open, in other words, it depends on a dichotomy of presence and absence. But once the will to power manifests itself openly or as eternal Becoming, it no longer needs allegory or any metaphysical language behind which to hide itself. The world of *Nineteen Eigthy-Four* is anti-allegorical; immediate power constantly destroys allegorical systems, and representations in general, as being ambiguous, superfluous and inimical to its goals. Smith's dream of meeting O'Brien in "the place where there is no darkness" is a good example of the constant destruction of allegory throughout the narrative. Smith "interprets" this phrase to mean "the imagined future, which one would never see, but which by foreknowledge, one could mystically share in" (92). However, after he is arrested and O'Brien proves to be not an ally but an enemy, the "place where there is no darkness" turns out to be, very literally, the cells of the thought police that are kept brightly lit day and night.

The mutability of the past is another anti-allegorical principle of unmediated power. Allegory, like truth, depends not only on a dichotomy of presence and absence, but also on a dichotomy of Being and Becoming. Unmediated power dispenses with the notion of Being and conceives of itself as an eternal play of simulacra. The mutability of the past implies endless Becoming as well as eternal return and joyful forgetfulness:

> The mutability of the past is the central tenet of Ingsoc. Past events, it is
> argued, have no objective existence, but survive only in written records and
> in human memories. The past is whatever the records and the memories
> agree upon. And since the Party is in full control of all records and in
> equally full control of the minds of its members it follows that the past is
> whatever the Party chooses to make it. It also follows that though the past
> is alterable, it never has been altered in any specific instance. For when it
> has been recreated in whatever shape is needed at the moment, then this
> new version *is* the past, and no different past can ever have existed. This
> holds good even when, as often happens, the same event has to be altered
> out of recognition several times in the course of the year. At all times the
> Party is in possession of absolute truth, and clearly the absolute can never
> have been different from what it is now. It will be seen that the control of
> the past depends above all on the training of memory. To make sure that
> all written records agree with the orthodoxy of the moment is merely a
> mechanical act. But it is also necessary to *remember* that events happened
> in the desired manner. And if it is necessary to rearrange one's memories
> or to tamper with written records, then it is necessary to *forget* that one has
> done so. The trick of doing this can be learned by the majority of Party
> members, and certainly by all who are intelligent as well as orthodox. In
> Oldspeak it is called quite frankly 'reality control'   (182-183).

Although Newspeak starts by having an allegorical structure required by
"double think," its ultimate goal is to do away with all ambivalence and
ambiguity, that is with allegory itself.

The Ministry of Love, of Truth, and of Peace may appear at first as
allegorical terms, since in Oldspeak (standard English) they mean exactly
their opposites. However, by the end of the novel, it becomes clear that
they are scrupulously literal, that they do not allow any double interpretation. In the Ministry of Love, the seat of the thought police, one learns how
to accept and love Big Brother; in the Ministry of Truth one learns how to
create truth without a guilty conscience; and in the Ministry of Peace one
learns how war is the only guarantee for an everlasting peace (cf. the
Roman dictum, also quoted by Nietzsche, according to which if you want
peace, you must prepare yourself for war). Newspeak itself is language
stripped of all its metaphorical accretions, all its ambiguities, and all its
allegorical possibilities. As Symes, an ardent supporter and creator of
Newspeak, says about the 11th edition of the Newspeak Dictionary, the
"definitive edition":

> You think, I dare say, that our chief job is inventing new words. But not a

bit of it! We're destroying words — scores of them, hundreds of them,
every day. We're cutting the language down to the bone. The Eleventh
Edition won't contain a single word that will become obsolete before the
year 2050 (48).

The destruction of Oldspeak would mean in the first instance the destruction of the literature of the past which is the allegorical discourse *par excellence*:

> By 2050 — earlier, probably — all real knowledge of Oldspeak will have
> disappeared. The whole literature of the past will have been destroyed.
> Chaucer, Shakespeare, Milton, Byron — they'll exist only in Newspeak
> vesions, not merely changed into something different, but actually changed
> into something contradictory of what they used to be. Even the literature
> of the Party will change. Even the slogans will change. How could you
> have a slogan like "freedom is slavery" when the concept of freedom has
> been abolished? The whole climate of thought will be different. In fact
> there will be no thought, as we understand it now. Orthodoxy means not
> thinking — not needing to think. Orthodoxy is unconsciousness   (50).

Orthodoxy as "unconsciousness" means a return to archaic values where
thinking does not mean self-reflection but doing or performing (scholars
have often noticed the "literal" character of Homeric language, for
instance).

One may wonder, with Smith, what are the objectives of the Will to
Power, what is to be achieved by such a radical change in human values.
O'Brien has a Nietzschean answer ready for us: nothing is to be achieved
but the perpetual enhancement of the feeling of power for its own sake:

> Now I will tell you the answer to my question. It is this. The Party seeks
> power entirely for its own sake. We are not interested in the good of
> others; we are interested solely in power. Not wealth or luxury or long life
> or happiness: only power, pure power. What pure power means you will
> understand presently. We are different from all oligarchies of the past, in
> that we know what we are doing. All the others, even those who resem-
> bled ourselves were cowards and hypocrites. The German Nazis and the
> Russian Communists came very close to us in their methods, but they
> never had the courage to recognize their own motives. They pretended,
> perhaps they even believed, that they had seized power unwillingly and for
> a limited time, and that just round the corner there lay a paradise where
> human beings would be free and equal. We are not like that. We know
> that no one ever seizes power with the intention of relinquishing it. Power
> is not means, it is an end. One does not establish a dictatorship in order to
> safeguard a revolution; one makes the revolution in order to establish the
> dictatorship. The object of persecution is persecution. The object of tor-

ture is torture. The object of power is power. . . (227).

The party will enact the eternally returning Dionysian drama of creation and destruction and all human beings will not only accept it but will ecstatically identify with and participate in it, the way they used to participate in the archaic mysteries of Dionysus:

> The heretic, the enemy of society, will always be there, so that he can be defeated and humiliated over again. Everything that you have undergone since you have been in our hands — all that will continue, and worse. The espionage, the betrayals, the arrests, the tortures, the executions, the disappearances will never cease. It will be a world of terror as much as a world of triumph. The more the Party is powerful, the less it will be tolerant: the weaker the opposition, the tighter the despotism. Goldstein and his heresies will live for ever. Every day, at every moment, they will be defeated, discredited, ridiculed, spat upon — and yet they will always survive. This drama that I have played out with you during seven years will be played out over and over again generation after generation, always in sub-, tler forms. Always we shall have the heretic here at our mercy, screaming with pain, broken up, contemptible — and in the end utterly penitent, saved from himself, crawling to our feet of his own accord. That is the world that we are preparing, Winston. A world of victory after victory, triumph after triumph after triumph: and endless pressing, pressing, pressing upon the nerve of power. You are beginning, I can see, to realize what that world will be like. But in the end you will do more than understand it. You will accept it, welcome it, become part of it (231).

Before I conclude my discussion of *Nineteen Eighty-Four*, I should like to meet certain objections that my argument will undoubtedly raise. Critics have often interpreted this novel as Orwell's warning against totalitarian political systems of the Nazi or the Communist type. But, as O'Brien himself points out, oligarchical collectivism far surpasses Nazi and Communist mentality. Thus, my argument has been that the model of this oligarchical collectivism is not fascism or Stalinism, but Nietzsche's race of the "masters of the earth." Just like O'Brien, Nietzsche would have dismissed the Nazis and the Communists as representatives of a "herd mentality," promoting petty bourgeois ideals, being motivated by *ressentiment*, and shying away from the aristocratic principle of "might is right." What distinguishes the O'Brien "masterly" type from a Nazi or a Communist dictator is *distance*, which, according to Nietzsche, precludes any danger of the master getting caught up in a mimetic relationship with the slave:

> Absurd and contemptible form of idealism that would *not* have mediocrity *mediocre* and, instead of feeling a sense of triumph at a state of exception-

alness, becomes *indignant* over cowardice, falsity, pettiness, and wretched-
ness. *One should not desire these things to be different!* and should make
the gulf *wider!*

    Chief viewpoint: establish *distances*, but *create no antitheses*. Dissolve
the *intermediate forms* and reduce their influence: chief means of preserving distances (Nietzsche 1968:475).

    On the sovereign types. — The "shepherd" as opposed to the "mas-
ter" (— the former a *means* of preserving the herd; the latter the *end* for
which the herd exists)   (479).

Getting mixed up in the herd mentality of the slave breeds guilt and *ressentiment*. These are precisely Smith's emotions toward the members of the
inner party. On the other hand, as we have seen, O'Brien preserves almost
a "divine" distance regarding Smith and therefore is free of any rancor
toward him. He transforms Smith into a toy which he manipulates for his
own pleasure, just as a guiltless cat plays with a mouse purely for the sake
of the game, rejoicing in its feeling of power. Moreover, insofar as Smith
represents the mentality of the outer party or an "intermediary form," his
elimination serves the purpose of preserving the distance between the inner
party and the proles, i.e., between the masters and the herd.

    I should also like to point out that, whereas the world of the novel
itself may be described as postmodernist (in the Nietzschean sense I have
discussed above), Orwell certainly does not share these postmodernist values. At the same time, however, it would be an error to assume that he
shares Smith's values instead. The latter are clearly as power-orientated as
those of O'Brien, and Smith appears to be little more than a mouse who
fancies himself to be a cat for a while. If Orwell's novel is a warning at all,
then it is a warning against the power-oriented mentality of man in general,
and in this respect it points far beyond any traditional Western, or for that
matter Eastern, values. The novel's dystopian and ironic nature renders
impossible any explicit statement as to what its positive standards of evalu-
ation are. In this sense, *Nineteen Eighty-Four* remains deliberately ambiguous: its purpose is not to offer a utopian solution of the type we may find,
e.g., in Voltaire's *Candide*, but, rather, to show the extreme consequences
of a kind of human mentality which has, for some time now, threatened to
take over the earth.

Conclusions

In this paper I have looked at allegory and hermeneutics as historical
categories: they come into being as instruments of literate or rational values

that are in turn the result of a mediated or disguised power mentality. When archaic or pre-rational values return in our culture — and it has been my contention that what we currently call "postmodernism" is precisely such a return — allegory and hermeneutics lose their utility or functionality, and therefore their cultural prestige as well. This loss explains, to a considerable extent, the anti-allegorical and anti-hermeneutical stand of much of postmodernist literature. As opposed to modernist texts which still support rational cultural values, even though they present these values in an ironical or parodic fashion, postmodernist texts shift their emphasis onto the world of the senses, discontinuity, decentering, play of surfaces, Becoming, and eternal return of the same. Thereby, they again bring pre-rational values to the foreground of our culture. "Modernism" and "postmodernism" are contemporary names for a very old cultural phenomenon: the relentless, inconclusive agon between the rational and the pre-rational values, which has been central to Western culture at least since the Hellenic classical period.

NOTES

1.   For a useful examination of the historical origins of the opposition between allegory and symbol in Romanticism, see Hans-Georg Gadamer (1975:65-73).

2.   The rehabilitation of allegory in modernism finds its clearest theoretical expression in Paul de Man (1979).

3.   One of the most influential critical statements indicative of the anti-hermeneutical orientation of postmodernism is Susan Sontag's short essay "Against Interpretation" (Sontag 1966).

4.   For a full development of this thesis, see my forthcoming book *Masks of Dionysus: Play, Imitation, and Power in Ancient Greece from Homer to Aristotle.*

5.   I am also aware that my interpretation of Nietzsche's *The Will to Power* goes against the commonly accepted one in Anglo-American letters. For a full exposition of this interpretation see the Nietzsche chapter in my forthcoming *Returns of the Repressed: The Play of Modern Philosophical and Scientific Discourse.*

REFERENCES

De Man, Paul. 1979. *Allegories of Reading: Figural Language in Rousseau, Nietzsche, Rilke and Proust.* New Haven: Yale University Press.
Gadamer, Hans-Georg. 1975. *Truth and Method,* trans. and ed. Garrett Barden and John Cumming. New York: Seabury Press.

Heidegger, Martin. 1958. *Der Satz vom Grund*. Pfullingen: G. Neske.

Lowry, Malcolm. 1947. *Under the Volcano*. Harmondsworth: Penguin, 1962.

-----. 1965. *Selected Letters*, ed. by Harvey Breit and Margerie Bonner Lowry. Philadelphia: Lippincott.

Nabokov, Vladimir. 1962. *Pale Fire*. Harmondsworth: Penguin, 1973.

Nietzsche, Friedrich. 1968. *The Will to Power*, trans. Walter Kaufmann. New York: Vintage Books.

Orwell, George. 1949. *Nineteen Eighty-Four*. Harmondsworth: Penguin, 1954.

Sontag, Susan. 1966. *Against Interpretation and Other Essays*. New York: Delta.

5

Postmodern Italy: Notes on the "Crisis of Reason", "Weak Thought," and *The Name of the Rose*

Stefano Rosso

1.   I have decided to discuss contemporary Italian thought, though it is not my usual field of study, not only to satisfy the kind request of the editors of this volume, but also because I think that the Italian debate on postmodernism differs from that of other countries such as the USA or France.[1] I will restrict myself here to a tentative outline of what I think is the most profound and articulated use of the terms "postmodern" and "postmodernity." I will concentrate on the question of "weak thought" (*pensiero debole*), in particular in the works of Gianni Vattimo. And in the last part of my paper I will refer to some "weak" elements in Umberto Eco's *The Name of the Rose* (*Il nome della rosa*, 1980). Since a large part of the Italian debate will not be considered, I have added a bibliographical note at the end of my text.

Before starting, let me give some information about the introduction of postmodernist concepts, themes, and interests in Italy: (a) the works of Jean-François Lyotard, especially *La Condition postmoderne*, have had an undoubtedly greater resonance in Italy than in France (see Ferraris 1983 and 1986); (b) essays on postmodernism by American scholars such as Ihab Hassan, William Spanos, Charles Altieri, Richard Palmer, Paul Bové, etc., have been translated into Italian between 1982 and 1984, which has given rise to increasing interest among scholars of literature; (c) some of the "classical" texts of postmodern American fiction — those that Fokkema saw as constituting the "hard core of Postmodernism" (1984:37) — were translated during the sixties and generally forgotten during the seventies, but are now experiencing a tepid revival in academic circles; (d) one can see a strong interest in the works of some French poststructuralists, who do not deal explicitly with the question of postmodernity, but whose perspective is deeply engrained in it (for example, Derrida's works, neglected in Italy during the seventies, are now being reimported, via the USA, accompanied by the works of American theorists such as Paul de Man, Richard Rorty, Stanley Fish and others); (e) however belatedly, a discussion has begun concerning the notion of postmodernism in philosophy, in literary theory and criticism, in the social sciences, and in architecture.[2]

2. In order to further specify the context in which the Italian debate on postmodernism has developed, it is necessary first of all to discuss briefly the "crisis of reason" and the question of "irrationalism." In Italy — according to Vattimo (1982:246) — one can speak of a first "crisis of reason" in the period following World War II. In that period, the "crisis of reason" represented above all a reaction against the dominant Crocean philosophy and, more generally, against "idealistic historical reason." Paradoxically, Marxism and Existentialism happened to be fighting against a common enemy; though their assumptions were very different, both were searching for a new kind of reason free from the influence of idealism. In the late fifties, Lukács popularized the term "irrationalism," referring retrospectively to the anti-historicist tradition of Kierkegaard, Schopenhauer, Nietzsche, etc. (Lukács' *Die Zerstörung der Vernunft*, 1954, was translated into Italian in 1959.) Thus Existentialism, which employed some arguments of anti-historicist philosophy against the Italian neo-idealism of Croce and Gentile, was labelled as "irrationalistic" by Marxist philosophers; the Marxists, in turn, were considered by the Existentialists as neo-idealists, since they seemed to share the historicist assumptions of neo-idealism.

On the other hand, the crisis of reason which has arisen during the last ten or fifteen years has radically called into question the "historical-dialectical reason" that still functioned as an alternative in the postwar period. The late "renaissance" of Heideggerian and Nietzschean studies, the dissemination of French poststructuralism, the renewed interest in the culture of Vienna of the first decades of our century and in some themes of the Frankfurt School, all coincide in contemporary Italy with the crisis of Marxist historicism, which had been a kind of common ground for most Italian thinkers in the fifties and sixties, prior to the pervasive diffusion of structuralism.

In Vattimo's view, the "irrationalistic" tendencies in Italian thought might therefore be understood as expressing a moment of crisis in historicism. This should explain why "the question of irrationalism, and the term itself, had a very limited echo outside the Italian context" (1982:245; unless otherwise indicated, all translations are my own). But what is more relevant here is that the ongoing crisis of Marxist historicism, particularly evident in the second half of the seventies, does not seem to come to resolution through the construction of a new and more comprehensive "rationality."

An emblematic expression of this "crisis of reason" — a term that at the end of the seventies somehow became fashionable and inflated — was a very successful collection of essays edited by A. Gargani (1979), entitled *Crisi della ragione* (The crisis of reason). The ten contributions to the volume are not homogeneous in terms of ideology or discipline. They all start, however, from the awareness of the crisis of classical reason — a mode of reason justified by a historical rational-real becoming — to which they oppose a "plurality of reasons" based on more or less heterogeneous reference to three fundamental "neoclassical modes of reason" (Ferraris 1983:41 and ff.): the critique of ideology, Heidegger's ontology and post-Wittgensteinian analytic philosophy. What all of these philosophical directions claim is that we can no longer speak of *one* way of thinking, but only of *many*. However, as G. Vattimo (1980a:19-20) pointed out in a review of *Crisi della ragione*, "the opposition 'reason'/'multiple modes of reasons' translates fully and completely the opposition between the metaphysical pretension of truth and the discovery of the practical character of rational procedures." It is not necessarily true — he argued — that "the discovery of reason as 'strategy' ... results in a multiplicity of modes of reason," and even less is it the case that the "affirmation of multiple modes of reason coincides with the recognition of reason as strategy and play of forces" (1980a:20).

It is evident that the authors of *Crisi della ragione* are still far removed from a philosophy of difference such as Vattimo's. These authors either maintain an idea of dialectics and inscribe their discourses within idealist-historicist schemes, or (as in the case of Rella's reading of Freud) simply assert the multiplicity of modes of reason, languages, idioms, giving each of them "the (however limited) hegemonic character that was acknowledged to belong to classical reason" (Vattimo 1980a:25). Vattimo, criticizing the still foundationalist perspective inherent in such projects, points to hermeneutics as the only non-metaphysical way of reflecting on the relationship between language and being and the problem of what lies "beyond language."

3.   The centrality of the "crisis of reason" and the important role played by the volume edited by Gargani is explicitly pointed out in the "Preface" by the editors of *Il pensiero debole* (Weak thought) (Vattimo and Rovatti 1983:9). Actually, *Il pensiero debole* is itself a sort of manifesto which takes the crisis of reason — as well as some versions of French poststructuralism, namely that of Deleuze and Foucault — as its negative point of reference.

Since "weak thought" is neither a school nor a systematic philosophical theory — as appears from the diverse approaches of the eleven contributors to the volume — an attempt at an analytic survey of their positions would be pointless. As I said before, I will limit myself to Vattimo's works, since he has most effectively tried to rescue the term "postmodern" from the vagueness which has accompanied it since its first appearance.

In his works before and after *Il pensiero debole*, one can find the juxtaposition of three terms, which at first may not seem so easy to relate to each other: hermeneutics, nihilism and postmodernity. The link between hermeneutics and nihilism is articulated in several essays, often devoted to long philological discussions of texts by Nietzsche and Heidegger, in which Vattimo tries to radicalize their anti-metaphysical perspective by unmasking their residual metaphysical assumptions. In his view, Nietzsche's and Heidegger's discovery of difference as what has been forgotten in the history of Being should not be allowed to become in turn a new "foundation" for thought. Rather, it should be radicalized as a weakening of the still metaphysical notion of being, to the point of conceiving being as an *event* (*Ereignis*) and no longer as a stable structure. To this "ontology of decline" corresponds an analogous weakening of thought. Only "weak thought" — a way of thinking which has attempted to give up any "strong" concept of reason and being as presence — can avoid falling back into the trap of metaphysical discourse. If, on the one hand, a hermeneutics of "unmasking" turns out still to be based on a foundationalist assumption, since it looks for an ultimate truth behind appearances, on the other hand the valorization of *simulacra* (as in Baudrillard's works or in Perniola 1980) is in the end no less foundationalist, since "an emphasis on simulation ... would assume the same centrality metaphysics granted to the *ontos òn*, the Foundation" (Ferraris 1981:119).

In his reading of Heidegger's nihilistic tendencies, Vattimo stresses the

role of two key concepts, *Andenken* and *Verwindung*. *Andenken* is defined
— especially in Heidegger's later works — as a recollecting or rethinking,
not so much of being as object or as what "has gone" (*vergangen*), but
rather as a recollecting of what "has been" (*gewesen*). *Verwindung* is a term
very seldom used by Heidegger (see *Identität und Differenz*) as an analogue
of *Ueberwindung* (overcoming), which is devoid of the dialectical elements
(as in the Hegelian *Aufhebung*) still at work in the latter. Consequently,
Vattimo claims, *Verwindung* should not be translated as "overcoming," but
rather as "distortion", "healing", "convalescence", "resignation," or "acceptance," thus clearly echoing Nietzsche's "philosophy of the morning"
(Vattimo 1985:172). Though *Andenken* and *Verwindung* have different
semantic spectra, they have a great deal in common: to distort/decline (*ver-
winden*) metaphysics is a way of recollecting it (*andenken*). Vattimo therefore disregards a possible interpretation of Heidegger which would lead
towards a mystical result, emphasizing instead those elements in Heidegger's thought which go against Heidegger's own reading of Nietzsche (Vattimo 1980:71-94).

The centrality of these two notions for postmodern thought is convincingly shown by Vattimo in his "The end of (hi)story" (1986b). In his view,
Lyotard's fundamental definition of the postmodern condition (especially
in the way it has been retrieved in Lyotard 1985) is still inscribed within
metaphysical assumptions. By claiming that "the *métarécits* by means of
which the philosophy of history of the 19th and 20th centuries used to
describe and legitimize historical existence have been confuted by decisive
events of our own time," Lyotard does not realize "that the dissolution of
the *métarécits* is itself a (paradoxical) kind of *métarécit*" (Vattimo 1986b) —
i.e. the *métarécit* of the dissolution of the *métarécits*. It is not my purpose
here to analyse the details of this argument. I just want to stress the "dis-
torting" and "parasitic" — one could say "deconstructive" — aspect of
postmodern thought, as defined by Vattimo.

Another term which — according to Vattimo — can help characterize
the weak thought of postmodernity, and which is strictly related to *Andenken* and *Verwindung*, is *pietas*. Since we can no longer refer to strong foun-
dational thought that provides us with rules and directions of behavior, we
are left to face our existence, as historically cast, towards death. But death
is actually what can provide us with some guidelines, since death is

> the coffer where values are deposited: the life-experiences of past genera-
> tions, the great and the beautiful of the past with whom we'd like to be and

to speak, the people we have loved and who have disappeared. Inasmuch as it is a crystallization of acts of the word and of modes of experience, language itself is deposited in the coffer of death. At bottom, that coffer is also a source of the few rules that can help us to move about our existence in a nonchaotic and undisorganized way while knowing that we are not headed anywhere (Vattimo 1981:10-11; here quoted from the English translation: 25).

Now *pietas* is the name for our attitudes of retrieving the forms of the past. Though these traces of "tradition" — Vattimo would rather say "trans-mission" (*Ueber-lieferung*) — no longer represent for us a *value* in the strong sense, still they are "the only kind of foundation which is at our disposal in the age of the end of metaphysics," such as "works of art, institutions, language, etc.," which are seen as inherited "monuments" (Vattimo 1986b).

Coming back to the problem of the continuity between Nietzsche and Heidegger and their relation to postmodernity, one should notice that the ontology of decline which is common to both philosophers does not come about as the consequence of a "pure movement of concepts," but rather "in relation to more general transformations in the conditions of existence," that is, the world of technology (Vattimo 1986a). Of course the Nietzsche-Heidegger continuity emphasized by Vattimo is not unproblematic and linear: in Nietzsche the "overcoming" of metaphysics is only outlined, whereas in Heidegger's notions of *Verwindung* and *Andenken* he sees a further step towards postmodernity.

On the very notion of technology, for instance, Vattimo sees a significant difference between the two thinkers. Nietzsche is still basically linked to an image of the engine (as something that can increase man's "capacity of 'mechanical' domination ... over nature" [Vattimo 1986a: 19]), whereas Heidegger, though in an ambiguous way, points to an idea of technology which is prophetically modelled on information theory. Information technology, Vattimo claims,

> seems to render subjectivity unthinkable for it is not given to one subject to possess or to manipulate, within a logic still bound to a master-slave metaphysics, the information from whose coordination and connections depend the true "power" of the late-modern world (Vattimo 1986a: 19).

The emphasis on a non-apocalyptic reading of computer society implies that postmodern (weak) thought should not be simply directed toward the past through a "pious" recollection, but should "distort" as well the complexity of present forms and values, thus pointing toward a "post-metaphysical" future.

Trying to summarize what has been described so far, one can say that: (a) in Italy, today, philosophical discourse cannot leave out of consideration the pervasiveness of the concept of dialectics, or, more precisely, its already "dissolute" forms (as in Adorno, Benjamin, Bloch and others); (b) in the last ten or fifteen years the philosophy of difference (as represented by the Nietzsche-Heidegger "renaissance") has radicalized the dissolute tendencies just mentioned; (c) the position taken by Vattimo — and, more or less, by the other contributors to *Il pensiero debole* — does not aim for an affirmative nihilism; rather, it goes in the direction of a weakening of both thought and being. Vattimo relates this parallel "decline" to the "postmodern condition," a condition in which we must take note that

> the intensification of social complexity, ... is not simplified, but is rendered more diffuse and pervasive by means of the technology that goes with information. This renders the conceiving of humanity in terms of multiple "subjective" poles, characterized by self-consciousness and by spheres of "conflictual" power, rather impossible (Vattimo 1986a: 19-20).

4. In the contemporary Italian debate, one can notice today an increasing tendency to homologize "postmodern" and "weak thought" (For an articulated "postmodern" perspective which argues *against* the "weakness" of "weak thought," see Perniola 1984.) It is possible (and desirable) that this more profound theoretical awareness may lead toward a deeper "philosophical" approach to postmodern literature. So far, the postmodern literary texts are still generally read and taught with a modernist approach, stressing neo-avant-gardistic features and forgetting the double bind inherent to the notion of postmodernity: "*post*modernity" as innovation in relation to "modernity," but at the same time postmodernity as *dissolution* of the pathos of the categories of "innovation," of the "new," and "progress." (On this important point see Vattimo 1985:12 and passim; Carchia 1982:117-19; and Ferraris 1986.) Besides, there seems to be a tacit agreement to avoid the question of postmodernism when Italian literature itself is at stake, except for the case of Calvino — officially "elected" a postmodern writer by John Barth — or of Carlo Emilio Gadda, who is considered by some to be one of the precursors of Italian postmodernism (Tani 1984:33-34 and passim).

If we consider Eco's best-seller *The Name of the Rose*, the situation is not very different. Eco's case is more complex since he himself, somewhat unexpectedly, contributed to the volume *Il pensiero debole* (Eco 1983b).

Now it is beyond my purposes to go into the details of Eco's actual position as theoretician within the "weak/strong" polemic (Eco's perspective on postmodernsim is clarified in Eco 1983a and Rosso 1983a). I will just note that in Eco's works (see Teresa de Lauretis 1981) — which no one ever accused of flirting with "irrationalism" — one can notice, after the beginning of the seventies, a kind of double tendency: on the one hand, a constant effort to categorize and systematize, excluding positions such as those of Lacan, Deleuze, Foucault and Derrida, and on the other hand an increasingly central role given to the concept of "unlimited semiosis" borrowed from Peirce.

This double tendency can be detected also in Eco's most recent works, such as his contribution to *Il pensiero debole*, entitled "L'antiporfirio." (For a "weak" reading of Eco's critical works see Marrone 1985; for a "strategic" reading see Bottiroli 1984.) If one considers *The Name of the Rose*, one can notice that, in the multitude of reviews devoted to it, Eco's "historical" novel has been linked with the problem of weak thought or, more generally, of postmodernism only quite seldom and merely tangentially. (To a lesser extent this is also the case, at least in Italy, for Calvino's works; for a "weak" reading of Calvino's *Palomar*, see Rovatti 1984.)

I am not trying to argue that *The Name of the Rose* is a more or less successful "postmodern" or even "weak" novel; neither am I arguing that "postmodern" or "weak" tendencies are the only or the most effective ones in this novel. I am only claiming that *some* tendencies which we could call "postmodern" — I have developed this argument in a more articulated way elsewhere (Rosso 1983b) — or even "weak" often emerge in Eco's text. Therefore — in the limited space left — I just want to touch upon another possible approach to this text, which too often has been read by critics in an apocalyptic key. Such apocalyptic critics were scandalized by the fact that "high literature" had abandoned the narrow codes of the literary elites and had entered the mass market and the discourse of the media. In such a reading, Eco's novel could even appear as the result of a "conscious and aggressive market strategy" (Ferretti 1983:70).

In *The Name of the Rose* the thematics of the "dissolution" of dialectics and of the "crisis of reason" at large are articulated with different names in the historical background which frames the narration, in the "motivations" that set the (anti)detective plot at work, in the endless discussions between William of Baskerville and Adso, in Adso's solitary reflections, etc. (In this general sense, the statement on the book jacket of the Italian edition that any reference to Italian current events is "unauthorized" is clearly ironic.) The questioning of the notion of "strong" thought in *The Name of the Rose* is apparent in its checkmating of the concepts of causality and "openness" of form, in its pervasive intertextuality, in its Rabelaisian-Bakhtinian opposition between "high" and "low" culture, in its explicit reference to a "rhizomatic" labyrinth, etc. Very broadly, I think one can easily perceive the pervasiveness in Eco's novel of the concept of *pietas* in a way similar to Vattimo's definition.

An explicit thematization of *pietas* can be found, for instance, near the end of the text, when Adso, coming back to the ruins of the abbey, several years after the tremendous fire, picks up the fragments of a few scorched manuscripts that he finds on the mouldy shelves:

> Often from a word or a surviving image I could recognize what the work had been. When I found, in time, other copies of those books, I studied them with love, as if destiny had left me this bequest, as if having identified the destroyed copy were a clear sign from heaven that said to me: Tolle et lege. At the end of my patient reconstruction, I had before me a kind of lesser library, a symbol of the greater, vanished one: a library made up of fragments, quotations, unfinished sentences, amputated stumps of books. (Eco 1980:502; here quoted from the English translation: 609)

One may object that both Adso and William, though moving from "strong reason" to "reasonability" (*ragionevolezza*) (Eco 1983a: passim, and Rosso 1983a: 4 and passim), still maintain a nostalgia for an "ancient mode of reason." Of course we cannot expect a medieval monk to be a "post-metaphysical thinker," and to accept with serenity a decentered world, as would Nietzsche's "good-tempered man." It is true, however, that both William and Adso perceive the world "nihilistically" — as lacking any foundation — and that they move towards the formulation of an ethical thinking which could be defined as "selectively tolerant."

But traces of *pietas* can also be perceived in the writing of the novel itself, in the fact that the text speaks lovingly about other texts, in the endless inventories, in the countless quotations, in the cult of the book and of whatever is written, including even the less significative *marginalia*, in the excessive codification and in the myriad of stereotypes. But isn't this "loving attitude" similar to what gives us pleasure when we watch — with postmodern eyes — John Wayne's or Humphrey Bogart's movies of the forties and fifties? As Teresa de Lauretis rightly observed (1981:86), a passage written by Eco himself in 1975 about Michael Curtiz' *Casablanca* is perhaps one of the most appropriate ways to approach *The Name of the Rose*:

When all the archetypes burst in shamelessly, we reach Homeric depths. Two clichés make us laugh. A hundred clichés move us. For we sense dimly that the clichés are talking *among themselves*, and celebrating a reunion. Just as the height of pain may encounter sensual pleasure, and the height of perversion borders on mystical energy, so too the height of banality allows us to catch a glimpse of the sublime. ... If nothing else, it is a phenomenon worthy of awe (Eco 1975; here quoted from the English translation: 38).

NOTES

1.   It is actually in France and the USA that one may find an increasing interest in recent Italian thought: I refer, for instance, to a long report in *Le Monde* (1984), devoted to the Italian philosophers, or to a recent issue of *Critique* entitled "Les philosophes italiens par eux-mêmes" (no. 442, 1985). Among American examples I could mention the international symposium on "Critique of Ideology and Hermeneutics in Contemporary Italian Thought," held at New York University in November 1983 and the issue of the journal *Differentia* (Queens College, New York, Autumn 1986), which is entirely devoted to the Italian literary and philosophical scene.

2.   Cf. further my bibliographical note.

REFERENCES

Blonsky, Marshall, ed. 1985. *On Signs*. Baltimore: Johns Hopkins University Press.

Bobbio, Norberto *et al*. 1982. *La cultura filosofica italiana dal 1945 al 1980*. Napoli: Guida.

Bottiroli, Giovanni. 1984. "Il pensiero metonimico," *Carte semiotiche* O:101-114.

Carchia, Gianni. 1982. *La legittimazione dell'arte*. Napoli: Guida.

De Lauretis, Teresa. 1981. *Umberto Eco*. Firenze: La Nuova Italia.

Eco, Umberto. 1975. "Ore 9: Amleto all'assedio di Casablanca," *Espresso*, August 17. Rpt. as "*Casablanca* o la rinascita degli dei," in Eco 1977:138-143. Eng. trans. by J. Shepley and B. Spackman, "*Casablanca*, or the Clichés Are Having a Ball," in Blonsky 1985:35-38.

-----. 1977. *Dalla periferia dell'impero*. Milano: Bompiani.

-----. 1980. *Il nome della rosa*. Milano: Bompiani. Eng. trans. W. Weaver, *The Name of the Rose*. New York: Harcourt Brace, 1983.

-----. 1983a. "Postille a *Il nome della rosa*," *Alfabeta* 49:19-22. Rpt. as a separate volume (1984) and as appendix to *Il nome della rosa* (1985), Milano: Bompiani.

-----. 1983b. "L'antiporfirio," in Vattimo and Rovatti 1983:52-80.

Ferraris, Maurizio. 1981. "Nichilismo e differenza: Una traccia," *Aut aut* 182-183:105-126.

-----. 1983. *Tracce: Nichilismo moderno postmoderno*. Milano: Multhipla.

-----. 1986. "Problemi del postmoderno," *Cultura e scuola* 97:104-115 and 98:106-118.

Ferretti, Gian Carlo. 1983. *Il best seller all'italiana*. Bari: Laterza.

Fokkema, Douwe. 1984. *Literary History, Modernism, and Postmodernism*. Amsterdam and Philadelphia: Benjamins.

Gargani, Aldo, ed. 1979. *Crisi della ragione: Nuovi modelli nel rapporto tra sapere e attività umane*. Torino: Einaudi.

Giovannoli, Renato, ed. 1985. *Saggi su "Il nome della rosa."* Milano: Bompiani.

Harrison, Thomas J., ed. 1983. *The Favorite Malice: Ontology and Reference in Contemporary Italian Poetry*. New York and Milano: Out of London Press.

Lyotard, Jean-François. 1985. "Histoire universelle et différences culturelles," *Critique* 456:559-568.

Marrone, Gianfranco. 1985. "Enciclopedie deboli e dizionari forti," *Aut aut* 205:115-125.

Perniola, Mario. 1980. *La società dei simulacri*. Bologna: Cappelli.

-----. 1984. "Lettera sul pensiero debole," *Alfabeta* 58: 24-25. (Republished in a longer version in *Aut aut* 201:51-64).

Rosso, Stefano. 1983a. "A Correspondence with Umberto Eco," trans. by C. Springer, *Boundary 2*, 12:1-13.

-----. 1983b. "*Il nome della rosa* tra nuova ragione e nichilismo." Paper read at the colloquium "Calvino and Company" (Brown University, April).

Rovatti, Pier Aldo. 1984. "Narrare un soggetto: Nota su *Palomar* di Italo Calvino," *Aut aut* 201: 32-37.

Tani, Stefano. 1984. *The Doomed Detective: The Contribution of the Detective Novel to Postmodern American and Italian Fiction*. Carbondale and Edwardsville: Southern Illinois University Press.

Vattimo, Gianni. 1980a. *Le avventure della differenza: Che cosa significa pensare dopo Nietzsche e Heidegger*. Milano: Garzanti. French trans. by J. Rolland *et al.*, *Les aventures de la différence*. Paris: Minuit, 1985.

-----. 1980b. "L'ombra del neorazionalismo: Note a *Crisi della ragione*,"

Aut aut 175-176:19-26.

-----. 1981. *Al di là del soggetto: Nietzsche, Heidegger e l'ermeneutica.* Milano: Feltrinelli. Partial translation by T. Harrison, "Bottle, Net, Truth, Revolution, Terrorism, Philosophy," *Denver Quarterly* 16, no.4 (1982):24-34.

-----. 1982. "Irrazionalismo, storicismo, egemonia," in Bobbio *et al.* 1982:243-262.

-----. 1983. "Dialettica, differenza, pensiero debole," in Vattimo and Rovatti 1983:12-28. Paper read at the symposium "Ideology and Hermeneutics in Contemporary Italian Thought" (New York University, November 1983). Eng. trans. by T. Harrison, "Dialectics, Difference, and Weak Thought," *Graduate Faculty Philosophy Journal* 10, no.1 (1984):151-164.

-----. 1985. *La fine della modernità: Nichilismo ed ermeneutica nella cultura postmoderna.* Milano: Garzanti. partial English translation by T. Harrison as "The Shattering of the Poetic Word" (in Harrison 1983:223-235) and "Myth and the Destiny of Secularization" (*Social Research* 52, no.2 (1985): 347-362; revised version, translated by J.R. Snyder, "Myth and the Fate of Secularization," *Res* 9, 1985:29-35).

-----. 1986a. "The Crisis of Subjectivity from Nietzsche to Heidegger," *Differentia* 1:5-21.

-----. 1986b. "The End of (Hi)story." Paper read at the symposium "Postmodernism: Society, Arts, Knowledge" held at Northwestern University, 17-19 October 1985. To appear in *Chicago Review* (Summer 1986).

Vattimo Gianni and Pier Aldo Rovatti, eds. 1983. *Il pensiero debole.* Milano: Garzanti.

BIBLIOGRAPHICAL NOTE

a) The "crisis of reason": *Crisi della ragione* (Gargani 1979) contains essays by Gargani, C. Ginzburg, G.C. Lepschy, F. Orlando, F. Rella, V. Strada, R. Bodei, N. Badaloni, S. Veca, C.A. Viano. About this volume, besides Vattimo (1980a), one should read the series of short essays entitled "Crisi della ragione?" published in *Alfabeta.* In no.9 (1980): U. Eco, "Cauto omaggio al modus ponens"; F. Leonetti, "Fine di un periodo e 'mossa del papa'"; P.A. Rovatti, "Il pretesto e il testo"; M. Spinella, "Crisi della ragione o crisi del sapere?"; P. Volponi, "La ragione immobile." In no.11 (1980): S. Veca, "I 'giochi' della ragione"; G. Giorello, "Il giglio, Milady e la dialettica"; F. Fistetti, "L'irriducibilità dei dialetti"; M. Ferraris, "Pluralismo di linguaggi o pluralità di differenze." By A. Gargani see also *Il sapere senza fondamenti* (Torino: Einaudi, 1978),

Stili di analisi (Milano: Feltrinelli, 1980) and *Lo stupore e il caso* (Bari: Laterza, 1985).
b) Postmodernism: Among the several Italian works on postmodernism — besides the excellent overview by Ferraris (1986) — see G. Bartolucci, M. Fabbri, M. Pisani, G. Spinucci, eds., *Paesaggio metropolitano* (Milano: Feltrinelli, 1982); it contains sixty-one short essays divided in five sections: "Metropolis and Aesthetics", "Metropolis and Technology", "Metropolis: Arts and Media", "Metropolis and Artistic Practices", "Performance on Performance." See also the collection of essays edited by R.C. Aldegheri and M. Sabini, *Immagini del post-moderno* (Venezia: Cluva, 1983) divided in two sections: "Culture and Post-industrial Society" and "Post-modern Architecture," and the volume by R. Barilli *et al.*, *Incontro con il postmoderno* (Milano: Mazzotta, 1984). Particular attention to literary American postmodernism can be found in C. Gorlier, "Il cerchio magico della nuova narrativa americana" (*Alfabeta*, 2, 1979), issue no.7 of *Calibano* (1982) and G. Carboni, *La finzione necessaria* (Torino: Tirrenia Stampatori, 1984). P. Carravetta and P. Spedicato, *Postmoderno e letteratura* (Milano: Bompiani, 1984) is an anthology of postmodern American theory and criticism. In *Alfabeta* see at least the series of articles under the heading "Postmoderno/Moderno." In no.22 (1981): J. Habermas, "Moderno, postmoderno e neoconservatorismo." In no.24 (1981): J.-F. Lyotard, "Regole e paradossi"; M. Ferraris, "Le legittimazioni postmoderne"; A. Illuminati and F. Montuori, "Piranesi e il fluire del nuovo"; P. Tanca, "L'architettura è morta a St Louis"; R. Barilli, "Boccioni e De Chirico"; F. Bolelli, "Come avere un mixer interiore." In no.26-27 (1981): S. Veca, "L'etica del moderno"; T. Maldonado, "Una ricerca retrospettiva"; F. Berardi Bifo, "Controllo totale e liberazione"; C. Formenti, "Il fascino dell'ombra." In no.29 (1981): G. Dorfles, "Ossia antimoderno"; A. Bonito Oliva, "Un'aperta inattualità"; A. Boatto, "Lo psiconauta." In no.32 (1982): J.-F. Lyotard, "Intervento italiano." In *Aut aut* 179-180 (1980) see the section "Sull'immagine postmoderna" (On the Postmodern Image): A. Dal Lago, "Metamorfosi del sociale e strategie di assoggettamento"; F. and R. Castel and A. Lovell, "La società psichiatrica avanzata"; G. Gozzi, "La distruzione del legame sociale: Da Wittgenstein a Luhmann"; C. Formenti, "La macchina, il cyborg, il mana: L'immaginario scientifico di Lyotard"; A. Casella, "L'ordine e le flutturazioni: *La nuova alleanza* di Ilya Prigogine"; D. Comboni, "La risposta è sì, ma fatemi ricordare qual era la domanda: Sul 'Rapporto' Nora-Minc"; R. Prezzo, "L'altrove della seduzione."
c) "Weak thought"; *Il pensiero debole* (Vattimo and Rovatti 1983) contains essays by L. Amoroso, G. Carchia, G. Comolli, F. Costa, F. Crespi, A. Dal Lago, U. Eco, M. Ferraris, D. Marconi, P.A. Rovatti, G. Vattimo. About "weak thought," one should read, again in *Alfabeta*, the series of essays entitled "debole/forte" (weak/strong). In no.58 (1984): M. Perniola (1984), and C. Formenti, "L'ultima similitudine." In no.60 (1984): P.A. Rovatti, "Una metafora necessaria." In no.62-63 (1984): F. Rella, "La figura che salva"; E. Greblo "L'esperienza dell'abbandono." In no.64 (1984): G. Jervis, "Le vecchie debolezze"; G. Bottiroli, "Labirinto di quarto tipo"; A. Illuminati, "Un equivoco terminologico." In no.65 (1984): G. Franck, "L'altro quotidiano." In no.66 (1984): C. Sini, "Impressioni." In no.67 (1984): G. Vattimo, "Le deboli certezze"; A. Sciacchitano, "Avere un debole"; D. Marconi, "Sei domande." In no.68 (1985): R. Gasparotti, "Il motivo dell'origine." In *Aut aut* 201 (1984) see R. Prezzo, "La macchina per fare il vuoto." M. Ferraris, "L'etnologia bianca: Decostruzionismo e scienze umane"; in

no.202-203 (1984) see G. Vattimo, "La filosofia del mattino" (later reprinted in Vattimo 1985), A. Dal Lago, "Il luogo della debolezza," P.A. Rovatti, "Tenere la distanza," F. Masini "Franz Kafka: Una distruzione che edifica." Among Gianni Vattimo's works after 1970, besides those listed in the References, one should see *Introduzione a Heidegger* (Bari: Laterza, 1971: French trans. by J. Rolland, *Introduction à Heidegger*, Paris: Cerf, 1985); *Il soggetto e la maschera: Nietzsche e il problema della liberazione* (Milano: Bompiani, 1974); *Introduzione a Nietzsche* (Bari: Laterza, 1985); in English: "Difference and Interference: On the Reduction of Hermeneutics to Anthropology," *Res* 4 (Fall 1982). By M. Perniola see also *Dopo Heidegger: Filosofia e organizzazione della cultura* (Milano: Feltrinelli, 1984) and *Transiti* (Bologna: Cappelli, 1985). For a "strong" polemic against "weak thought" see A. Viano, *Va pensiero* (Torino: Einaudi, 1985). The Italian speakers at the symposium "Ideology and Hermeneutics in Contemporary Italian Thought" (New York University, 1983) were: G. Agamben, R. Bodei, A. Gargani, M. Perniola, G. Vattimo; there were also papers by F. Rossi-Landi and C. Sini. The American respondents were: F. Jameson, M. Jay, A. Mandelbaum, R. Rorty, E.W. Said, R. Schürmann, H. Silverman, W. Spanos, Hayden White. So far only the contributions by Agamben, Bodei, Perniola, Vattimo, Schürmann and White have appeared in *Graduate Faculty Philosophy Journal* 10, no.1 (1984).

d) *The Name of the Rose*: Besides the collection of thirty-five essays edited by Giovannoli (1985) and the bibliography there included (pp.443-446), see the bibliography in De Lauretis 1981 (pp.103-106). *Sub-stance* 47 (1985) contains the proceedings of the symposium on *The Name of the Rose* held at Austin, Texas, 20-22 September 1984. See also Tani 1984:68-75 and passim. For a sociological approach to the reception of Eco's novel, dominated by apocalyptic overtones, see Ferretti 1983:63-71 and passim.

Analytical Criticism

6

New Nouns for Old: "Language" Poetry, Language Game, and the Pleasure of the Text

Marjorie Perloff

> — When words are, meaning soon follows.
> Ron Silliman, "For L=A=N=G=U=A=G=E"

One of the anomalies of criticism in the late twentieth century is that the lyric poem, the great genre of the Romantics, as of the High Modernists, no longer seems central to its discourse. Take the case of Roland Barthes, himself an extraordinarily "poetic" writer, if by "poetic" we mean that his writing foregrounds the metaphoric, syntactic, and sound properties of language, exploiting these linguistic relationships at the expense of "plot" or "character" or "thematics." Given Barthes' passion for what he calls the "wounds" and "seductions" of language (1973:62), and given his interest in such diverse texts as those of Racine and Balzac, Sade and Fourier, Flaubert and the Goethe of *Werther*, and in such diverse media as photography and film, landscape design and architecture, it seems puzzling that he should have paid so little attention to poetry.

Or is it? Perhaps the difficulty is that discourse about poetry, for a writer of Barthes' generation, is inevitably colored by the image of The Poem laid down by the great Modernist poets from Baudelaire to Valéry, whose claim it was, so Barthes argues in *Le Degré zéro de l'écriture*, that poetry is an autonomous language, arriving at truths that are above and beyond Nature:

> ... sous chaque Mot de la poésie moderne gît une sorte de géologie existentielle, où se rassemble le contenu total du Nom.... Le Mot n'est plus dirigé *à l'avance* par l'intention générale d'un discours socialisé; le consom-

> mateur de poésie, privé du guide des rapports sélectifs, débouche sur le
> Mot, frontalement, et le reçoit comme une quantité absolue, accompagnée
> de tous ses possibles. Le Mot ... accomplit donc un état qui n'est possible
> que dans le dictionnaire ou dans la poésie, là où le nom peut vivre privé de
> son article, amené à une sorte d'état zéro.... Cette faim du Mot, commune
> à toute la Poésie moderne, fait de la parole poétique une parole terrible et
> inhumaine (Barthes 1953: 37-38).

"Terrible and inhuman," that is to say, in its overdetermination of the sign.
"La poésie contemporaine" [i.e. Modernist], writes Barthes in *Mythologies*,
"est *un système sémiologique régressif*. Alors que le mythe vise à une ultra-
signification ... la poésie au contraire tente de retrouver une infrasignifica-
tion, un état présémiologique du langage; bref, elle s'efforce de retrans-
former le signe en sens: son idéal — tendanciel — serait d'atteindre non au
sens des mots, mais au sens des choses mêmes" (Barthes 1957: 219-220).

To reach the meaning of things themselves — it is this desire to bypass
the signifier that makes much neo-Romantic and neo-Symbolist poetry
written today seem so "regressive." For, as Barthes remarks in a 1975 interview, literature can no longer coincide with the function of *mathesis*, which
he defines as "un champ complet de savoir." In our time, "Le monde est
planétaire" and "ce que l'on sait du monde, on le sait tout de suite, mais on
est bombardé d'informations parcellaires, dirigées... Pendant des siècles, la
littérature a été à la fois une *mathésis* et une *mimésis*, avec son métalangage
corrélatif: le reflet. Aujourd'hui, le texte est une *sémiosis*, c'est-à-dire une
mise en scène du symbolique, non pas du contenu, mais des détours, des
retours, bref des jouissances du symbolique" (Barthes 1981: 224-225).

The text as *semiosis*, as "*mise en scène de signifiance*" (1981: 225). In
the late seventies, on both the East and West Coasts of the United States
(but notably not, at least to begin with, in the center), a "poetry" movement has erupted that takes what Barthes calls *arthrologie* (literally, the
study of joints, used ironically by Barthes [1981: 125] to designate the study
of how unlike or discontinuous items are combined) quite seriously. Its
name, "Language Poetry," immediately prompted, and continues to
prompt, scorn and suspicion on the part of the traditional poetry community. For isn't all poetry made of language? And isn't the visual appearance
of the name of the group's founding magazine, $L=A=N=G=U=A=G=E$,
merely pretentious? Since when, after all, are the letters of the alphabet
equal?

Not coincidentally, the first major journal to publish an anthology of the young American "Language poets" was the Paris journal *Change* in March 1981. This selection was followed by Charles Bernstein's "Language Sampler" in *The Paris Review* (1982: 75-125), and since then, editions, anthologies, and critical essays by and about the Language poets have multiplied. As I was writing this essay, a magazine from New Zealand arrived called *Splash* (1985), its whole issue, edited by Wystan Curnow, devoted to Language Poetry. Indeed, the New Zealanders, anxious to demonstrate their familiarity with this new American avant-garde, refer to the 1984 *L=A=N=G=U=A=G=E Book*, edited by Charles Bernstein and Bruce Andrews quite casually as the *L-Book*.

What, then, are the distinguishing features of "L" poetry? Let me try to sketch in the most salient ones. In his Introduction to the *Paris Review* "Language Sampler," Charles Bernstein — probably the most articulate spokesman of the group and, to my mind, a truly original and exciting poet — writes:

> What we have here is an insistence to communicate. Not, perhaps, where communication is schematized as a two-way wire with the message shuttling back and forth in blissful ignorance of the (its) transom (read: ideology). There are no terminal points (me → you) in a sounding of language from the inside, in which the dwelling is already / always given" (Bernstein 1982: 75).

And again, "The trouble with the conduit theory of communication (me → you) is that it presupposes individuals to exist as separate entities outside language and to be communicated *at* by language" (1982: 78).

Since the rejection of the "conduit theory of communication" is at the very heart of Language Poetry, the concept needs clarification. In an essay called "Reading Cavell Reading Wittgenstein," Bernstein writes:

> The distortion is to imagine that knowledge has an "object" outside of the "language games" of which it is a part — that words refer to "transcendental signifieds" ... rather than being part of a language which itself produces meaning in terms of its grammar, its conventions, its "agreements in judgement." Learning a language is not learning the names of things outside language, as if it were simply a matter of matching up "signifiers with signifieds," as if signifieds already existed and we were just learning new names for them.... Rather we are initiated by language into a (the) world, and we see and understand the world through the terms and meanings that come into play in this acculturation.... In this sense, our conventions (grammar, codes, territorialities, myths, rules, standards, criteria) are our nature (Bernstein 1981: 229).

This is not, Bernstein is quick to insist, a Derridean skepticism about the very possibility of referentiality:

> What Derrida ends up transforming to houses of cards — shimmering traces of life, as insubstantial as elusive — Wittgenstein locates as *meaning*, with the full range of intention, responsibility, coherence, and possibility for revolt against or madness without. In Wittgenstein's accounting, one is not left sealed off from the world with only "markings" to "decipher" but rather *located* in a world with meanings to *respond* to.... The lesson of metaphysical finitude is not that the world is just codes and as a result that presence is to be ruled out as anything more than nostalgia, but that we can have presence, insofar as we are able, only *through* a shared grammar (Bernstein 1981: 304).

Let me try to sort out these distinctions. Proposition #116 of the *Philosophical Investigations* reads:

> When philosophers use a word — "knowledge", "being", "object", "I", "proposition", "name" — and try to grasp the *essence* of the thing, one must always ask oneself: is the word ever actually used in this way in the language-game which is its original home?
> What *we* do is to bring words back from their metaphysical to their everyday use (Wittgenstein 1958: 48e).

There are no "transcendental signifieds" outside and beyond language — no fixed entities designated by terms like "truth" and "beauty." On the contrary, Wittgenstein argues in the *Lectures on Aesthetics*, words like "beautiful", "fine," and lovely," are first taught as substitutes for facial expressions or gestures. "Lovely!" we say to the child holding out a peach, while smiling and patting our tummies. When, that is to say, we hear someone say "This is lovely" or "This is beautiful," we concentrate, not on the subject and predicate of the proposition, but "on the occasions on which they are said — on the enormously complicated situation in which the aesthetic expression has a place." And further, "What belongs to a language game is a whole culture (Wittgenstein n.d.: 2-3, 8).

Nature, that is to say, gives way to culture; the exploration into "the nature of things" has gradually given way to the exploration into human modes of response to the world. As the Language poet Joan Retallack puts it: "The status of metaphysics (how things are) was successively eclipsed by epistemology (how we know), philosophy of mind (how we think), philosophy of science (how we describe), and philosophy of language (how language, with which we describe and otherwise structure our experience in the world, works)" (1984: 222).

But, it will be objected, how is this philosophical perspective to be "translated" into poetry? The answer is that, for the Language poets, there is no real distinction between the two. Wittgenstein's aphoristic fragments, after all, have many "poetic" features. Conversely, as Bernstein puts it in the Introduction to the "Language Sampler":

> The work collected here can be characterized in the negative as writing that does not privilege any single mode, including the expository logic and speech-derived syntax that dominate contemporary writing practice. Distinctions between essays and lyrics, prose and poetry are often not observed.... Issues of poetics, when not explicitly determining the genre of the work, often permeate its mode of address — a tendency that can pull the poem out of the realm of purely personal reference and into a consideration of the interaction among the seemingly competing spheres of politics, autobiography, fiction, philosophy, common sense, [or] song (Bernstein 1982: 76).

Consider the following examples. First, the opening stanza of Galway Kinnell's "Memory of Wilmington," from the prize-winning *Mortal Acts, Mortal Wounds* (1980: 55):

> Thirty some years ago, hitchhiking
> north on Route 1, I stopped for the night
> at Wilmington, Delaware, one of those American cities
> that start falling apart before they ever get finished.
> I met, I remember, an ancient hobo — I almost remember
>   his name — at the ferry — now dead,
> of course, him,
> and also the ferry —
> in great-brimmed hat, coat to his knees,
> pants dragging the ground, semi-zootish rig
> plucked off various clotheslines. I remember....

From the vantage point of Language poetics, the implicit assumptions that inform a poem like this one are questionable. For Kinnell's premise is that there was a particular event (the meeting with a hobo) that took place at a particular moment in time (thirty-some years ago) in a particular place (Wilmington, Delaware), and that theses "realities" exist outside language and, in Bernstein's words, "to be communicated *at* in language." That is to say: experience is prior to the language that communicates it; the story of the hobo exists in a mental realm waiting to be activated by the words of the poet who can somehow match signifier to signified, can assert confidently that Wilmington is "one of *those* American cities" [my italics], and can characterize the hobo's outfit as a "semi-zootish rig / plucked off various clotheslines."

The "language game," we might say, is prescribed for us, the control-ling "I" assuming (the "conduit theory of communication") that *we* con-strue the meaning of the proper name "Wilmington, Delaware" or the piece of clothing, "zoot suit" precisely as he does. Indeed, Kinnell's portrait of the hobo, a critic like Bernstein would argue, depends upon the "fitting [of] words into a pattern" rather than "actually letting it happen" (Andrews and Bernstein 1984: 39). Or, as Lyn Hejinian puts it in "If Written is Writ-ing", poetry is a matter of seeking "a vocabulary for ideas" rather than "ideas for vocabularies" (Andrews and Bernstein 1984: 29). In positing the self as the primary organizing feature of writing, Kinnell is bound by the inevitable restrictions of such watchwords as "I feel", "I see", "I know", "I remember," authenticity of feeling or memory being guaranteed by the poet's ability to specify, to match "image" to "idea":

> After he ate, I remember, the old hobo
> — *Amos*! yes, that was his name! — old Amos sang,
> or rather laughed forth a song or two, his voice
> creaking out slower and slower
> like the music in old music boxes, when time slows itself
>   down in them (1980: 56).

Compare this memory of "old Amos" to the following passage from Ron Silliman's long prose poem of 1981 called *Tjanting*:

> Performance piece: on a 5 buck dare my father sinks his hand into a vat of hot tar. In every telephone there were rooms. An audible marks the quar-terback's despair. Day gradually steamd into night. Toothless man in a tweed cap, from wch a pigeon feather sticks. How before the new view soon bobbd into world. Anything might come next. The damp on the sit-ting steps finally soakd in. This is a weather report. Why remind it was important his shoelaces matchd himself? The violence of charm. To these almost too far apart bridges seemed instant (1981: 110).

Here what Charles Bernstein calls "the idea of individual voice as a privileged structure" gives way to "a sounding of language from the inside"; the poet's "voice" has become no more than a marginal presence, splicing together the given "data" so as to articulate their meanings. A sentence like "Day gradually steamd into night," for example, is a stock "literary" phrase that expresses, not Silliman's uniqueness, but his familiarity with particular literary codes — in this case, the "language game" of the Victorian pulp novel. There are kernels of similar cliché phrases in "How before the new view soon bobbd into world" and "The damp on the sitting steps finally soakd in." In the latter example, what looks like a citation from a hackneyed novel is ironized by the transferred epithet: "sitting on the damp steps" becomes "The damp of sitting steps." Again, the language of media communication appears in sentences like "This is a weather report," or, once again in transposed form, in "In every telephone there were rooms."

Interestingly, when a particular moment in the poet's own past is recalled — "on a 5 buck dare my father sinks his hand into a vat of hot tar" — the memory prompts, not personal revelation (Kinnell's "I remember those summer nights / when I was young and empty, / when I lay through the darkness, wanting, wanting..."), but the absorption of the subjective image into the larger field of public discourse: the "audible [that] marks the quarterback's despair" and the "rooms" (of vocal despair) inside "every telephone." The "Toothless man in a tweed cap, from wch a pigeon feather sticks" is itself a stock image to be found in novels like *Studs Lonigan*, novels in which old men whose shoelaces don't match sit on the back steps at night until the damp has "finally soakd in." But Silliman's "Performance piece" will not allow us to read his text as a novel with a cast of characters, having such and such psychological traits. The talk of the "damp" that "finally soakd in" may, after all, be part of the "weather report." "Anything," as he reminds himself, "might come next." Indeed, the "real" and the "imaginary" inevitably fuse: "To these almost too far apart bridges seemed instant."

II

"A *tjanting*," Barret Watten explains in his Introduction to Silliman's long prose poem, "is a drawing instrument used for handwork in batik. The pun is exact: *Tjanting* (chanting) would seem to follow its predecessor as an oral form (*Ketjak*), but is in fact written toward writing considered as itself" (Silliman 1981: iii).

This is an important point. For Modernist poets from Pound and Williams to Olson and O'Hara, the goal was to simulate direct, impassioned speech. A man on his feet, talking — this was Olson's description of the poet. In the sixties, when Zukofsky was first read seriously by younger poets and when Gertrude Stein became a major influence, we witness a gradual shift from a speech-based poetics to a renewed emphasis on the writerly, indeed, on artifice and manner. The poetry of John Ashbery, as I have argued elsewhere (Perloff 1987), provides a significant bridge to the *fin de siècle* "language-games" of Charles Bernstein, Ron Silliman, Lyn

Hejinian, Susan Howe, Rae Armantrout, Michael Palmer, Bob Perelman, and a score of other young Language poets. But since I began with Barthes, let me point to what may seem the surprising link (*arthrology* indeed!) between a text like *Roland Barthes par Roland Barthes* and Silliman's *Tjanting*.

The fragments that constitute Barthes' mock-autobiography are introduced by short titles arranged in alphabetical order, from the *A* of "Actif / réactif" to the *T* of "Le monstre de la totalité," a fragment that ends with the passage:

> Autre discours: ce 6 août, à la campagne, c'est le matin d'un jour splendide: soleil, chaleur, fleurs, silence, calme, rayonnement. Rien ne rôde, ni le désir, ni l'agression; seul le travail est là, devant moi, comme une sorte d'être universel: tout est plein. Ce serait donc cela, la Nature? Une absence ... du reste? La *Totalité*? (Barthes 1975: 182)

And of course the question is left open, the final page of the book containing a pictograph called "La graphie pour rien," followed by an illegible line of writing labelled "... ou le signifiant sans signifié."

Between A and T (notice that Barthes does not give us the expected A to Z sequence with its inevitable move toward closure), the fragments are arranged so as to prevent them "de se solidifier" (Barthes 1981: 198). Not that anarchy, Barthes is quick to point out, is the signified of the system. "Peut-être," he remarks, "... le meilleur moyen d'empêcher cette solidification est-il de feindre de rester à l'intérieur d'un code apparemment classique, de garder les apparences d'une écriture soumise a certains impératifs stylistiques, et d'atteindre ainsi la dissocation du sens final à travers une forme qui n'est pas spectaculairement désordonnée" (1981: 198).

By "un code apparemment classique," Barthes is evidently referring to the alphabetical order of titles, each followed by a paragraph or two of what seems to be commentary, as in a Commonplace Book. But consider the choice of the thirteen "A" titles: *Actif / réactif, L'adjectif, L'aise, Le demon de l'analogie. Au tableau noir, L'argent, Le vaisseau Argo, L'arrogance, Le geste de l'aruspice, L'assentiment, non le choix, Vérité et assertion, L'atopie, L'autonymie*. No two are quite parallel: *Actif* is an adjective, *L'adjectif* a noun. In *Actif* the A is the first letter, in *L'adjectif* it follows the article, in *L'aise* it isn't sounded at all, and in the fourth title, the A appears in the fourth word. Again, some of the titles are abstractions (*Vérité et assertion*) while others designate a specific place (*Au tableau noir*), or a proper name (*Le vaisseau Argo*). The seemingly orderly sequence of parallel items is thus no more than a form of etiquette, as if to say that once these codes are established, the text is free to move in a variety of directions.

Consider what happens in a relatively long text under *F* (juxtaposed to the tiny "Fourier ou Flaubert?") called "Le cercle de fragments." It begins with an infinitive: "Écrire par fragments; les fragments sont alors des pierres sur le pourtoir du cercle; je m'étale en rond: tout mon petit univers en miettes; au centre, quoi?" (Barthes 1975: 96-97). But then the "je" whose universe is dispersed in little "miettes" becomes an "il": "Son premier texte ou à peu près (*1942*) est fait de fragments." A little narrative of Barthes' career follows: its Gidean beginnings, the lexias of *S/Z*, the fact that "Le catch, il le voyait déjà comme une suite de fragments," and at this point the author pauses to cite himself in *Mythologies*. Here is what Barthes calls "le romanesque" without the continuity of "le roman," the narrative that presents its subject from different pronominal perspectives and then, once removed, in his own earlier writings. But in the fourth paragraph, narrative gives way to rumination on the word:

> Non seulement le fragment est coupé de ses voisins, mais encore à l'intérieur de chaque fragment règne la parataxe. Cela se voit bien si vous faites l'index de ces petits morceaux; pour chacun d'eux, l'assemblage des référents est hétéroclite; c'est comme un jeu de bouts rimés: "Soit les mots: *fragment, cercle, Gide, catch, asyndète, peinture, dissertation, Zen, intermezzo*; imaginez un discours qui puisse les lier." Eh bien, ce sera tout simplement ce fragment-ci. L'index d'un texte n'est donc pas seulement un instrument de référence; il est lui-même un texte, un second texte qui est le *relief* (reste et aspérité) du premier: ce qu'il y a de délirant (d'interrompu) dans la raison des phrases" (Barthes 1975: 97).

Here Barthes' "Jeu de bouts rimés" links together nine nouns that stand synecdochically for the poet's "cercle": the "fragments," first learned from Gide and observed in the "catch," the "figure de l'interruption et du court-circuit" which is "l'asyndète," and which operates in Barthes' "naive" attempt at "peinture" — these lead to "des 'arrivées' inattendues" and to "l'ouverture abrupte, separée rompue" of Zen (paragraph 7) (98). In Zen Buddhism, says Barthes, "Le fragment (comme le haiku) est *torin*; il implique une jouissance immédiate: c'est un fantasme du discours" (98). This "fantasme du discours" — a discourse that might link the magic words in Barthes' lyric string of paragraph 4 — can, says Barthes, come to you anywhere: "au café, dans le train, en parlant avec un ami (cela surgit latéralement à ce qu'il dit ou à ce que je dis); on sort alors son carnet, non pour noter une 'pensée,' mais quelque chose comme une frappe, ce qu'on eût appelé autrefois un 'vers'" (98).

And, indeed, the whole "circle of fragments" has now taken a *verse* "turn." The last of Barthes' key words is *intermezzo*, and in paragraph 8 we read:

> ... le fragment est comme l'idée musicale d'un cycle ... chaque pièce se suf-
> fit, et cependant elle n'est jamais que l'interstice de ses voisines: l'oeuvre
> n'est faite que de hors-texte. L'homme qui a le mieux compris et pratiqué
> l'esthétique du fragment (avant Webern), c'est peut-être Schumann; il
> appelait le fragment "intermezzo"; il a multiplié dans ses oeuvres les *inter-
> mezzi*: tout ce qu'il produisait était finalement *intercalé*: mais entre quoi et
> quoi? (98)

The musical analogy leads into the coda of what is surely a poetic discourse, even if Barthes never allows it to "solidify" into the prose poem which is its intertext:

> Le fragment a son idéal: une haute condensation, non de pensée, ou de
> sagesse, ou de vérité (comme dans la Maxime), mais de musique: au "dé-
> veloppement," s'opposerait le "ton," quelque chose d'articulé et de
> chanté, une diction: là devrait régner le *timbre*. *Pièces brèves* de Webern:
> pas de cadence: quelle souveraineté il met a *tourner court*! (98)

In citing Webern's *small pieces*, Barthes' text does, so to speak, *turn short*, returning us to the "petit univers en miettes" of the opening paragraph, to the stones on the perimeter of the writer's circle. And indeed, the speaking subject is dispersed in the circle of fragments: pronouns and tenses shift, abstraction alternates with image, and bits of narrative are *intercalated* into the meditative structure. The form of the whole is in Barthean parlance, "discontinuous and combinatory"; the "juxtaposition of things," what Barthes calls in *L'Empire des signes* "l'à côté de," creates a postmodern analogue to the definition poem or riddle. The prose, highly condensed, alliterative, and assonantal (e.g., "les pierres sur le pourtoir du cercle") mimes "le circle des fragments," moving, as it does, from writing to reading to wrestling, from parlor game to painting to Zen koan, to the musical phrase. There are nine key words and nine paragraphs: in the ninth, we read that the musical fragment has a "'ton,' quelque chose d'articulé et de chanté, une diction." And of course "diction" is Barthes' own domain.

In *Roland Barthes par Roland Barthes*, number series and alphabets thus function as markers to identify the "language game" in question. And further, these quantitative structures replace the self as the primary organizing feature of writing. "A poem," as Charles Bernstein puts it, "exists in a matrix of social and historical relations that are more significant to the formation of an individual text than any personal qualities of the life or voice of an author" (Andrews and Bernstein 1984: 41).

Now let us come back to Silliman's *Tjanting*. As the poet explains in a recent interview with Tom Beckett (Silliman 1985: 35-36), the number of sentences per paragraph in *Tjanting* is determined by the Fibonacci number series, which is to say, by the rule that each term is the sum of two previous terms: 1, 1, 2, 3, 5, 8, 13, 21, 34... n. But because he wanted to have "two oppositional series of paragraphs" (Silliman's somewhat naive way of paying homage to Marxian dialectic and "the class struggle ... viewed as a form") he construes the series so that one line of development goes 1, 2, 5, 13 ... 4181, while the second or "response" goes 1, 3, 8, 21 ... 2584. (The total of 4181 and 2584 is 6765, the last Fibonacci term under 10,000).

Why such an elaborate number system? Having done away with "the received tradition of a writing that presumes and imposes a stable 'voice'," the "problem," says Silliman, is simply how to proceed. "What motivates the next line, the next sentence, the next paragraph or stanza? Without syntax, what justifies the existence of even the next word?" (1985: 34). All poetry, in other words, is, in some sense, "procedure," the important thing being not to let "procedure," whether the "rule-governed behavior of the sonnet" or the numerical constraints of the Fibonacci system, become an ingrained habit, a cookie-cutter to be used again and again.

Since the final paragraph of *Tjanting* goes on for 87 pages (and the penultimate one for 50), the Fibonacci scheme has more to do with the poet's scheme of construction than with our reading habits. More important, from the reader's point of view, is Silliman's repetition rule. "Each paragraph," he explains, "repeat[s] each sentence of its previous occurrence.... However, the repeats [are] rewritten so as to reveal their constructedness, their artificiality as elements of meaning, their otherness" (Silliman 1985: 36).

To illustrate, here is the opening of *Tjanting* (1981: 11) with the number of sentences per paragraph written in parentheses.

> Not this. (1)
> What then? (1)
> I started over & over. Not this. (2)
> Last week I wrote "the muscles in my palm so sore from halving the rump roast I cld barely grip the pen." What then? This morning my lip is blisterd. (3)

Of about to within which. Again & again I began. The gray light of
day fills the yellow room in a way wch is somber. Not this. Hot grease has
spilld on the stove top. (5)
     Not that either. Last week I wrote "the muscle at thumb's root so taut
from carving that beef I thought it wld cramp." Not so. What then? Wld I
begin? This morning my lip is tender, disfigurd. I sat in an old chair out
behind the anise. I cld have gone about this some other way. (8)
     Wld it be different with a different pen? Of about to within which
what. Poppies grew out of the pile of old broken-up cement. I began again
& again. These clouds are not apt to burn off. The yellow room has a sober
hue. Each sentence accounts for its place. Not this. Old chairs in the back
yard rotting from winter. Grease on the stove top sizzled & spat. it's the
same, only different. Ammonia's odor hangs in the air. Not not this. (13)

Silliman's "tjanting" ("chanting") consists of tightly interwoven repeats and
numerical structures so as to foreground what Barthes calls "the work of
the signifier." The dialectic of oppositional paragraphs is never one of obvious contrast; Silliman himself points out that such "separation…would have
made the work seem too ping-pong like" (1985: 36). Thus, the relationship
between the two series is contrapuntal rather than oppositional: "Not this"
— the phrase appears and reappears in both series, each time in a slightly
different context, in what we might call a different language game. Further,
the repeated phrases become part of a network of parallels and antitheses:
"Not this" / "Not that either"; "I started over & over" / "I began again &
again"; "Wld it be different with a different pen?" / "It's the same, only different"; "Hot grease had spilld on the stove top" / "Grease on the stove top
sizzled & spat"; "I sat in an old chair out behind the anise" / "Old chairs in
the back yard rotting from winter."
     Like *Roland Barthes par Roland Barthes*, but in much more extreme
form, *Tjanting* thus takes as its starting point the autobiographical convention only to turn it inside out. The reader cannot get absorbed in the personal "story," because the repetitions and permutations call attention to the
mise en scène of *signifiance* rather than on what is recounted. Further, the
foregrounding of rhyme ("Again & Again I began," "The gray light of day
fills the yellow room in a way") — and of song rhythms ("Wld it be different with a different pen?"; "Grease on the stove top sizzled & spat", "Ammonia's odor hangs in the air") calls attention to "the work of the signifier,"
to the refusal of words, morphemes, and phonemes to provide what Joan
Retallack calls a "squeegee-cleaned window on transcendent Truth", "a
self-effacing medium to a world fully furnished and ready for inspection"
(1984: 218).

Indeed, so prominent is sound patterning in a text like *Tjanting* that Silliman's "prose" is quite literally more "poetic" (if we remember that "verse" derives from "versus" or "return") than, say, Galway Kinnell's "Memory of Wilmington," with its loose free-verse rhythms. "Poetry," for Kinnell, means draping an otherwise normal sentence over a series of lines, for example:

> Thirty-some years ago, hitchhiking north on Route 1, I stopped for the night at Wilmington, Delaware, one of those American cities that start falling apart before they ever get finished.

I am not at all sure that lineation improves this sentences, but, in any case, it strikes the ear as much less obviously a poem than does a passage like the following:

> Humidity of the restroom. Half-heard humor. Old rusted hammer head sits in the dust. Clothespins at angles on a nylon line. Our generation had school desks which still had inkwells, but gone were the bottles of ink. Green glass broken in the grass. Every dog on the block began to bark. Hark. Words work as wedges or as hedges to a bet. Debt drives the nation (Silliman 1981: 15).

Here a fairly routine childhood memory — the clothesline in the backyard, the old schooldesks with inkwells, the humid school restroom — is transformed by what Charles Bernstein calls "a recharged use of the multivalent referential vectors than any word has" (Andrews and Bernstein 1984: 115). Thus "humidity" generates "humor" and "hammer," and if "Words work as wedges," there is no reason, given the power of rhyme and the meaning of the business cliché "to hedge one's bets," that they should not also act as "hedges to a bet" that inevitably produces "Debt." Which is another way of saying that to understand the meaning of "hedges," we must know in what language game it is being used.

"Fragmentation," writes Bruce Andrews, "doesn't banish the references *embodied* in individual words; merely — they are not placed in a *series*, in grammar, in a row, *on a shelf*" (Andrews and Bernstein 1984: 34). To put it another way, we might say that in Language poetry, T.S. Eliot's "fragments" "shored against" the poet's "ruin" give way to a delight in the very discontinuity and re-combination of the fragments. As in the Chinese scroll that the Barthes of *L'Empire des signes* takes as his paradigm, it is the "next to" (*l'à côté de*) that provides the pleasure of the text.

REFERENCES

Andrews, Bruce and Charles Bernstein. 1984. *The L=A=N=G=U=A=G=E Book*. Carbondale and Edwardsville: Southern Illinois University Press.

Barthes, Roland. 1953. *Le Degré zéro de l'écriture*. Paris: Seuil.

-----. 1957. *Mythologies*. Paris: Seuil.

-----. 1973. *Le Plaisir du texte*. Paris: Seuil.

-----. 1975. *Roland Barthes par Roland Barthes*. Paris: Seuil.

-----. 1981. *Le Grain de la voix: Entretiens 1962-80*. Paris: Seuil.

Bernstein, Charles. 1981. "Reading Cavell Reading Wittgenstein," *Boundary 2*,9: 295-306. Excerpted in Andrews and Bernstein 1984: 60-62.

-----. 1982. "Language Sampler," *Paris Review* 86: 75-125.

Kinnell, Galway. 1980. *Mortal Acts, Mortal Wounds*. Boston: Houghton Mifflin.

Perloff, Marjorie. 1987. "Ashbery and *fin de siècle*." Forthcoming.

Retallack, Joan. 1984. "The Meta-Physick of Play: L=A=N=G=U=A=G=E U.S.A," *Parnassus* 12: 213-244.

Silliman, Ron. 1981. *Tjanting*. Berkeley, Ca.: The Figures.

-----. 1985. "Interview with Tom Beckett," *The Difficulties (Ron Silliman Issue)*: 34-46.

Wittgenstein, Ludwig. 1958. *Philosophical Investigations*. 3rd ed., trans. G.E.M. Anscombe. New York: Macmillan.

-----. no date. *Lectures & Conversations on Aesthetics, Psychology, and Religious Belief*. Compiled from Notes taken by Yorick Smythies, Rush Rhees, and James Taylor, ed. Cyril Barrett. Berkeley and Los Angeles: University of California Press.

7

Samuel Beckett and the Postmodernism Controversy

Breon Mitchell

I am not at all sure that controversy is the right word in my title. Postmodernist critics offer up their ideas so modestly, so tentatively, so playfully, that they cannot be caught in a controversy, simply because their convictions are, like Postmodernism itself, often self-subversive and indeterminate. Ihab Hassan lists five characteristics of Postmodernism, or ten, or twice that number, depending upon the time available, and always with the warning that they all are given to "provide a start — but only a start." We are warned that "the list can prove deceptive. For differences shift, defer, collapse" (1980: 123-124). He seems perfectly open to altering his list and including in it any suggestion of our own if it would make us feel better.

Douwe Fokkema is less playful, but equally circumspect in advancing his linguistic codes: "Lotman distinguished at least two codes. I, however, would suggest that there are at least five codes that are operative in virtually all literary texts (my five codes are quite different from the five codes distinguished by Roland Barthes)." Not only does Fokkema decline to defend his own set of codes against any other previous set, he doesn't even claim a special status for them: "It is due largely to the habitual interests of the student of literature and the state of our discipline that I do not mention more than five codes, but the number is far from sacred" (1984: 8,9). Presumably the state of our discipline and the quality of our students is such that neither can cope with more than five items at a time. At any rate, in such an atmosphere polemics in the old sense disappears, and controversy no longer seems the appropriate word. As Umberto Eco put it not too long ago, "I realize, as I say this, that perhaps I use 'modern' and 'postmodern' in a different sense from that in which you and others use it. Well, this seems to me a very postmodern attitude — don't you agree?" (Rosso 1983:

5). And indeed it is.

But even if controversy is muted, the resulting critical plurality leads to a general confusion which is surely widespread and at least some cause for concern in a group which proposes to publish a volume on Postmodernism in the ICLA series. To take one very minor but symptomatic example: a recent review in the *German Quarterly* of a book entitled *Peter Handke and the Postmodern Transformation* includes this passage:

> And then there is the problem raised by the authors' assumption about literary history. For them, there "was" (sic) a movement called "Modernism" to which "Postmodernism" in theory and practice stands in opposition... (The authors') authority for this sort of poetics is Ihab Hassan; I am not sure they have Hassan quite right since I understand Hassan to regard "Postmodernism" as a change or development in "Modernism" rather than a decisive break with it. The synthesis of the two movements is for the authors the so-called New Sensibility, which they describe and define by quoting six criteria established by the West-German germanist Hans-Gerhard Winter — figural perspective, merger of inner and outer world, self-referentiality, theme of identity, open form demanding that the reader "think out the story." There is, I think, nothing "sensibly new" in these strategies and themes since they represent the conventions of modernist art in general (Voris 1985: 485).

I've quoted this passage at some length because it seems to me typical of what happens more often than not — the book is confused, the reviewer is confused, and I am confused. And I don't think that things go off track in this book, or in this review, just because Winter exceeds the five categories that our discipline and students can handle. There is something instead in our very way of going about discussing Postmodernism which contributes directly to the problem. The postmodernism dialogue is attractive in many ways — open, entertaining, and free from cant. On the other hand it is becoming more and more difficult to distinguish critical plurality from mass confusion.

The problem is not made any easier by the terms we have to work with. Suppose we could start all over. Surely no one would argue seriously for retaining the words Modernism and Postmodernism if we could think of anything better. And what does it say about us that we can't? As terms, Modernism and Postmodernism are something we have to live with. Thus the urge to define, redefine, stretch the limits, all in an effort to make the terms, in themselves so pitifully limited in expressive power, cover developments in the arts which seem of crucial importance. Some of the more recent efforts, including the suggestion "Paramodernism" for the period between Modernism and Postmodernism (assuming we know what those are) simply continue a tendency with which we are all too familiar.

But it seems to me that little hope lies in the direction of new prefixes. In a *New Yorker* essay entitled "Modernist, Postmodernist, What Will They Think of Next?", John Updike calls such literary labelling "innocent fun, which helps not only us but, more to the point, college English majors to get a grip on things." He himself doubts that postmodernist will acquire the canonical permanence of "Post-Impressionist or post-Kantian, for the reason that Impressionism and Immanuel Kant were phenomena more distinct and limited than Modernism was. We still live in modern (from the Latin *modo*, "just now") times, and so will our descendants, until the dictionary falls to dust" (Updike 1984: 136). Of course Updike has reason to take special interest in such matters, since his own novels are persistently excluded from the postmodernist camp in critical discussions.

The various attempts which have been made to differentiate Modernism from Postmodernism by Barth, Hassan, Lyotard, Fokkema, Eco and others are familiar to the narrow audience they address. Even among these critics, however, there is little specific agreement as to the nature, scope or historical boundaries of the terms, and little likelihood there ever will be. Of course there is just as much disagreement about such concepts as Expressionism, Surrealism, and Romanticism. But whereas earlier literary historians often believed they were arguing about something real, critics in the postmodern era are perfectly willing to call into question their own enterprise, to deny essentialist concepts, to suggest even more inventive prefixes and suffixes for Modernism, all with the modest intention of entertaining themselves and others, raising questions of serious intellectual interest while simultaneously demonstrating the postmodernist aesthetic in their own work. Almost every critic who seeks to define Postmodernism is willing to agree that the definition he or she offers is of merely heuristic value.

In the meantime the terms have taken on a life of their own, and, not surprisingly, they bear little resemblance to the ideas proposed by literary critics. Postmodernism has already escaped us, and is widely used by any number of people who are demonstrably innocent of any knowledge of the specifics or world view which supposedly underlie the concept. Matei Calinescu has pointed out that the word modern has long since ceased to be synonymous with "contemporary" in the arts (1977: 86). But by an ironic compensation of the public mind, Postmoderism has taken on this very function. As generally used today, postmodern simply means what's happening now, and it is likely that we all may be forced to accept this broader application whether we like it or not.

But if there is little specific agreement as to exactly what has happened, and even less as to how and why it occurred, it is generally recognized that a major shift has taken place, that the modernist enterprise has come to an end, and that a new postmodernist era has arrived. It is this general sense which has permeated the public mind as well. And now it is our task to try to understand that shift more clearly.

II

It is at this point that models of one sort or another are often helpful. One such suggestive, tentative model was advanced some ten years ago by Ihab Hassan. It links the general movement from Modernism to Postmodernism with two major literary figures of our age — James Joyce and Samuel Beckett:

> Joyce and Beckett represent two ways of the imagination in our century. Joyce and Beckett, two Irishmen. They divide the world between them, divide the Logos, the world's body. One, in high arrogance, invents language anew, and makes over the universe in parts of speech. The other, in deep humility, restores to words their primal emptiness, and mimes his solitary way into the dark. Between them they stretch the mind's tether until it begins to snap (Hassan 1975a: 183).

In Hassan's view, Beckett's Bloomian anxiety in the face of Joyce's accomplishment pushes the younger Irishman inexorably toward silence: "Beckett redefines originality as a flight from originality, imagination as an escape from amplitude, language as silence. In the anxiety of genius, Beckett does not attempt to surpass Joyce; he 'negates' him by his own example. Negates? Yes. Beckett redirects the endeavor of literature and turns Joyce into a 'classic'" (Hassan 1975a: 185). But by *Finnegans Wake*, in Hassan's view, Joyce himself has developed into a postmodernist: "The quest for a total verbal consciousness in Joyce, the quest for a minimal verbal consciousness in Beckett — both express a postmodern will to dematerialize the world, to turn it into a gnostic reality, a fantasy" (196). And finally, we face the postmodern condition:

> The contrasts between Joyce and Beckett also hold every new writer in an invisible grip; the literary predicament is continual. For the difficulties that

Beckett encountered in relation to Joyce are compounded in the case of the young writer who must cope with *both* Beckett and Joyce. There they stand at the antipodes of language, defining the outer limits of contemporary literature. How, then, can a postmodern genius exceed these limits? (Hassan 1975a: 185)

Hassan's model is thus essentially linear. First Joyce the Modernist, then Joyce and Beckett the postmodernists, then Postmodernism itself. Such a model seems to have a good deal of explanatory power. Literary history is made concrete through major figures, the progression from Modernism to Postmodernism seems visible, the motivating force which underlies the shift appears psychologically probable (Beckett's anxious swerve away from Joyce). Nevertheless there are a few problems with the progression which may be worth discussing for the light they shed on our topic. In the remainder of this paper, then, I would like to reexamine the Joyce-Beckett-Postmodernism model.

Let us begin with *Finnegans Wake*. Hassan suggests that "The monstrous effort of *Finnegans Wake* strains, beyond its puns and infinite sounds, beyond its noise, toward a region of articulate silence; that, of course, is the region which the works of Beckett occupy, and around which much of postmodern literature circles" (1975a: 186). The rhetoric of this sentence leads a little too easily to its conclusion: *Finnegans Wake* strains toward silence (how?), Beckett's work centers around silence, so does much postmodern literature, (thus) *Finnegans Wake* is postmodern. Taken on purely logical grounds, that argument doesn't go very far. Moreover, even if we grant the late Joyce and *Finnegans Wake* postmodernist status, what now explains the shift? We know, or think we can understand, a shift in Beckett's attitude toward art and language, but what caused that same shift in Joyce? We are left with an assertion which dangles without convincing. And when what dangles before us is Joyce and *Finnegans Wake* that's no small matter.

The assertion of any major shift in Joyce's own creative drive also runs counter to anything we know from Joyce's letters and essays, and counter to the evidence of the texts themselves. Joyce's constant enterprise from *Dubliners* on remained one which could reasonably be called Modernist: to stretch the limits of his art as far as he could, to recreate the world in language, to fulfill Flaubert's dream of a book spinning like a world in the emptiness of space. *Finnegans Wake* is the logical continuation of the Joycean aesthetic, an expanding universe of language. Certainly no shift or reversal was ever implied by Joyce. He called *Ulysses* his day book, *Finne-*

gans Wake his night book. One led logically, in terms of the Joycean aesthetic, into the other, the seeds of the *Wake* being clearly present in *Ulysses*. Joyce's enterprise was, from first to last, surprisingly constant and unified. And it seems only reasonable to call that enterprise Modernist, at least until we find some better word.

After Beckett's early experiments with the prose style of *Work in Progress*, his aesthetic too remains strikingly constant, from the late 1930's to the present. Like Joyce, that aesthetic is given form in works which change and develop, without, however, offering evidence of any fundamental shift in the way Beckett feels about his art.

Beckett is, of course, a particularly interesting case for postmodernist critics. Because his work continues to push further and more relentlessly to the edge of the sayable than any other writer, he makes any discussion of Postmodernism which omits him seem pallid. And indeed, he is generally enlisted in the ranks of the postmodernists without further ado. Lyotard's definition of the postmodern sounds like a paraphrase of Beckett's aesthetics: "The postmodern would be that which, in the modern, puts forward the unpresentable in presentation itself; that which denies itself the solace of good forms, the consensus of a taste which would make it possible to share collectively the nostalgia for the unattainable; that which searches for new presentations, not in order to enjoy them but in order to impart a stronger sense of the unpresentable" (1983: 340). While Julia Kristeva notes: "As far as writing is concerned, it has since set out to blaze a trail amidst the unnamable; Beckett is the best example with his derisory and infernal testimony" (1980: 141).

And yet there is something in the deep seriousness of Beckett's attitude toward art which looks suspiciously modernist. The least that can be said is that he does not fit in comfortably with the playful self-reflexivity of many of his present-day colleagues. The recent controversy over the American Repertory Theatre's production of *Endgame* in Cambridge, Massachusetts (and here the word controversy is indeed in order) was really not all that surprising. Robert Brustein, wanting to bring what he described as "new values to an extraordinary play," had set *Endgame* in an underground subway tunnel, with a bombed-out, vandalized subway car extending halfway across the stage. What resulted was summarized in the pages of the *New York Law Journal*:

> In the rear, a wall rises the full height of the stage, with long, narrow iron
> ladders climbing to the top in the places where the "windows" are sup-

posed to be. Instead of two plain "ashbins," the ART production substitutes seven beat up oil drums.

Where Mr. Beckett's *Endgame* demands silence, the ART production gives us an overture composed by Phillip Glass to precede the play, open the play and accentuate lines of the dialogue. . . . Advised of the changes, Mr. Beckett insisted that the production be halted. . . . A complaint, with an order to show cause seeking a temporary restraining order and preliminary injunction halting the ART production, had been prepared for filing. . . . Under the terms of an extraordinary settlement agreement, the ART production opened, as planned. But in exchange for mutual releases, ART agreed to insert in all playbills for its production of *Endgame* a written statement by Beckett and Rosset together with a page of the text of *Endgame*. . . . Mr. Beckett's statement reads: "Any production of *Endgame* which ignores my stage directions is completely unacceptable to me. My play requires an empty room and two small windows. The American Repertory Theatre production, which dismisses my directions, is a complete parody of the play as conceived by me. Anybody who cares for the work couldn't fail to be disgusted by this." . . . On behalf of ART, Mr. Brustein wrote ". . . to insist on strict adherence to each parenthesis of the published text — not only robs collaborative artists of their respective freedom, but threatens to turn the theatre into waxworks" (Garbus and Singleton 1984: 1-2).

It is difficult to conceive of Beckett's reaction as the expression of a postmodernist aesthetic, or of a postmodernist mind. In fact it sounds quite conservative — the sort of anger one might expect from an old-fashioned modernist. And this was no mere aberration. It's well known that the primary reason Beckett takes so many of his works to West Germany for their first performance is that there he is accorded total control of the production, down to each step and breath.

Is it possible that rather than an early postmodernist, Beckett was (is) the last of the great modernists? Was the anxious swerve that took him away from Joyce's aesthetics a truly new departure, a shift from the modernist enterprise? Or was it rather the other side of the modernist drive toward total art, toward the exploration of the exact limits of what can and cannot be said?

There is no question that Beckett stood in awe of Joyce, and that he soon needed to clear imaginative space for himself. But even in taking a diametrically opposed path, he still seems to have thought of himself as engaged in a fundamentally similar enterprise. The recent publication of Beckett's letter of 1937, in German, to Axel Kaun, is unusually revealing:

Es wird mir tatsächlich immer schwieriger, ja sinnloser, ein offizielles Englisch zu schreiben. Und immer mehr wie ein Schleier kommt mir meine Sprache vor, den man zerreissen muss, um an die dahinterliegenden Dinge (oder das dahinterliegende Nichts) zu kommen. Grammatik und Stil. Mir scheinen sie ebenso hinfällig geworden zu sein wie ein Biedermeier Badeanzug oder die Unerschüttlichkeit eines Gentlemans. Eine Larve. Hoffentlich kommt die Zeit, sie ist ja Gott sei dank in gewissen Kreisen schon da, wo die Sprache da am besten gebraucht wird, wo sie am tüchtigsten missbraucht wird. Das wir sie so mit einem Male nicht ausschalten können, wollen wir wenigstens nichts versäumen, was zu ihrem Verruf beitragen mag. Ein Loch nach dem andern in ihr zu bohren, bis das Dahinterkauernde, sei es etwas oder nichts, durchzusickern anfängt — ich kann mir für den heutigen Schriftsteller kein höheres Ziel vorstellen.

Oder soll die Literatur auf jenem alten faulen von Musik und Malerei längst verlassenen Wege allein hinterbleiben?. . .

Selbstverständlich muss man sich vorläufig mit Wenigem begnügen. Zuerst kann es nur darauf ankommen, irgendwie eine Methode zu erfinden, um diese höhnische Haltung dem Worte gegenüber wörtlich darzustellen. In dieser Dissonanz von Mitteln und Gebrauch wird man schon vielleicht ein Geflüster der Endmusik oder des Allem zu Grunde liegenden Schweigens spüren können.

Mit einem solchen Programm hat meiner Ansicht nach die allerletzte Arbeit von Joyce gar nichts zu tun. Dort scheint es sich vielmehr um eine Apotheose des Wortes zu handeln. Es sei denn, Himmelfahrt und Höllensturz sind eins und dasselbe. Wie schön wäre es, glauben zu können, es sei in der Tat so (Beckett 1937: 52-53).

(It is indeed becoming more and more difficult, even senseless, for me to write an official English. And more and more my own language appears to me like a veil that must be torn apart in order to get at the things (or the Nothingness) behind it. Grammar and Style. To me they seem to have become as irrelevant as a Victorian bathing suit or the imperturbability of a true gentleman. A mask. Let us hope the time will come, thank God that in certain circles it has already come, when language is most efficiently used where it is being most efficiently misused. As we cannot eliminate language all at once, we should at least leave nothing undone that might contribute to its falling into disrepute. To bore one hole after another in it, until what lurks behind it — be it something or nothing — begins to seep through; I cannot imagine a higher goal for a writer today. Or is literature alone to remain behind in the old lazy ways that have been so long ago abandoned by music and painting?. . .

Of course, for the time being we must be satisfied with little. At first it can only be a matter of somehow finding a method by which we can represent this mocking attitude towards the word, through words. In this dissonance between the means and their use it will perhaps become possible to feel a whisper of that final music or that silence that underlies All.

With such a program, in my opinion, the latest work of Joyce has nothing whatever to do. There it seems to be matter of an apotheosis of the word. Unless perhaps Ascension to Heaven and Descent to Hell are somehow one and the same. How beautiful it would be to be able to believe that that indeed was the case (Beckett 1937: 171-172).

An astounding letter, about which one or two points should immediately be made. First, behind Beckett's rejection of the Joycean method is a clear longing to believe that in a deep sense he and Joyce are approaching the same goal by different paths. Secondly, the phrases with which he describes this goal remain astonishingly apt for Beckett's work even today. Thirdly, he is not alone. The remark about circles in which "the time has already come" for discarding the masks of grammar and style almost certainly refers to the group Eugene Jolas gathered around the avant-garde periodical *transition* — Beckett had already signed a literary manifesto in its pages which included some of the same points. But perhaps most interestingly, Beckett sees his goal as already achieved in music and the visual arts, a remark which points back toward early Modernism much more clearly than it points forward to Postmodernism. Beckett's interest in the relationship between language and reality reflects a broader cultural crisis which had already been evident in the work of the young Hugo von Hofmannsthal, whose Lord Chandos letter of 1902 outlined his own despair at expressing anything significant at all about life through language. One has only to think of Rilke and Kafka on the one hand, or Mauthner and Wittgenstein on the other, to recall the extent to which this question permeated early twentieth-century thought.

Joyce and Beckett thus represent two major parallel tendencies in literature during the first half of this century: one which stresses the creative and infinite power of the word, and another which sees language as impotent in the face of reality, incapable of expressing anything of fundamental importance. The drive to push language to its limits, and to identify those limits, is essentiality a modernist drive. Once those limits have been charted by writers of great power, however, the postmodern era sets in. Joyce did indeed engage in a quest for total verbal consciousness, as Hassan suggests, and Beckett in a quest for a minimal verbal consciousness, but rather than a postmodern will which has grown mysteriously out of Modernism, this represents the culmination of Modernism itself.

The postmodernist condition, then, consists in the recognition of the modernist achievements of Joyce and Beckett, who, in Hassan's words, have divided the world between them. They represent two poles on the surface of the literary globe which every writer will inevitably encounter if he or she goes far enough. The anxiety of influence lives on, and nowhere is it more clearly in evidence than in John Barth's claim that "The postmodernist has the first half of our century under his belt, but not on his back" (quoted by Updike 1984: 142). Barth has both Joyce and Beckett looking over his shoulder, and that's not nearly so comfortable a feeling as he would have us believe. The postmodernist dilemma involves the recognition that the boundaries of literary expression have already been charted by artists of genius and true integrity. Such a recognition also entails a burden of freedom — for within this finite universe all paths are now equally open.

III

I am painfully aware that the end result of this brief re-examination of the Joyce-Beckett-postmodernist model may appear to be little more than switching nametags on the parties involved. I deny that *Finnegans Wake* is postmodern, I view both Joyce and Beckett as modernists, I characterize Postmodernism as a recognition of being situated *between* the limit cases of Joyce and Beckett. So what? Well, such an analysis does have certain implications. Because it describes a condition only, rather than a set of particular stylistic features or a certain period code, it maps out a truly open field for postmodernist writing. The only prerequisite for inclusion among the postmodernists is an author's consciousness of the postmodern situation, and his or her willingness to produce texts under that sign. In this sense, such recent novels as Norman Mailer's *Tough Guys Don't Dance*, William Gaddis' *Carpenter's Gothic*, and Umberto Eco's *The Name of the Rose* are all equally postmodern, in spite of the enormous differences among them in style and structure.

To suggest such a view is something quite different from reducing the notion of Postmodernism to a simple matter of dates. Hundreds of novels still appear each year which show little sign of the struggle out of which our best writers create their texts. But it is equally worth stressing that such signs may be effectively submerged. Eco's *The Name of the Rose*, for example, does not carry its present critical credentials as a postmodern work by virtue of its stylistic features, its narrative strategies, or the way in which it plays upon received generic forms, all of which are relatively traditional and might pass more or less unheralded under another author's name.

Instead, we grant the novel postmodern status because we know that Eco is spinning his tale in full consciousness of his predicament. As Eco puts it in "Reflections on *The Name of the Rose*", "The writer... always knows what he is doing and how much it costs him. He knows he has to solve a problem," one which begins with the opening sentence of the novel: "Is it possible to say 'It was a beautiful morning at the end of November' without feeling like Snoopy?" (1985: 8,9). Eco finds the answer to this question in the creation of ironic distance by "quoting" both plot and genre, but it is worth noting again how closely such ironic quotation may end up resembling an old-fashioned novel. It is, in fact, only the metatext of Eco's "reflections" which clearly reveals the postmodern sensibility behind the novel. Thus Eco concludes, "I believe that post-modernism is not a trend to be chronologically defined, but, rather, an ideal category — or better still, a *Kunstwollen*, a way of operating" (1985: 16). Does this not raise authorial intention, or at least consciousness, to the status of a criterion for postmodernist writing? Indeed it does. Yet what strength remains in the intentional fallacy argument for the contemporary theorist of today, in a world of interlocking texts including the letters, memoirs, prefaces and published reflections of the author?

The broader view of literary Postmodernism I have outlined also mitigates against importing hidden value judgments under the guise of analyzing style and structure. The present party game of dividing contemporary authors into modernists and postmodernists is fun to play, but raises serious issues. If we call Barth, Barthelme and Pynchon hardcore postmodernists (to use Fokkema's term) while calling Updike and Styron modernists, what exactly are we claiming? Isn't what we want to say simply that the latter seem to us old-fashioned in a pejorative sense? That they have not kept with the times, and that we can thus take them less seriously? Have we not surreptitiously reintroduced value judgments based on style alone? — implying that there are certain things writers *ought* to be doing these days, certain ways they *should* be writing, and that if they don't they will have to content themselves with a smaller share of our time and attention? In short, are we not simply calling those texts postmodern which we like most, because they appeal most strongly to our own preconceptions about the sorts of playful, self-reflexive moves an author ought to make to keep us entertained?

But the fact of the matter is that some of the most interesting writing today shows few of the stylistic features we have come to call postmodern, while the work of many postmodernists seems to offer little but the formal trappings which allow us to apply the label with a minimum of effort. Opening up the postmodernist canon to writers who do not easily fit the mold allows us to concentrate instead upon the broad family of resemblances which link all serious attempts to contemporary prose. In such a world, *The Witches of Eastwick* and *Waiting for the Barbarians* appear as postmodern as *The Twofold Vibration*. And the author who opts for a path more closely tied to earlier traditions of the novel will bear as little resemblance to Dickens or Kafka as Pierre Menard does to Cervantes.

REFERENCES

Beckett, Samuel. 1937. Letter to Axel Kaun, in Cohn 1984: 51-54, trans. Martin Esslin: 170-173.

Calinescu, Matei. 1977. *Faces of Modernity: Avant-Garde, Decadence, Kitsch*. Bloomington: Indiana University Press.

Cohn, Ruby. 1984. *Disjecta: Miscellaneous Writings and a Dramatic Fragment by Samuel Beckett*. New York: Grove Press.

Eco, Umberto. 1985. "Reflections on *The Name of The Rose*," *Encounter* 64: 7-19.

Fokkema, Douwe W. 1984. *Literary History, Modernism, and Postmodernism*. Amsterdam and Philadelphia: Benjamins.

Garbus, Martin and Gerald E. Singleton. 1984. "Boston Production of Endgame Raises Controversy," *Newsletter of the Samuel Beckett Society* 6 (1985): 1-2. Originally printed under the title "Playwright-Director Conflict: Whose Play Is It Anyway?" *New York Law Journal* 192: 1-2.

Garvin, Harry R., ed. 1980. *Bucknell Review: Romanticism, Modernism, Postmodernism*. Lewisburg, Pa.: Bucknell University Press.

Hassan, Ihab. 1975a. "Joyce, Beckett, and the Postmodern Imagination," *TriQuarterly* 34: 179-200.

-----. 1980. "The Question of Postmodernism," in Garvin 1980: 117-126.

Hassan, Ihab and Sally Hassan, eds. 1983. *Innovation/Renovation: New Perspectives on the Humanities*. Madison: The University of Wisconsin Press.

Kristeva, Julia. 1980. "Postmodernism?" in Garvin 1980: 136-141.

Lyotard, Jean-François. 1983. "Answering the Question: What is Postmodernism?" in Hassan and Hassan 1983: 329-341.

Rosso, Stefano. 1983. "A Correspondence with Umberto Eco," *Boundary 2*, 12: 1-13.

Updike, John. 1984. "Modernist, Postmodernist, What Will They Think of Next?" *The New Yorker*, 10 September: 136-142.

Voris, Renate. 1985. Review of Jerome Klinkowitz and James Knowlton, *Peter Handke and the Postmodern Transformation, The German Quarterly* 58: 483-486.

8

The Intrusive Author in British Postmodernist Fiction: The Cases of Alasdair Gray and Martin Amis

Richard Todd

Mention of the "intrusive author" in the context of British postmodernism almost certainly calls to mind what has become one of Britain's few "canonic" postmodernist texts: John Fowles's *The French Lieutenant's Woman*, which first appeared in 1969. In this essay I want to discuss two much more recent British texts, Alasdair Gray's *Lanark: A Life in Four Books* (1981) and Martin Amis's *Money: A Suicide Note* (1984). My purpose is to argue that each represents a significantly distinct approach to what I have elsewhere argued is a perceived threat of solipsistic closure that may be particularly urgent in contemporary British fiction (Todd 1986). In these texts the device of the intrusive author is examined in a peculiarly self-reflexive manner. Because Fowles's text became widely known internationally during the 1970s, it may now be thought of as having become misleadingly stratified into some kind of definitive statement of postmodernism in British fiction, and thus as a relatively rare phenomenon, illustrating as it does an examination not only of the intrusive author but of other postmodernist concerns such as ontological indeterminacy and the multiple potential of endings in fiction. I wish therefore in presenting these texts by Gray and Amis to enter a protest at the *exclusiveness* of the premature canonic status *The French Lieutenant's Woman* has gained in discussions of British postmodernism during the past fifteen years or so.

The French Lieutenant's Woman is too well-known to warrant detailed examination of what its narrator terms the "impresario" figure (Fowles 1969: 395) — glimpsed at times during the preceding text — who reappears in its last chapter to readjust his watch in order to allow an alternative replay of the novel's closing moments. Despite the clear distinction in ontological status between this impresario figure and that of the unpleasantly overknowledgeable, purveyingly informative narrator,[1] it is evident in the book's last chapter that the narrator is being accorded privileges strictly speaking above his station as he observes the impresario at work. From across a street the narrator is able to see that the impresario sets his watch back by fifteen minutes, and to speculate patronisingly (and wrongly) on his reasons for doing so. "Wrongly," that is to say, in terms of the very existence of the closing pages of the narrative we then proceed to read. Although the distinction in ontological status between impresario and narrator is insisted upon, therefore, the reader is left with the uncomfortable impression that as persons they are remarkably similar to each other in character.

This similarity is seen by many of Fowles's critics, in Britain's literary-journalistic world at least, as evidence of a flawed and limited creative imagination. I believe, however, that it is more enlightening to suggest that the similarity is deliberately fostered by Fowles, and I suggest further that we can usefully describe its effect in terms of our impression that both impresario and narrator are characters that are deliberately presented as aspects of a composite selfhood. In what follows, therefore, I want to pursue these suggestions, and to do so through discussion of the chosen texts of Alasdair Gray and Martin Amis. For one of my assumptions will be that Gray and Amis, far more insistently than Fowles or any of his more tentative imitators such as Malcolm Bradbury (in *The History Man*, 1975), use the device of the intrusive author to exploit self-reference and self-reflexiveness in a number of interesting and noteworthy ways. If the uses of Gray and Amis may guide us here, it would seem that the more intrusive the authorial presence becomes, the less dominant is the need for an historical or topographical registration, such as we find in *The French Lieutenant's Woman*, that subverts the conventions of realism by asserting its closeness to realism's standards, and the more clearly we may discern a stylistic virtuosity foregrounded *in its own right* rather than as a form of parody or pastiche. In short, the more intrusive the authorial conscription of the text becomes, the closer the text moves towards an exploitation of the self-referent and the self-reflexive. I would argue that the historical and (more apparently still) topographical registrations in both *Lanark* and *Money* do something other than assert their subversive relationship to realism's conventions. I should prefer to say that these registrations have become autonomous, and that they assert their independence of any relationship to recognizable convention: in their different ways, they are surrealistic, and argue various kinds of innovation, including even innovations of genre, rather than the subversion we might have been led to expect from our ability to claim for them the status of postmodernist. As far as stylistic foregrounding is concerned there is more evident virtuosity, as will be seen, in *Money*, but this is not to say that *Lanark* is without its noteworthy stylistic attributes.

Lanark: A Life in Four Books is the first significant — and remains to date the major — publication of a writer who was immediately hailed as one of the most original and fascinating to come out of Scotland this century. At the time of its publication in 1981, Alasdair Gray was in his late 40s, and was known primarily as a painter. But the work had clearly been gestated for more than two decades, part of it having appeared in print as early as 1958, as the acknowledgements page (of which more below) testifies. In view of the time it took to appear itself, *Lanark* has been followed by a remarkable flurry of activity. There have been two more novels, *1982, Janine* (1984) and *The Fall of Kelvin Walker* (1985), as well as a collection of shorter fiction, *Unlikely Stories, Mostly* (1983), three of these pieces also having first appeared in print during the 1950s.

   Lanark is constructed on an epic scale, and is unusual in Gray's work so far, at least in this respect. In not only its scale but also its structure it is in interesting ways clearly examining the claims of the vernacular epic tradition. As the subtitle suggests, *Lanark* consists of four Books. At first sight their numbering, in the order three, one, two, four, appears subversive, but a completed reading reveals that what we have is recognizable as a double epic in which the epic convention of commencement *in medias res*, and the use of flashback, have been subjected to unusually close scrutiny. For Books one and two are not simply a flashback but comprise an impacted narrative in their own right, a narrative that looks at first very much like a *Bildungsroman*. Thematically, at least, these Books seem to owe a certain amount to James Joyce, before gradually attaining more nightmarish and fantastic dimensions than anything to be found in *A Portrait of the Artist as a Young Man*. Books one and two, then, relate the life of Duncan Thaw, in a Glaswegian portrait of the young man as an art student, up until his mysterious death, disappearance or suicide (if it is that). The narrative of Books one and two is told to the titular consciousness Lanark (who is never

given a first name) during a crucial point in his purgatorial afterlife in the
city-world of Unthank — a world on which the sun never shines — by the
voice of an "oracle." The briefly included life-history of this Beckettian
unnamable relates, in a transitional passage between Books three and one,
how he rejected his body and indeed the entire physical world. The oracle
tells Lanark:

> By describing your life I will escape from the trap of my own. From my sta-
> tion in nonentity everything existent, everything *not me*, looks worthwhile
> and splendid ... . Your past is safe with me (Gray 1981: 116).

The oracle's non-existence is typographically reinforced by an absence of
quotation marks whenever he speaks.

I suggest that the main question persistently posed, and ultimately left
unanswered, by the form and content of *Lanark* has to do with the relationship between its two halves. Even though Books one and two are impacted
within them, Books three and four offer a continuation *and* a mirroring of
the "earlier" books. The purgatorial and surrealistic afterlife Lanark
experiences first in Unthank, and then Provan, to which he journeys, both
reflect and refract the experiences Duncan Thaw has undergone in Glasgow. I can point only to selected examples. The world of Unthank and Provan bears a nightmarish relation to the deprived topography of Thaw's
Glasgow, yet after Thaw's disappearance Lanark achieves the consummation with Rima that Thaw had failed in with Marjory Laidlaw, who is the
last in Thaw's series of admired but unavailingly lusted-after *princesses loin-
taines*. More interestingly and significantly, Thaw's private, domestic, dissi-
dent and even anti-social or anti-societal concerns are replaced by Lanark's
increasingly publically- and municipally-minded ones. Despite this, there
remains a distinctly anarchic streak in Lanark's behavior, a characteristic
that at times achieves the paranoia of the dreaming world, and towards the
progressively quest-like end of Book four it becomes evident that Lanark's
struggle has been against an established system or order that he has discovered during the course of Books three and four but — like the reader —
has been unable to make much sense of. Thaw, obviously a highly talented
painter, is afflicted not only by sexual frustrastion, masturbatory solitude,
and a lack of evident worldly success, but by asthma and, later, eczema,
both conditions intermittent but virulent in nature. Lanark, like many in
the unsunlit world of Unthank, is afflicted by "dragonhide," a condition
shown to be curable, although at a cost, and variable in its effects. Much of
the most impressive parts of the Thaw narrative concern Thaw's commis-

sion, at the behest of the minister at one point hospitalised in the same ward as Thaw, to paint a mural in a presbyterian church in Cowcaddens, initially in an attempt to stave off the church's threatened closure. But once embarked on this project, Thaw gradually alienates his allies at the church, overextends both himself and his deadline, and becomes increasingly obsessive about his ability to complete the work in the allotted time, or indeed at all. Thaw appears to lose his reason, and prior to his disappearance there is an obscurely-presented but brilliant account of an unsolved murder Thaw may have committed in his frustration at being unable to interest Marjory sexually. At a crucial point in the opening Book three, Lanark descends through a mouth: the figure inverts that of birth, but also gives point to the repeated mentions, in the Thaw part of the narrative, to the Glaswegian topographical feature of "the mouth of a close"; in suggesting the obsessive way dream-topography can "take off," as it were, from the faintest of clues in real life, this detail argues a continuous imagination running through the consciousnesses of Thaw, Lanark and the author. Emerging more or less intact into some kind of institute Lanark finally encounters Rima, and it is after they have more or less therapeutically made love that the oracle recounts Books one and two. In Book four, Lanark and Rima embark on their journey towards Provan through a so-called "intercalendrical zone" where the normal passage of time is suspended. Rima shows the signs of pregnancy with alarming speed, and both are billeted in an occupied and apparently no longer consecrated cathedral where Rima gives birth to a son, Alexander. The passage of time is in fact greatly accelerated from this point on until the end of the novel.

To what extent, then, is Lanark's life to be seen as a linear continuation of Thaw's, and to what extent a cyclic purgatorial re-enactment? I have drawn attention to a few of the text's features that strongly encourage the temptation to see duplication. The oddities of nomenclature should be mentioned here: those pertaining to characters and places in the text's two halves seem to be deliberately unmatched, so that the topographical name Lanark is applied to a character whose name elsewhere, Thaw, possesses some kind of significatory potential. Similarly we seem invited to pair off the topographical name Glasgow with the resonances offered by the names Unthank and Provan. And it is surely significant, or susceptible of interpretative significance, that Lanark's son's name, Alexander, is etymologically related to Alasdair. Thus although we may speak of duplication, the entire structure of the text, in which the Thaw narrative — recounted by an

oracle — is impacted within Lanark's, militates against a purely cyclic, du-
plicative reading, and in this way forces us to hold such a reading in an
uneasy equilibrium as we attempt to balance it against the arguable legitimacy of a linear reading. In itself the experience may not represent an innovation — we may be faced with something rather comparable in the case
(say) of *Paradise Lost* — but its immediacy is compounded by the
encounter, during the course of Book four, between Lanark and his author,
who is named Nastler.

As precedent for his appearance Nastler cites, not *The French Lieutenant's Woman*, but — requesting Lanark not to feel embarrassed — "Vonnegut [who] has it in *Breakfast of Champions* and Jehovah in the books of
Job and Jonah" (Gray 1981: 481). The entire section is termed "Epilogue"
but actually forms the conclusion to chapter 40, and is followed by four
more chapters. At first presented as Provan's king, Nastler is revealed also
as a conjurer as the bookshelves and canvasses Lanark impetuously over-
turns in the studio-like room in which the encounter takes place mysteriously right themselves. (Nastler's powers may remind us of those exerted
by Miles Green in Fowles's *Mantissa* [1982].) Nastler is attended by a girl
who is completing some of the more tedious detail to one of Nastler's canvasses: she leaves after a short altercation about her remuneration, an
exchange in which Nastler's stinginess becomes evident, and Nastler and
Lanark begin the discussion that forms the bulk of the Epilogue. Lanark's
predicament is compared and contrasted with those of the heroes of what
are called the Greek book about Troy, the Roman book about Aeneas, the
Jewish book about Moses, the Italian book that shows a living man in
heaven, the French book about babies, the Spanish book about the Knight
of the Dolorous Countenance, the English book about Adam and Eve, the
German book about Faust (to which Nastler shows unusual antipathy), the
honest American book about the whale, and the Russian book about war
and peace. Meanwhile, in the margins of this discussion, we find an unattri-
buted "Index of Plagiarisms." Claiming systematic status — three kinds,
"block", "imbedded," and "diffuse" plagiarisms are distinguished — the
Index is in fact completely capricious in nature, possessing some of the
comprehensive unhelpfulness of the Notes to T.S. Eliot's *The Waste Land*,
or (to show that the quality is not exclusive to the modernist or postmodernist periods) "E.K."'s commentary to Spenser's *The Shepherd's Calendar*
(1579). Under BURNS, ROBERT, for instance, we find:

> Robert Burns' humane and lyrical rationalism has had no impact upon the
> formation of this book, a fact more sinister than any exposed by mere
> attribution of sources. See also Emerson (Gray 1981: 487).

But the discussion between Nastler and Lanark, and the indexed marginalia, are not all. The text fractures further, as throughout the Epilogue
we find a series of footnotes comprising a petulant commentary that not
only sabotages the discussion comprising this part of the narrative, but
sabotages the Index as well. It is impossible to determine to whom the various voices in this fragmentation belong, as they are not named in the
Epilogue. The contents page, however, adds some information, describing
the Epilogue as "annotated by Sidney Workman, with an index of diffuse
and imbedded Plagiarisms" (block plagiarisms are not mentioned). The textual fracturing in the Epilogue is made more compound still by a series of
running captions at the top of each page which, in their own way, provide a
summary of the narrative formed by the discussion taking place between
Nastler and Lanark.

   The author's apparent perversity in placing the entire Epilogue four
chapters away from the end of *Lanark* is justified by having the encounter
it so complexly recounts set in 1970, some ten years or so before what we
take to have been the book's completion. As a result, what Nastler says
about its composition makes us face the self-referent, self-reflexive nature
of the text as a whole with particular scrutiny:

> During my first art school summer holiday I wrote chapter 12 and the mad-
> vision-and-murder part of chapter 29. My first hero was based on myself.
> I'd have preferred someone less specialized but mine were the only entrails
> I could lay hands upon. I worked poor Thaw to death, quite cold-
> bloodedly, because though based on me he was tougher and more honest,
> so I hated him. Also his death gave me a chance to shift him into a wider
> social context. You [Lanark] are Thaw with the neurotic imagination trim-
> med off and built into the furniture of the world you occupy (Gray 1981:
> 493).

In a curious way, then, the acknowledgements page forms part of *Lanark's*
textual self-reflexiveness. And a querulous footnote to the last sentence in
the above quotation reads:

> But the fact remains that the plots of the Thaw and Lanark sections are
> independent of each other and cemented by typographical contrivances
> rather than formal necessity. A possible explanation is that the author
> thinks a heavy book will make a bigger splash than two light ones (Gray
> 1981: 493 n.8).

The question of relationship between the two halves of *Lanark* is therefore raised, and left unanswered and indeed not determinable in view of, and because of, the textual fracture surrounding and accompanying the encounter between the character Lanark and his author Nastler, so that the various voices all sabotage each other. A note comments on the Index of Plagiarisms that it "proves that *Lanark* is erected upon an infantile foundation of Victorian nursery tales, though the final shape derives from English language fiction printed between the 40's and 60's of the present century," and goes on to attribute to Nastler — and undermine — the claim that he has been "summarizing a great tradition which culminates in himself!" (Gray 1981: 489-490, n.6). Much more could be said: early in the interview Nastler remarks, concerning his proposed explanation to Lanark: "The critics will accuse me of self-indulgence, but I don't care" (Gray 1981: 481), a remark footnoted thus: "To have an objection anticipated is no reason for failing to raise it [sic]" (Gray 1981: 481 n.1). The last of the Epilogue's footnotes is perhaps worth special mention in view of the little episode in which the girl, who has been assisting Nastler with the more tedious details of a particular canvas, leaves after a short argument about payment:

> As this "Epilogue" has performed the office of an introduction to the work as a whole (the so-called "Prologue" being no prologue at all but a separate short story), it is saddening to find the "conjurer" omitting the courtesies appropriate to such an addendum. Mrs Florence Allan typed and retyped his manuscripts, and often waited many months without payment and without complaining ... (Gray 1981: 499 n.13).

At what really is the end of *1982, Janine*, Alasdair Gray provides an "Epilogue for the discerning critic," in which various literary debts are mentioned. The role both Epilogues play is comparable in that what purports to be exegetical assistance serves to raise more questions than it answers. James Joyce spoke with pride of the way his work would keep the exegetes in business for years to come: we may be faced here with a distinction between modernism and postmodernism that deserves some scrutiny, since it seems evident that Gray's way of keeping the exegetes in business is different, in kind and not just in degree, from the obscurity offered by a Joycean text such as *Ulysses* or *Finnegans Wake*; in Gray's *Lanark* the various interpretations provided by the fracturing of the text during the confrontation between Lanark and Nastler are uttered by different voices whose authority cannot be determined, so that they resonate against each other internally, perpetually and inconclusively.

Martin Amis's *Money: A Suicide Note* offers further evidence of the peculiarly postmodernist character of the task of keeping the exegetes in business, and it seems insufficient to describe the experience his text provides as merely "tiresome" and as an "artistic trick" (Bayley 1985: 13). I wish to present this text, too, in such a way as to argue that its use of the device of the intrusive author is integrally related to its self-reflexiveness.

The self-reflexiveness of *Money* takes on especially interesting dimensions as we consider the high public profile Martin Amis has maintained in Britain since emerging as a novelist of some stature as early as 1975, while still in his mid-twenties. We may contrast this with Alasdair Gray's reclusiveness, a quality that — while it may not be as obsessively guarded as that of writers such as Thomas Pynchon or J.D. Salinger — is reflected in the subversive blurbs he has provided for *Unlikely Stories, Mostly* and *1982, Janine*. In the former case, instead of a Jerry Bauer portrait on the flap there is a child's line-drawing ("James Bliss drew this picture of Alasdair Gray 9 August 1981"). In contrast, Martin Amis, the son of a famous literary father, has not only had no difficulty in achieving notoriety but has seemed actively to court it, and it has proved hard for London's literary establishment to speak rationally of his work and personality. To his enemies (and there seem to be many) he is seen as the leader of one of the most powerful and influential literary cliques of this or any other age: he has recently been vilified in an extraordinarily embittered piece in *Time Out* and appears to have been the victim of a spoof letter to the satirical magazine *Private Eye*. But to his admirers Amis is (among many panegyrics) the finest prose stylist of his generation. The title and subject-matter of his third novel, *Success* (1978), might thus be regarded as fascinatingly self-reflexive. *Money* is Amis's fifth novel, and he is still only in his mid-thirties: the prolific output forms another obvious point of contrast with Gray.

It has been argued by Karl Miller that Amis's last three novels, *Success, Other People* (1981), and *Money*, all share a common interest or even theme, in that all three are "fictions ... turmoils, in which orphan and double meet" (Miller 1985: 409). This is certainly true, although one might well develop the point by noticing that Amis has increasingly obsessively started to explore the relationship between what one can only call the different orders of reality to which orphan and double belong. The first of this group of three novels catalogues the transfer of that elusive quality, success, from double to orphan and cunningly manipulates the reader's sympathies in

doing so. *Other People* presents, in the awaking consciousness of the reson-
antly-named Mary Lamb (there are connotations of both nursery-rhyme
innocence and the matricidal insanity of Charles Lamb's twin sister), what
may be a nightmarish afterworld in which she is a resurrected murder victim, named Amy Hide is a previous existence; however, in a characteristic
surprise ending Amis makes it uncertain as to whether what we have
experienced in *Other People* is an afterlife so much as a time-warp, reversal
or simply hiccup, during which Amy has lost her reason and identity, and
after which life begins as normal again. The problem is rendered still more
complex by the presence of a clue-planting detective, John Prince, who may
or may not have been related to Amy Hide, and by the presence of a voice
(is it the author's?) who begins the narrative with the words: "I didn't want
to have to do it to her" (Amis 1981: 9).

I draw attention summarily and inadequately to these characteristics of
Money's immediate predecessors in order to point to the way in which this
text turns the screw until further. The orphan in this urban satire is named
John Self, and describes himself as "200 pounds of yob genes, booze, snout
and fast food" (Amis 1984: 35). This overweight, hard-living media slickster
spends almost the entire novel commuting between London (where he has
been making TV commercials that have had to be taken off the air on
grounds of obscenity) and New York (where he is casting and scripting a
high-earning feature film first entitled *Money*, then *Good Money*, then *Bad
Money*). Self in fact meets two versions of the double: in London he
encounters a writer named Martin Amis, whom he eventually coerces into
rewriting the script of *Money* after the previous script-writer's failure to
make it sufficiently attractive to the four leads, all of whom have refused
their roles; in New York he is pursued by Martina Twain, who introduces
the largely unread Self to works such as *Animal Farm, Nineteen Eighty-
Four*, and takes him to see Verdi's *Otello* — meanwhile we discover that
Martina's husband Ossie has been having an affair with Self's girlfriend
Selina Street.

Self is not, in fact, strictly speaking, an orphan, and one of the components of the rather complex denouement of *Money* concerns his discovery
of his true paternity. On his own account Self was born "upstairs" in a London pub called the Shakespeare. Believing himself to be the son of Barry
Self, he eventually discovers that his true father is Fat Vince, "beer-crate
operative and freelance bouncer at the Shakespeare," who has "been in and

out of this place every day for thirty-five years" (Amis 1984: 140). Martin Amis, also 35 in the year of *Money*'s publication (although of course younger in the year — 1981 — in which the narrative is set), is introduced gradually into the narrative, and, on the first occasion they meet, Self, not notably literate, asks Amis: "Your dad, he's a writer too, isn't he? Bet that made it easier." Amis's reply is worth recording: "Oh, sure. It's just like taking over the family pub" (Amis 1984: 87). The *TLS* reviewer of *Money* reminded its readers that one fat Englishman had crossed the Atlantic a generation before (Korn 1984: 1119). It seems to me that we are presented in *Money* with a number of instances of self-reflexiveness being confronted so explicitly (the nomenclature is clearly to be seen as part of the process) that we are forced to examine the extent to which the novel's various voices both are and are not claiming to be aspects of a single consciousness. One of the fascinating features of *Money* is, indeed, the voice of the narrator, a voice that, stylistically speaking, is explicitly virtuoso, yet whose owner is at pains to tell us that he has read little and absorbed less. This feature of the narrative is closely related to the interesting mis-hearings that are dotted around the text: Self, who in any case suffers from a "fresh disease ... called tinnitus" (Amis 1984: 7), is often "hearing things" as well as frequently blacking out on account of powerful combinations of drink and drugs and *not* (as he discovers to his cost at the novel's end) hearing or recalling or being capable of taking in information that really matters. In a brothel in Manhattan he tells a girl called Moby that his name is Martin and that he is a writer: he is flummoxed by her reply: "John roar mainstream?" (Amis 1984: 99). Talking to his sinister agent Fielding Goodney, Self makes a note of a possible substitute star, Nub Forkner:

> "That's o-r-k, Slick," said Fielding. I glanced down at the page. "That's what I've got." " ... You read much, John?" "Read what?" "Fiction." "Do you?" "Oh sure. It gives me all kinds of ideas. I like the sound and the fury," he added enigmatically (Amis 1984: 208).

At one of the points of the denouement Self beats up the person he thinks has been persecuting him throughout the novel, and thinks he hears its final words as: "Oh damn dear go ... Oh and you man dog" (Amis 1984: 326).

Yet when all this is said, the voice, with its hectic pace and tone — even the violence and the profuse and candid sexuality, the urban satire mediated through a flaunted stylistic virtuosity such that the only semi-colon in something like 200,000 words of text occurs in the last sentence,

after a figurative allusion to their absence (in terms of the novel's pace)
some 80 pages earlier — despite all this, the voice of Self is very much the
voice Amis uses elsewhere; and this seems to me to represent an explicitly
considered solution to the problem of how, in a text of this kind, one conveys a narrator of Self's philistinism, whose final discovery is that all the
money he believes himself to have been earning forms part of an operation
he has been tricked into financing himself, a rip-off Martin Amis admits his
complicity in. Perhaps emblematic of the difficulty such a text presents is
the chess game Self and Amis play towards the end. Self is in fact an excellent player, surely a deliberate and flagrantly unexpected attribute, and he
is "zugzwanged" by Amis after a cliff-hanging game. Despite Self's having
used the word earlier in his narrative (Amis 1984: 117), he now, at the end
of their game, has to ask Amis for a definition of it ("What the fuck does
that mean?"); Martin Amis replies: "Literally, *forced to move*. It means
that whoever has to move has to lose. If it were my turn now, you'd win.
But it's yours. And you lose" (Amis 1984: 353). Elsewhere, both Martin
and Martina severally explain aspects of what we must call the experience
of literature to Self. Thus Martina:

> talked of the vulnerability of a figure knowingly watched ... . The analog-
> ous distinction in fiction would be that between the conscious and the
> reluctant narrator — the sad, the unwitting narrator (Amis 1984: 128).

And Martin tells Self:

> The further down the scale [the hero] is, the more liberties you can take
> with him. You can do what the hell you like to him, really. This creates an/
> appetite for punishment. The author is not free of sadistic impulses (Amis
> 1984: 233).

It is in the light of this self-reflexive complexity of "voice" in *Money* that we
should also see the pervasively arresting topographical description of both
Manhattan and London. Here are two examples selected virtually at random, the first reminding us that Amis has also published a work of nonfiction entitled *The Invasion of the Space Invaders*:

> I spent an improving four hours on Forty-Second Street, dividing my time
> between a space-game arcade and the basement gogo bar next door. In the
> arcade the proletarian ghosts of the New York night, these darkness-wor-
> shippers, their terrified faces reflected in the screens, stand hunched over
> their controls. They look like human forms of mutant moles and bats,
> hooked on the radar, rumble and wow of these stocky new robots who play
> with you if you give them money. They'll talk too, for a price. *Launch Mis-*

sion, Circuit Completed, Firestorm, Flashpoint, Timewarp, Crackup, Blackout! The kids, tramps and loners in here, they are the mineshaft spirits of the new age. ... In the gogo bar men and women are eternally ranged against each other, kept apart by a wall of drink, a moat of poison, along which the mad matrons and bad bouncers stroll (Amis 1984: 28-29).

I walked back to my sock in the thin rain. And the skies. Christ! In shades of kitchen mists, with eyes of light showing only murk and seams of film and grease, the air hung above and behind me like an old sink full of old washing-up. Blasted, totalled, broken-winded, shot-faced London, doing time under sodden skies (Amis 1984: 153).

Readers familiar with recent developments in British literature will notice something of the so-called "Martian" school of bizarrely figurative expressiveness, a characteristic use of the English language that has been suggestively compared to the "metaphysical" style of the late sixteenth and early seventeenth centuries. My point in drawing attention to this characteristic of *Money*'s topographical descriptions is to insist that in devising a voice for John Self, the extra-fictional Martin Amis has, it seems to me, quite explicitly chosen to use his own, a voice that is clearly recognizable from his own other published fiction. I am convinced that we should see Amis's strategy as a deliberate choice that illustrates a self-conscious confrontation of the problem of solipsistic "closure" and not — instead — as illustrating any kind of limitation of which no awareness has been shown.

This claim, applicable in different ways, as I hope to have shown, to both the texts I have been discussing, leads me to my conclusion, which I shall attempt to summarize as follows: *Lanark* and *Money* each represent different ways of responding self-reflexively to a perceived threat of solipsistic closure, a threat that — as I have argued elsewhere — may be particularly urgent in contemporary fiction in Britain because of the perceived weight and multiplicity of traditional approaches to realism. Gray and Amis have pushed the postmodernist device of the intrusive author to a point where stylistic and topographical elements have become practically autonomous of any reference to that tradition. But the way each writer has used the device in the texts I have been considering demonstrates individual preoccupations as much as it illustrates the variety of possible approaches to self-reflexiveness.

Gray both examines the vernacular epic tradition and subversively claims a place in it. The subversiveness of that claim is integral to his use of the device of the intrusive author for, in true postmodernist fashion, Gray fragments his narrative at the point of Nastler's introduction in order to show us that the two parts of his "A Life in Four Books" are indeterminably connected, and that neither a cyclic nor a linear reading will wholly suffice. It is topographical rather than stylistic elements that combine with *Lanark*'s self-reflexive theme to assist us to this conclusion. Amis offers us what may be, as Miller has claimed, generically innovative in its linking of the device of the intrusive author to an obsession with orphan and double in a tradition whose roots can be traced at least as far as a Gothic text such as James Hogg's *Confessions of a Justified Sinner* (1824) (Miller 1985: 411). There has not been room in my account for stress to be laid on the way the draft script for Self's feature film *Money* mirrors his account (in Amis's *Money*) of his own circumstances (Amis 1984: 62), nor have I been able to draw attention to Self's repeated claims that he feels "invaded": even so, it should be clear that Amis's treatment of his self-reflexive theme is combined with a stylistic virtuosity (to which topographical elements are *subordinated*) that suggests a yet more thoroughgoing fragmentation than does Gray's. Such fragmentation confirms, more strongly still than in Amis's previous fiction to date, our sense of a single selfhood complexly refracted through the existence of various, duplicitously conflicting, voices.

NOTE

1.   Fowles's most recent novel, *A Maggot* (London: Cape, 1985) comes closer than any of his intervening fictions to recapturing the narrative voice of *The French Lieutenant's Woman*. It ends with some interesting reflections on Fowles's conception of historical fiction.

REFERENCES

Amis, Martin. 1981. *Other People: A Mystery Story*. Harmondsworth: Penguin, 1982.
-----. 1984. *Money: A Suicide Note*. London: Jonathan Cape.
Bayley, John. 1985. "Being Two is Half the Fun," *London Review of Books* (7/12), 4 July: 13.
Fokkema, Douwe and Hans Bertens, eds. 1986. *Approaching Postmodernism*. Amsterdam and Philadelphia: Benjamins.
Fowles, John. 1969. *The French Lieutenant's Woman*. St Alban's: Granada/Panther, 1971.

Gray, Alasdair. 1981. *Lanark: A Life in Four Books*. London: Granada/ Panther, 1982.

Korn, Eric. 1984. "Frazzled Yob-gene Lag-jag," *The Times Literary Supplement*, 5 October: 1119.

Miller, Karl. 1985. *Doubles: Studies in Literary History*. London: Oxford University Press.

Todd, Richard. 1986. "The Presence of Postmodernism in British Fiction: Aspects of Style and Selfhood," in Fokkema and Bertens 1986: 99-117.

9

Postmodern Characterization and the Intrusion of Language

Hans Bertens

My point of departure is a remark made by Lord Peter Wimsey, the aristocratic and debonair amateur detective who operates so successfully in the novels of Dorothy L. Sayers. In *Whose Body* Lord Peter faces a baffling case. A body has turned up in the bathtub of an unsuspecting architect and the police are at a loss to identify it; no one of that description would seem to be missing. Lord Peter, however, is unruffled. As he says to his friend, police inspector Parker, murder always has its motive and in the absence of other clues motive will very well do as the starting-point for an investigation. And of course this murder, too, turns out to have its motive, a psychological motive which then appears to be centrally bound up with what is presented as the character of the criminal. In other words, Lord Peter believes in causality and Dorothy Sayers adds characterological consistency in the criminal to enable Lord Peter to come up with one of his brilliant insights. As is always the case in the classic detective novel, the workings of the human mind are understood within a framework of causality and consistency.

Now for all critics who have written on the subject, Postmodernist literature rejects that framework — which is of course the framework of the nineteenth-century Realist novel — although there is not much agreement on the kind of characterization that we may expect in texts that are considered to be Postmodernist.

First, there are those critics who take a formidable distance from the genre practice by Dorothy L. Sayers and see Postmodernism as its antipole. Let me quote William Spanos: "It is...no accident that the paradigmatic.

archetype of the postmodern...literary imagination is the anti-detective story (and its anti-psychoanalytical analogue), the formal purpose of which is to evoke the impulse to 'detect' and/or psychoanalyze in order to violently frustrate it by refusing to solve the crime (or find the cause for neurosis)" (Spanos 1972: 154). For Spanos and for others who use the same terminology of the anti-detective — for instance Michael Holquist (1971) — Postmodernist characterization explicitly refuses to commit itself to psychological causality and presents characters as unknowable. Gerald Graff expresses the same view in different terms: "In postmodern fiction, character, like external reality, is something 'about which nothing is known,' lacking in plausible motive or discoverable depth" (Graff 1979: 53). David Lodge, too, speaks of the "uncertainty" of Postmodernist writing, an "uncertainty, which is endemic, and manifests itself on the level of narrative rather than style" (Lodge 1977a: 226). Giving an example of uncertainty in characterization, Lodge remarks elsewhere that "the characters of postmodernist fiction are often sexually ambivalent" (Lodge 1977b: 43).

For some rather annoyingly prescriptive critics such as Thomas Docherty (1983) and Alan Singer (1983), Postmodernist characters are radically inconsistent and if they are not inconsistent they should be, for all consistency smacks of essence and thus of metaphysics. It goes without saying that their Postmodernist characters act gratuitously, for motivation, too, suggests metaphysics. The radical discontinuity that many critics have found in Postmodernist fiction — either at the thematic or at the formal level, or at both (see, for instance, Hassan 1975, Hoffmann 1982, Fokkema 1984) — has here entered characterization as well.

In other cases it is argued that Postmodernist character is neither unknowable nor inconsistent and gratuitous, but simply absent. Gerald Graff sees this disappearance of character in what he calls the celebratory mode of Postmodernism, a mode that rejoices in a "dissolution of ego boundaries" (Graff 1979: 57), and Daniel Bell sees in the various kinds of Postmodernism "simply the decomposition of the self in an effort to erase the individual ego" (Bell 1976: 29). But this position may well be another way of looking at inconsistency and gratuitousness. Alan Wilde, for instance, discusses in his *Horizons of Assent* the fiction of Federman and the other Surfictionists and claims that they see the "self" as "non-existent" (Wilde 1981: 180), a charge which they would hotly deny and probably at the same time endorse, arguing that such a notion of a "self," with all its implications of essentiality, belongs to a traditional realistic framework and has therefore rightly been given up in favor of a concept of character that excludes essence. In other words, Graff, Bell, and Wilde might well refuse to see character where for critics such as Docherty and Singer it is very much in evidence.

To round off this rather selective survey of critical positions on Post-modernist characterization — I will, for instance, omit Norman Holland's interesting "theme-and-variations concept" of Postmodernist identity (Holland 1983: 304) — I will now turn to two observations made respectively by Gerhard Hoffmann et al. and by Ihab Hassan. In their "'Modern', 'Post-modern' and 'Contemporary' as Criteria for the Analysis of 20th Century Literature", Hoffmann, Hornung and Kunow suggest that "a radical gap between modern and postmodern literature is reflected in the opposition of two épistémès: subjectivity versus loss of subjectivity" (Hoffmann et al. 1977: 20), and Hassan seems to tap a similar intellectual vein in observing, a propos of Postmodernist fiction, that for structuralists and post-struc-turalists the self "is really an empty 'place' where many selves come to mingle and depart" (Hassan 1977: 845).

It is this notion of a non-subjective, pluralist (or potentially pluralist) Postmodernist character that I will explore in this article, paying particular attention to the intrusion of language into character or, to put the matter differently, to the extent that we are not dealing with character at all in Postmodernist characterization, that is, with character in the traditional representational sense, but with various kinds of discourse that are not grounded in what Alan Wilde calls a "self," but that seem to be floating into and out of certain fictional structures that are endowed with proper names. Perhaps I should be more precise because the two contemporary texts I propose to discuss — Peter Handke's Die Angst des Tormanns beim Elfmeter (1970), translated into English as The Goalie's Anxiety at the Penalty Kick, and Norman Mailer's The Executioner's Song (1979) — do to my mind aim to be representational, also in their characterizations. However, as I will argue, both texts, partly in spite of themselves, primarily represent the impossibility of traditional representation. They turn out to be at least in part metalinguistic acts that represent language, especially in their characterizations.

Let me now go back to Lord Peter Wimsey, who has not only provided the starting-point for this article, but who also functions as my guiding light. I propose to do some detecting myself and will examine four celebrated murder cases, three of them fictional, the last one, involving a double murder, only too real. My choice of these murders does not reflect an ill-controlled sensationalism on my part, but is motivated by the admittedly unproven notion that murder, as an extreme instance of human behavior, calls for more narrational motivation than everyday actions such as eating, fishing, or having a drink. If that notion is correct fictional murders will highlight the issue of motivation.

I must admit that in one way I am far ahead of the traditional detective: in my cases the identity of the murderer poses no problem. In André Gide's *Les Caves du Vatican* (1914) the murderer is a youth called Lafcadio Wluiki who, apparently for no reason at all, pushes a man he has never seen before out of a speeding train. In Albert Camus' *L'Etranger* (1942) the murderer, Meursault, narrates the story himself and tells us in detail how he happens to shoot a man whom he has met only half an hour before on a deserted beach. In Peter Handke's *Die Angst des Tormanns beim Elfmeter* the narrator tells us how the protagonist, Bloch, kills a girl he has only met once, a couple of days before. Finally, in Mailer's *The Executioner's Song*, we are told how Gary Gilmore on two consecutive days in 1976 killed two men whom he had never seen before.

What these murders have in common is that there is very little, if anything at all, connecting the murderers with their victims. They would seem to be crimes that are either wholly without motive or that are seriously undermotivated by traditional, realistic standards. The murders would seem to be gratuitous and seem to invite Postmodernist readings (which is my reason for selecting these particular murders — I do not want to make things too easy for myself). This gratuitousness is, in fact, what André Gide himself calls attention to in an amusing *mise en abyme* which reflects on his own purposes in *Les Caves du Vatican*. One of his characters, Lafcadio's half-brother, who is a writer, has this in mind for the protagonist of a novel he is planning to write: "'I mean to lead him into committing a crime gratuitously — into wanting to commit a crime without any motive at all'" (Gide 1914: 195). I shall concentrate, then, on motive, which of course belongs to characterization, and try to demonstrate that in spite of superficial similarities there is a world of difference between murder as presented by Gide and Camus on the one hand and Mailer and Handke on the other. In Gide and Camus murder and motive can easily be placed within a (fairly) traditional representational framework. In Handke and Mailer representation is highly problematic; motivation is not so much linked up with what may be seen as *essential* character, but with *provisional* character, with character that is not really grounded but in last instance appears to consist of discourse. It is this that gives the characterizations of Handke's and Mailer's protagonists a distinctively Postmodernist character.

Les Caves du Vatican, published in 1914 as the third and last of Gide's so-called *soties*, is a curious novel. First of all, it offends through its crazy improbabilities both the conventions of Realism and Modernism; we find for instance a very Postmodernist conspiracy theory that claims that the true Pope has been replaced by a false one and is kept imprisoned in the Castle of St Angelo. Then, it is openly self-reflexive and the narrator's persistent irony has a strong decentering effect. In short, we would not be surprised to find gratuitous acts in such an apparently proto-Postmodernist novel and indeed the novel's interest in the *acte gratuit*, to use Gide's term, is obvious, as in the self-reflexive passage that has just been quoted.

On the face of it, young Lafcadio's behavior seems completely inconsistent and it is not surprising that a critic like Wylie Sypher, in his *Loss of the Self in Modern Literature and Art* claims that "Gide bases his characters on the discontinuity principle" (Sypher 1962: 64). Early in the novel Lafcadio enters a burning house and endangers his life in order to save two children; perhaps a month later he kills with great equanimity a man by pushing him out of a train, only to confess his crime afterwards to his half-brother and the latter's daughter. He calls himself apparently quite correctly "a creature of inconsequence" (Gide 1914: 82).

But this is misleading. If we look closer at Lafcadio's behavior it becomes less incomprehensible and the narrator's commentary helps us to get a clearer focus. We are informed that Lafcadio "prized above all things the free possession of his soul" (Gide 1914: 56), that he has "a horror of owing anything to anyone" (60), that he has "a naturally aristocratic disposition" (175), and that he has a "passionate curiosity...against which nothing — not even his personal safety — had ever been able to prevail" (218). The narrator, who is by the way markedly less ironic toward Lafcadio than towards his other characters, reveals, intentionally or not, Lafcadio's character, his essence. Or, to put the matter in other terms, he allows the reader to impose a totalizing interpretation on the characterization that he presents. Throughout the novel we see Lafcadio safeguarding the freedom that he values so highly. He desires to be totally impenetrable, totally unknowable, hiding both his emotions and his intellectual accomplishments and living in a room that reveals nothing about its occupant. Significantly he destroys his diary and even the only photograph he possesses of his mother when he discovers that a stranger has tampered with them. Lafcadio wants to frustrate all attempts at interpretation of what might be called his inner self and punishes himself by stabbing a sharpened penknife into his thigh (a so-called "punta") when he has carelessly allowed himself to drop his mask. To quote from the diary:

> For having beaten Portos at chess   . . . . 1 punta
> For having shown that I spoke Italian . . . . . 3 punta
> For having answered before Protos   . . . . . . 1 p.
> For having had the last word   . . . . 1 p.
> For having cried at hearing of Faby's death   . 4 p. (50)

This obsessive fear of interpretation is one side of Lafcadio's concept of freedom. The other side is his equally strong desire, spurred on by his passionate curiosity, to test its limits and expand it, not only in theory but also in practice. As he has noted in his diary: "Do you understand the meaning of the words, 'STOP AT NOTHING'?" (51) This desire to explore the limits of his freedom, not checked by any respect for the human race, provides then the motive for the murder he commits. True, the murder is to a certain extent gratuitous, in that time, place, and victim are arbitrarily selected. Even at the last moment Lafcadio decides that he will call off his project if he sees a light in the countryside before he has counted up to twelve. But that does not mean that this murder has no motive, that it is a true *acte gratuit*. It is not surprising that after the crime Lafcadio does not regard himself as a criminal, but as an adventurer. He sees himself as an adventurer of the spirit, an explorer who has crossed a new frontier. It is also not surprising that the next day his adventure appears to be compromising and grotesque. The murder has been too easy and he feels resentment against his victim for not having defended himself any better. In other words, nothing much has been gained and when someone else is arrested for the murder Lafcadio feels that he will "never rest content till he had set Fate at defiance more rashly still" (229).

True enough, there are moments in the novel when Lafcadio seems different and shows great emotion, but these moments all have to do with his newly found aristocratic family — early in the novel he discovers that he is the illegitimate son of a French nobleman — and are in line with what the narrator calls his "aristocratic disposition"; perhaps unintentionally Gide has endowed Lafcadio with a good deal of rather snobistic sentimentality.

However, that greatly prized family tie does not prevent Lafcadio from transgressing another boundary in the novel's closing scenes where he sleeps with the virgin daughter of his half-brother, violating two taboos at the same time.

Summarizing this, Lafcadio's *acte gratuit* turns out to be not so gratuitous at all and his seemingly inconsistent behavior is not at all inconsistent. It is governed by a hidden essence that provides a constant motive for the most diverse actions. Although Gide's novel is highly self-conscious and self-reflexive, very much aware of its status as language, Lafcadio's characterization may very well be interpreted within a realistic framework of causality and consistency. Although Lafcadio every now and then refers to the testing of his freedom as a game he is playing, there is little doubt that the game is serious and that this playing is bound up with his essential self. It is never suggested that he could be different, that he is playing a role he has temporarily assumed. His behavior is not dictated by a "self" that is eventually exposed as language. This does of course not exclude the possibility that he is part of a larger, purely linguistic game that Gide is playing in his *sotie* and that he is therefore in no way representational, but given Gide's interest in the *acte gratuit* as "an antidote to social and psychological determinism" (Fokkema 1986: 90) — we may assume that Lafcadio, as his characterization suggests, is meant to be representational and to function on an epistemological level.

Just as André Gide's novel returns again and again in critical discussions of gratuitousness, Camus' *L'Etranger* figures prominently in discussions of the so-called loss of the "self" in twentieth-century literature. Whereas Lafcadio is seen to expand character, in breaking through the conventions of realistic characterization, Camus' Meursault is seen as an emptying of realistic characterization. Wylie Sypher, for instance, claims that Meursault exists "in a condition that is amnesic or numbed" (Sypher 1962: 161) and if he is not anonymous — Sypher calls the "self" in our day "an anonymous self" (6) — then his existence is certainly "minimal" (68).

One might argue that Gide, because of the self-reflexiveness of his novel, leaves the matter of representation at least partly up to his readers, but that is certainly not the case in *L'Etranger*. In his afterword to the novel, Camus declares that Meursault is for him "not a reject, but a poor and naked man, in love with a sun which leaves no shadows. Far from lacking all sensibility, he is driven by a tenacious and therefore profound passion, the passion for an absolute and for truth" (Camus 1942: 119). As Hoffmann has recently argued, "the absurd...is a rigorous epistemological attitude toward the problem of signification with all its metaphysical aspects" (Hoffmann 1986: 189). Clearly, Meursault is meant to be representational; he becomes the vehicle for what Camus calls a "negative truth," a truth that he finally grasps when, condemned to die, he is able to make peace with the indifference of the world and the absurdity of life: "I looked up at the mass of signs and stars in the night sky and laid myself open for the first time to the benign indifference of the world. And finding it so much like myself, in fact so fraternal, I realized that I'd been happy, and that I was still happy" (117). Meursault's characterization is meant to mirror the indifference and absurdity of the world and his unflinching acceptance of that world — and of his kinship with it — makes him for Camus "the only Christ we deserve" (119).

Since indifference and absurdity pervade the world that Meursault's characterization is meant to reflect, we may expect them to appear in the circumstances surrounding the murder and they do, but within a realistic or even naturalistic framework. Two important facts about Meursault are established early in the novel. Right from the start Meursault complains about the glare of the sky reflecting off the road, the blinding light in the mortuary, again the unbearable glare of the sky, the sunshine that hits him like a slap in the face, etc. The other fact is his indifference, which is inextricably bound up with a deep perplexity as to the true nature of things; "you can never tell," is what Meursault keeps repeating through the novel. Examples of this baffled indifference abound. His mother's death does not affect him; "nothing has changed" as he puts it himself. He is not interested in the job in Paris that his boss tentatively offers him because "none of it really mattered" (Camus 1942: 44), and he reacts in a curiously indifferent way to his lover Marie's proposal of marriage: "Marie came round for me and asked me if I wanted to marry her. I said I didn't mind and we could do if she wanted to. She then wanted to know if I loved her. I replied as I had done once already, that it didn't mean anything but that I probably didn't" (44). In an equally indifferent way — "I had no reason not to please him" (36) — he gets involved in a scheme of a fellow lodger, Raymond, who wants to revenge himself on his Arab mistress, an involvement which will eventually cost him his life, because the prosecutor will construct his involvement as premeditation.

The murder is the direct result of Meursault's sensitivity to the sun and his indifference and is made possible by his chance possession of Raymond's gun. On the beach, Meursault, Raymond, and a friend meet two Arabs who have followed them there and who are obviously related in some way to Raymond's mistress. A scuffle ensues and one of them wounds Raymond with a knife. After the wound has been dressed there is a second confrontation near a little spring behind a rock during which Meursault, who so far has not been involved, persuades Raymond, who appears to be trigger-happy, to hand over his gun: "'if he doesn't draw his knife, you can't shoot'" (Camus 1942: 57). The Arabs retreat and disappear and Meursault goes with Raymond back to the beach-house where the others are waiting. However, he can't bring himself to climb the stairs leading up to the house in the excessive heat and to face the tearful women inside and, thinking of the cool spring, he walks down the beach again, pressed on by the blinding heat. When he finds one of the Arabs at the spring, he knows that all he has to do is turn around, but "the whole beach was reverberating in the sun and pressing against me from behind" (59). So he stays and when the Arab, who is still sitting, draws his knife, Meursault shoots:

> The light leapt up off the steel and it was like a long, flashing sword lunging at my forehead. At the same time all the sweat that had gathered in my eyebrows suddenly ran down over my eyelids, covering them with a dense layer of warm moisture. My eyes were blinded by this veil of salty tears. All I could feel were the cymbals the sun was clashing against my forehead and, indistinctly, the dazzling spear still leaping up off the knife in front of me. It was like a red-hot blade gnawing at my eyelashes and gouging out my stinging eyes. This was when everything shook. The sea swept ashore a great breath of fire. The sky seemed to be splitting from end to end and raining down sheets of flame. My whole being went tense and I tightened my grip on the gun. The trigger gave... (60).

As Meursault later tells his lawyer, "by nature my physical needs often distort ... my feelings" (65). His feelings, fairly indifferent at the best of times, have been no match for the unbearable onslaught of the sun, reflected by the Arab's knife. Meursault is at the moment of the murder primarily a biological mechanism that is forced to protect itself and he shoots to kill.

The murder, then, is fully motivated in terms of causality and consistency — almost excessively so — and although we may consider some of the elements that make it possible absurd, such as Meursault's rather curious oversensitivity to the sun, his initial involvement in the case, and the fact that Meursault who has earlier taken the gun to protect the Arab now shoots him with it, there is nothing absurd or gratuitous about the murder itself. Absurd as the world may be, we are dealing in Meursault's characterization with essence and language functions in that essentialistic characterization as an epistemological tool that is able to probe the world and to arrive at the negative truth I mentioned earlier. Meaningfulness, truth, and the hypocrisy of social conventions are all subjected to investigation in *L'Etranger*, but the ability of language to describe and even penetrate the world is not. Meursault is representational and the matter of representation is never problematized by Camus.

This brings me to my two contemporary texts, *Die Angst des Tormanns beim Elfmeter* and *The Executioner's Song*. Both texts are very much aware of the fact that language may be highly problematic. They draw our attention to language in a number of ways. The first one is through the not so Postmodernist suggestion that character is unknowable and cannot be penetrated by language. There is a long and respectable tradition of ultimately unknowable characters in fiction, from Stendhal's alter ego in *Vie de Henri Brulard*, through Conrad's Lord Jim and Kurtz, to Faulkner's Sutpen in *Absalom, Absalom!* More interesting for my purposes is the suggestion that language is not only unable to penetrate behind the surface of things — as it still can do in the characterizations of Lafcadio and Meursault — but that it is also unable to describe that surface adequately. The third suggestion, and the most radical one, is that character *is* language.

This needs some clarification because obviously every literary character is language. What I have in mind, however, is that in a good many contemporary cases in which language is still able to probe character what is revealed is not characterological essence, as in the cases of Lafcadio and Meursault, but language. In such cases language reveals merely another language, or, to use a broader term, discourse, beyond which there is nothing, no essence at all. And since discourse is by its nature public, such characters are, properly speaking, not subjects, but part of the language that surrounds them.

Such a Postmodernist characterization in terms of discourse may, in spite of the views of Docherty, Singer, and others, very well make use of causality and consistency. After all, causality and consistency are in such cases not connected with an essentialistic character, but with provisional discourse, a discourse that may at any time be replaced by another type of discourse — even if such a replacement does not actually take place. To ground a character in discourse is to indicate its fragility, its potential for

total discontinuity, and implicitly undermines the *principles* of characterological causality and consistency, even if in actual practice causality and
consistency seem to reign.

I will first examine Handke's novel. I realize that I have not been able
to do full justice to the two novels that I have already discussed, but in the
case of Handke's extraordinarily complex text doing full justice is simply
out of the question within the scope of this article. This proviso made, let
me begin with the statement that the murder that Handke's protagonist
Bloch commits is the result of his problematic relationship with language
and I propose to examine that relationship first.

At one point in the novel, in a state of exhaustion, Bloch's usually
troubled relations with the outside world are perfectly harmonious: "He
saw and heard everything with total immediacy, without first having to
translate it into words, as before, or comprehending it only in terms of
words or word games. He was in a state where everything seemed natural to
him" (Handke 1970: 80). What we have here is an immediacy of experience
that by-passes language, that is, in fact, only possible because of the exclu-
sion of language. We are dealing here with a Bloch who wants to merge
with the object world, to enter a pre- or extra-linguistic state where the subject is able to experience without articulating that experience. For this
Bloch language can only present a threat.

But these states of perfect ease are rare for Bloch. Far more usual for
him is the following experience:

> Everything he saw was cut off in the most unbearable way....as though the
> things around him had all been pulled away from him. The wardrobe, the
> sink, the suitcase, the door: only now did he realize that he, as if compel-
> led, was thinking of the word for each thing. Each glimpse of a thing was
> immediately followed by its word....he had seen the things as though they
> were, at the same time, advertisements for themselves. In fact, his nausea
> was the same kind of nausea that had sometimes been brought on by cer-
> tain jingles, pop songs, or national anthems... (Handke 1970: 43-44).

Here language robs things of their true being and makes them false and
unreal. Here we are dealing with a second Bloch, a Bloch who cannot get
rid of language, who experiences language as a source of total alienation
but is unable to escape it. As Frank Kermode puts it, "Bloch...is sick, and
what makes him nauseated is language" (Kermode 1983: 131). However,
this Bloch, who is kept apart from the world by language, at times also
experiences language as a source of relief. At those times language func-

tions as a protective screen that keeps the world at a safe distance.

Let me illustrate this paradoxical state of affairs. At certain points in the novel this second Bloch, who cannot escape language, resorts to a nominalistic, early Wittgensteinian attitude toward language in his attempts to describe the world:

> ...when he talked about an indirect free kick, he not only described what an indirect free kick was but explained, while the girls waited for the story to go on, the general rules about free kicks. When he mentioned a corner kick that had been awarded by a referee, he even felt he owed them the explanation that he was not talking about the corner of a room. The longer he talked, the less natural what he said seemed to Bloch. Gradually it began to seem that every word needed an explanation. He had to watch himself so that he didn't get stuck in the middle of a sentence (Handke 1970: 49).

As usual the failure of language as a means of description and thus of communication causes in Bloch a strong sense of the disconnectedness of everything around him and only because the girls he is talking with use words casually and unproblematically is Bloch able to see things in their connections and in their totality again: "Bloch once again became aware of contours, movements, voices, exclamations, and figures all together" and a moment later he bites into a sandwich one of the girls holds out to him "as though this was the most natural thing in the world" (50). Language, which a moment before was extremely threatening, has now become safe, a place of refuge.

Sometimes the distance between word and world becomes so great for Bloch that he moves beyond his nominalist attempts at naming the world to a post-structural, Derridean view of language in which words do not refer to the world of facts anymore, but only to themselves, so that he feels compelled to put them between quotation marks even when looking at the objects that suggest them: "'Suds' 'poured' 'over' 'the doorsteps'. 'Featherbeds' 'were lying' 'behind' 'the windowpanes'" (Handke 1970: 93). At other times he is convinced of the non-referentiality of language used by others, but is not prepared to admit that his own language is meaningless as well until he is forced to recognize its meaninglessness:

> Now the loathsome word-game sickness had struck even him, and in broad daylight. "Broad daylight"? He must have hit on that phrase somehow. That expression seemed witty to him, in an unpleasant way. But were the other words in the sentence any better? If you said the word "sickness" to yourself, after a few repetitions you couldn't help laughing at it. "A sick-

ness strikes me": silly. "I am stricken by a sickness": just as silly. "The
postmistress and the mailman"; "the mailman and the postmistress"; "the
postmistress and the mailman": one big joke. Have you heard the one
about the mailman and the postmistress? "Everything seems like a heading," thought Bloch... (70).

And then, right at the point where language has totally deserted him, he
paradoxically invokes it to regain a sense of normalcy: "'The mailman hits
the bag and takes it off,' thought Bloch, word for word. 'Now he puts it on
the table and walks into the package room.' He described the events to
himself like a radio announcer to the public, as if this was the only way he
could see them for himself. After a while it helped" (71).

Throughout the novel this Bloch, who cannot get rid of language, is
alternately repelled by language because of its inability to describe the
world, or, worse, because of its self-referentiality, or he is attracted by it
because it provides connections and explanations, deceptive as these are,
and thus makes everything seem "natural," which is a keyword in Bloch's
mental vocabulary.

It is such an alternation in attitudes towards language that makes Bloch
commit his murder. His victim, a young cashier in a cinema attracts his
attention through "the perfectly natural manner" (Handke 1970: 5) in
which she responds "to the wordless gesture with which he'd put his money
on the box-office turntable" (5). There is, in other words, perfect communication without language. When Bloch remembers this the next day he
decides to look her up and a couple of days later he goes with her to her
apartment, sleeps with her and strangles her the next morning. During their
first and last breakfast together, Bloch notices

> that she talked about the things he'd just told her as if they were hers, but
> when he mentioned something she had just talked about, he either quoted
> her exactly or, if he was using his own words, always prefaced the new
> names with a hesitant "this" or "that", which distanced them, as if he were
> afraid of making her affairs his (16).

The cashier takes language for granted, but Bloch cannot do so. Sure
enough, as the narrator informs us, "From time to time...the conversation
became as natural for him as for her" (17), but again and again Bloch slips
back into his feeling that language is unnatural and treacherous. He gets
more and more irritated until a perfectly normal question makes him lose
all control and he suddenly finds himself choking the girl.

Bloch's sometimes unbearable awareness of the inadequacy of language is indirectly responsible for the murder. Furthermore, it is obvious that the failure of language is so threatening to Bloch because what he experiences as his identity, his hold on himself and the world, is bound up with language so that the awareness of that failure acutely threatens his sense of himself as a coherent subject. If language's supposed competence in dealing with the world is a fiction, then Bloch as he knows himself and the world is a fiction as well.

Clearly, Bloch's characterization may be seen within a framework of causality and consistency. Sure enough, Bloch shows three rather different attitudes towards language, but all three of them are internally consistent and they are obviously interrelated. Language either fails him completely or reveals, in so far as it can reveal anything at all, only disconnectedness, so that only through bad faith or through abandoning language altogether can Bloch possibly achieve the peace of mind that so persistently escapes him. Yet this evidence of causality and consistency does not place Bloch's characterization within a realistic framework. Handke's novel does not suggest that we are dealing with essence in his protagonist's character. Bloch's *Angst* is simply conditioned by discourse: a logocentric discourse that has great faith in the powers of language. And the exposure of that discourse *as* discourse is so threatening because Bloch's sense of himself is based upon language; whatever truths he has assumed about himself will dissolve in ungrounded discourse if language does not have the powers ascribed to it.

So far I have discussed Bloch in representational terms. However, there are a number of indications in the novel that seriously undercut its representational side. On a metafictional level the narrator clearly faces the same problems with language that he has Bloch struggling with. Let me offer some examples. There are, for instance, nominalistic passages such as the following one:

> After a while he stopped, then immediately broke into a run from a stand-
> ing position. He got off to a quick start, suddenly stopped short, changed
> direction, ran at a steady pace, then changed his step, changed his step
> again, stopped short, then ran backward, turned around while running
> backward, ran forward again, again turned around to run backward, went
> backward, turned around to run forward, after a few steps changed to a
> sprint, stopped short, sat down on a curbstone, and immediately went back
> to running from a sitting position (Handke 1970: 74).

Such passages, which Alan Thiher very appropriately calls examples of "hyperrealism," are minute descriptions that reveal nothing and only stress the inadequacy of language to represent more then "a positivistic reduction of the world to intolerably trivial limits" (Thiher 1984: 147). At other times the narrator, apparently aware of the futility of such descriptions, calls attention to their futility by explicitly refusing to continue them: "Next to him on the bench there was a dried-up snail spoor. The grass under the bench was wet with last night's dew; the cellophane wrapper of a cigarette box was fogged with mist. To his left he saw . . . To his right there was . . . Behind him he saw . . . He got hungry and walked away" (57). The strongest suggestion that language cannot really have a representational function, however, is offered by a passage in which all nouns are replaced by crude drawings, obviously not Bloch's but the narrator's (90). If we may read *Die Angst des Tormanns beim Elfmeter* then as representational, we may also read it as representing the impossibility of representation.

In a different way the same holds for the last text I want to examine, Norman Mailer's *The Executioner's Song*. But whereas Handke is clearly aware of the danger of non-representation threatening his own language, it is far less clear whether Mailer — whom we may identify with the narrator of *Song* — is beset by the same doubts. It is more probable that in the case of *Song* we are dealing with what Alan Thiher has called a "schizo-text," that is, a text that intends to reveal that the world has to a certain extent been replaced by discourse, but still considers itself grounded outside discourse, on firm ground.

But let me begin my discussion of Mailer with the murder, in this case murders, committed by ex-convict Gary Gilmore, three months after his release on parole. Gilmore, who is having serious trouble with his girl friend, Nicole, first robs and shoots a gas station attendant and then, the following night, robs and kills the desk clerk of a nearby motel. The murders are cold-blooded, but the stupidity of the murderer is almost beyond belief: both murders are committed in an area where Gilmore, an ex-con, is pretty well known, the proceeds are negligible, and while getting rid of his gun after the second murder Gilmore accidentally shoots himself through his hand. And this from a criminal who according to psychological reports is of good to superior intelligence.

This is not the only contradiction that the character of Gilmore offers. In fact, of the four murderers discussed here Gilmore is by far the most mysterious; he is the only one who remains unknowable and whose motivation is never completely cleared up. After his arrest Gilmore claims again and again that he does not know why he found it necessary to kill his victims. Once, in a letter to Nicole, he suggests that his irritation with the fact that he could not afford a certain pick-up truck was responsible for his outburst of violence; at another time he tells an interviewer that he went out killing in order to avoid killing Nicole. But that is about as close as we can get. And the psychiatrists who refuse to declare him insane do not get any closer. In fact, the more his lawyers search the reports on Gilmore "the less they encountered madness, and the more he appeared grim, ironic, practical" (Mailer 1979: 383). Mailer, who surprisingly and much to his credit does not take Gilmore into his hipster cosmology, is the first to admit this. In his afterword he tells us that although his story is "as accurate as one can make it" and is based upon interviews that in transcript would run to fifteen thousand pages, it has not necessarily "come a great deal closer to the truth than the recollections of witnesses" (1051). Mailer's often nominalistic language reflects this state of affairs, as for instance in the description of the first murder:

> It was a bathroom with green tiles that came to the height of your chest, and tan-painted walls. The floor, six feet by eight feet, was laid in dull gray tiles. A rack for paper towels on the wall had Towl [sic] Saver printed on it. The toilet had a split seat. An overhead light was in the wall.
>
> Gilmore brought the Automatic to Jensen's head. "This one is for me," he said, and fired.
>
> "This one is for Nicole," he said, and fired again (224).

Mailer's reluctance to interpret Gilmore's motivation and his character are all the more conspicuous because so many characters in his story are looking for totalizing interpretations. Lawrence Schiller, the media agent who buys the exclusive rights to the stories of Gilmore and his girl-friend, is explicit about this in a telegram he sends Gilmore in prison: "I am thoroughly convinced that as I go deeper the meaning of your life becomes more clear..." (763). Gilmore's mother is reported thinking that "from the time Gary was 3 years old, she knew he was going to be executed. He had been a dear little guy, but she had lived with that fear since he was 3. That was when he began to show a side she could not go near" (494). There is Barry Farrell, a journalist who is convinced that the key to Gilmore's character must be found in childhood beatings, a suggestion that Gilmore persistently denies. This process of interpretation, of looking for essence, even goes on after the execution, when during the memorial service for Gilmore people who knew him well come together with the intention, as one of them says, "to expose the real Gary Mark Gilmore" (1019).

But in spite of all attempts, Gilmore stays out of reach. Still, this is nothing new, as I have already pointed out. We find much the same mystery and much the same baffled attempts at understanding in a comparable book, Truman Capote's *In Cold Blood*, although admittedly Capote moves further in the direction of psychological explanations than Mailer is prepared to do in *The Executioner's Song*. However, in *Song* we also find an important new element. Late in the book, Lawrence Schiller is said to have decided for himself that "Much of human motivation...came from the idea of behavior that movie plots laid into your head. When you could make remarks that brought back those movie plots, people acted on them" (Mailer 1979: 933). We are reminded of Jean-François Lyotard's view of the role that the media ("l'informatique") play in shaping individual character in postmodern society and it is this notion of character shaped by discourse or, to put it differently, character replaced by discourse, that gradually moves to the center in the last part of Mailer's book.

The first hint that Gilmore may be merely playing roles is given through his cellmate Gibbs: "Gilmore had a quality Gibbs could recognize. He accomodated. Gibbs believed he, himself, could always get near somebody — just use the side that was like them. Gilmore did the same" (Mailer 1979: 358). After Lawrence Schiller has made his entrance into the Gilmore case, and Gilmore is on his way to become a national celebrity, this impression is strengthened. Schiller sees Gilmore "selling himself as a tough con" (693) and to Barry Farrell, brought into the case to construct an interview with *Playboy* out of Gilmore's answers to the questions he sends him, it looks "as if Gilmore was now setting out to present the particular view of himself he wanted people to keep. In that sense, he was being his own writer" (793). The same Farrell later thinks that if less attention had been paid to the case by the media Gilmore might have wanted to avoid execution. As it is he becomes, according to Farrell, "trapped in fame" (831), in other words, trapped in discourse.

But the real extent to which Gilmore is playing roles is only revealed when Farrell begins to analyse Gilmore's answers to the questions and the letters he has sent Nicole after his imprisonment:

> Rereading the interviews and letters, Farrell began to mark the transcripts

> with different-colored inks to underline each separate motif in Gilmore's
> replies, and before he was done, he got twenty-seven poses. Barry had
> begun to spot racist Gary and Country-and-Western Gary, poetic Gary,
> artist manqué Gary, macho Gary, self-destructive Gary, Karma County
> Gary, Texas Gary, and Gary the killer Irishman. Awfully prevalent lately
> was Gilmore the movie star, awfully shit-kicking large-minded aw-shucks
> (Mailer 1979: 830).

A closer look at the letters reveals the same pattern: "The mood...often
changed at the beginning of a new page. In effect, each sheet was being
worked on as a separate composition" (836). No wonder Gilmore has
everybody confused. Even a last tape recording, made for his girl-friend
Nicole, is totally decentered; it is nothing but a collection of voices:

> The voice in this recording was unlike anything Ron had heard coming out
> of Gary before, a funny voice, fancy and phony and slurred. Every now
> and then it would be highly enunciated. It was as if each of his personalities
> took a turn, and Ron thought it was like an actor putting on one mask, tak-
> ing it off, putting on another for a new voice (941).

Yet we are not dealing with a schizophrenic, but with a man who emerges
from the psychiatric reports as a grim, ironic and practical personality.

Gilmore, then, has not a "character" in the traditional sense of the
word — that is, in the way that Mailer has chosen to present him. His
behavior is absolutely unpredictable and often at odds with his statements.
To give a last example of this, he insists again and again that he loves and
admires his impoverished mother, yet he leaves no provisions for her in his
will while leaving three thousand dollars to Nicole's baby-sitter. As the prosecutor in his case observes, "It was like dealing with a crazy pony who was
off on a gallop at every wind. Then wouldn't move" (Mailer 1979: 431).

It is by no means accidental that the impression that Gilmore is made
up out of voices, out of roles that he either consciously or subconsciously
adopts, becomes so strong in the last part of the book. By then Gilmore,
waiting for his execution, is severely restricted in his movements and is
indeed almost reduced to a voice, speaking to us through the tapes that are
smuggled out of the prison. It is also not accidental that it is Farrell who discovers Gilmore's various voices. Farrell waits for the tapes to be typed up
and then reads the transcripts, without hearing Gilmore's actual voice.
Schiller, on the other hand, feels that listening to each new tape is his "creative experience of the day. He'd have an immediate reaction. At such
times, he felt he understood Gilmore at a moment-by-moment level"
(Mailer 1979: 837-38). In other words, Schiller is deceived by presence, by

his belief that voice and essence are identical, even if the voice is only taped. Later, Schiller, too, realizes that he has heard only language, a language either divorced from Gilmore's essential character or a language that has come to replace that character as movie plots have come to replace authentic behavior.

The language with which Mailer probes Gilmore's character certainly has epistemological pretensions — he calls his book a *"true life story"* (1979: 1053) — but what is uncovered is not anything belonging to a world of characterological essence but only various types of discourse. Mailer must be aware of this, as he appears also to be aware of the problems involving representation. His language is at times excessively nominalistic, just as Handke's language, as for instance in his minute description of the room in the Holiday Inn where Gilmore spends the night after the first murder. And it is surely not accidental that he quotes a letter from Gilmore to Nicole in which Gilmore seems to be pushing against the limits of language in an effort to do justice to his feelings — *seems* to be pushing, because we may as well be dealing with one of the voices that Farrell will later discover.

If it is clear that Mailer is aware that with Gilmore he has not penetrated beyond Gilmore's voices, it is far less clear to what extent he sees the other characters in his *"true life story*, with its real names and real lives" (1979: 1053), in terms of language. True enough, he describes them by giving each of them his or her own language, complete with appropriate metaphors, and he even calls the two parts of his story "Western Voices", respectively "Eastern Voices." But he may as well refer here to the fact that he worked primarily from taped interviews; voices provided the material out of which his book is constructed.

In any case, and no matter what Mailer's intentions may have been, in Gary Gilmore we have what I would call an example of Postmodernist characterization. Just as in the case of Handke's Bloch we have an attempt at representing character that calls attention to the impossibility of representation and, at the same time, to the fact that what is finally represented may very well be nothing but discourse. It seems to me that such attempts at characterization reveal more tellingly the inadequacy and at the same time the omnipresence of language — and thus the difference with characterizations such as those of Lafcadio and Meursault — than those Postmodernist characterizations, as for instance in the work of the American Surfictionists, that have abandoned representation altogether and present a rather artificial discontinuity and absence of causality. As Alan

Thiher has pointed out, "Not the least interesting" — and I would add: revealing — "aspect of contemporary culture is that many believe simultaneously that language articulates the world and that language cannot reach the world" (Thiher 1984: 93).

REFERENCES

Bell, Daniel. 1976. *The Cultural Contradictions of Capitalism*. New York: Basic Books.

Camus, Albert. 1942. *The Outsider*, trans. Joseph Laredo. Harmondsworth: Penguin, 1983. Translation of *L'Etranger*.

Docherty, Thomas. 1983. *Reading (Absent) Character: Towards a Theory of Characterization in Fiction*. Oxford: Clarendon Press.

Fokkema, Douwe W. 1984. *Literary History, Modernism, and Postmodernism*. Amsterdam and Philadelphia: Benjamins.

-----. 1986. "The Semantic and Syntactic Organization of Postmodernist Texts," in Fokkema and Bertens 1986: 81-98.

Fokkema, Douwe and Hans Bertens, eds. 1986. *Approaching Postmodernism*. Amsterdam and Philadelphia: Benjamins.

Gide, André. 1914. *The Vatican Cellars*, trans. Dorothy Bussy. Harmondsworth: Penguin, 1969. Translation of *Les Caves du Vatican*.

Graff, Gerald. 1979. *Literature Against Itself: Literary Ideas in Modern Society*. Chicago: University of Chicago Press.

Handke, Peter. 1970. *The Goalie's Anxiety at the Penalty Kick*, trans. Michael Roloff, in *Three by Handke*. New York: Avon/Bard, 1977. Translation of *Die Angst des Tormanns beim Elfmeter*.

Hassan, Ihab. 1975. *Paracriticisms: Seven Speculations of the Times*. Urbana: University of Illinois Press.

-----. 1977. "Prometheus as Performer: Toward a Posthumanist Culture," *Georgia Review* 31: 830-850.

Hassan, Ihab and Sally Hassan, eds. 1983. *Innovation/Renovation: New Perspectives on the Humanities*. Madison: University of Wisconsin Press.

Hoffmann, Gerhard. 1982. "The Fantastic in Fiction: Its 'Reality' Status, Its Historical Development and Its Transformation in Postmodern Narrative," *REAL* (*Yearbook of Research in English and American Literature*) 1: 267-364.

-----. 1986. "The Absurd and Its Forms of Reduction in Postmodern American Fiction," in Fokkema and Bertens 1986: 185-210.

Hoffmann, Gerhard, Alfred Hornung and Rüdiger Kunow. 1977. "'Modern', 'Postmodern' and 'Contemporary' as Criteria for the Analysis of 20th Century Literature," *Amerikastudien* 22: 19-46.

Holland, Norman N. 1983. "Postmodern Psychoanalysis," in Hassan and Hassan 1983: 291-309.

Holquist, Michael. 1971. "Whodunit and Other Questions: Metaphysical Detective Stories in Post-War Fiction," *New Literary History* 3: 135-156.

Kermode, Frank. 1983. *Essays on Fiction 1971-82*. London: Routledge and Kegan Paul.

Lodge, David. 1977a. *The Modes of Modern Writing: Metaphor, Metonymy, and the Typology of Modern Literature*. London: Arnold.

-----. 1977b. "Modernism, Antimodernism and Postmodernism," *The New Review* 4, 38: 39-44.

Mailer, Norman. 1979. *The Executioner's Song*. London: Arrow, 1980.

Singer, Alan. 1983. *A Metaphorics of Fiction: Discontinuity and Discourse in the Modern Novel*. Gainesville: University Presses of Florida.

Spanos, William V. 1972. "The Detective and the Boundary: Some Notes on the Postmodern Literary Imagination," *Boundary 2*, 1: 147-168.

Sypher, Wylie. 1962. *Loss of the Self in Modern Literature and Art*. New York: Random House.

Thiher, Allen. 1984. *Words in Reflection: Modern Language Theory and Postmodern Fiction*. Chicago and London: University of Chicago Press.

Wilde, Alan. 1981. *Horizons of Assent: Modernism, Postmodernism, and the Ironic Imagination*. Baltimore and London: Johns Hopkins University Press.

10

Popular Genre Conventions in Postmodern Fiction: The Case of the Western

Theo D'haen

Of late, the contribution of the detective novel to literary Postmodernism has received detailed attention (Cawelti 1976: 136-138, Holquist 1971, Spanos 1972, Tani 1984). Tani, the most recent commentator on the issue, discusses Leonardo Sciascia's *A ciascuno il suo* and *Todo modo*, John Gardner's *The Sunlight Dialogues*, Umberto Eco's *Il nome della rosa*, Thomas Pynchon's *The Crying of Lot 49*, William Hjortsberg's *Falling Angel*, Italo Calvino's *Se una notte d'inverno un viaggiatore*, and Nabokov's *Pale Fire* as examples of postmodern detectives. Next to these, he refers in passing to a whole host of other contemporary writers. This leads him to conclude that "good contemporary fiction and anti-detective fiction [i.e. what he sees as the typically postmodern variant of the genre — T.D.] are for the most part the same thing" (1984: 149) and that "any recent good novel that holds the attention of the reader through suspense, undermines his expectations, and offers a revelation (often unpleasant), is largely drawing on anti-detective fiction's techniques. These techniques are in turn the inversion of detective fictional techniques, that is, the postmodern negation of the centeredness and reassurance typical of the genre" (1984: 149).

Yet, this particular (sub)genre's surfacing is only part of a more general flooding in of popular (sub)genres into the center of the literary system in Postmodernism. In fact, most of what Tani says with regard to detective and anti-detective fiction holds for Cawelti's general definition of formula stories and their inversion in Postmodernism. Corrected and expanded in this way, Tani's claim can be backed up by adding to his list some more examples of anti-detective novels, such as Robbe-Grillet's *La Jalousie* and

La Maison de rendez-vous, but also Jean Echenoz's recent *Cherokee*, John Hawkes's *The Lime Twig*, and even Norman Mailer's *Tough Guys Don't Dance*. Looking at some other formulaic genres we might refer to works in the sado-masochist and pornographic tradition, such as Hawkes's *The Passion Artist* and *Virginie: Her Two Lives*. Using the formula of science-fiction are Doris Lessing, in her Canopus in Argos-series, Anthony Burgess in *The End of the World News*, Don DeLillo in *Ratner's Star*, John Fowles who in *A Maggot* mixes the formulas of the historical, the detective, and the science-fiction novel, and Hugo Raes in *De Lotgevallen* and *De Verwoesting van Hyperion* (For a case in support of the thesis of the increasing centrality of popular forms in contemporary fiction see Waugh 1984: 79-86.)

We can see this process of literary change as the replacement of the canonical socio-psychological novel prevalent until the nineteen-fifties by noncanonical fictional forms: hitherto muted genres become dominant and vice versa (Jakobson 1978: 82-87). However, as polysystem theory has demonstrated, the literary system operates in conjunction with other systems and within the larger system of culture (national or international) in general (Even-Zohar 1979, Lefevere 1985). Hence, the particular direction literary evolution takes is functionally related to concomitant changes in these other systems and in the cultural system at large. Conversely, the shift to the center of hitherto peripheral genres affects them too. I will first try to account for this shift in general, and then illustrate it with a discussion of some examples from a genre that has hitherto received less attention than the detective: the western. Here, I will concentrate on E.L. Doctorow's *Welcome to Hard Times* (1960), Richard Brautigan's *The Hawkline Monster* (1974), and the Dutch author Louis Ferron's *De ballade van de beul* (1980, The Hangman's Ballad).

Taking our cue from Michel Foucault (1966) we might postulate, in our recent past, an epistemic caesura. This caesura marks the end of the "humanist" world view linked to scientifically progressive and economically liberal capitalist bourgeois ideology. The new episteme posits man not as individual consciousness but rather as meeting point of pre-existing social practices and — especially — discourses. Poststructuralist thought would have it that the "individual" in the humanist world view is fully as much a creature of coded discourse as any post-humanist is, but that it is part and parcel of the humanist world view to veil this fact by *projecting* the ideal of the "individual." The difference, and hence the epistemic caesura, is then to be located in the post-humanist's *awareness* of his being a coded creature of his time and society's discourses. This is what Jean-François Lyotard (1979) diagnoses as *la condition postmoderne*.

For Lyotard the corollary to this postmodern *prise de conscience* is "l'incrédulité à l'égard des métarécits" (1979: 7), where these "metanarratives" (Hassan & Hassan's translation, 1983: 26) stand for the kind of codes that allowed man to make sense of his world within the context of the humanist world view. As far as fiction is concerned, these codes (religion, science, psychology, history, economics, politics, law, class codes) were always articulated by "serious" fiction in the sense that the novel typically portrays the individual working his way through to insight into his very own individual and unique relation to his world and its codes. The change-over from Modernism (in its late-, high-, or limit-Modernist variant, see McHale 1986) to Postmodernism, then, marks the epistemic caesura from the humanist to the post-humanist world view in four ways. To begin with, it problematizes the systemic centrality of the "serious" novel exemplarily reflecting the humanist ideal. Second, the (sub)genres challenging the "serious" novel implicitly attack "high art," the last avatar the humanist world view resorted to for bolstering its claims. Third, by their very nature and function these (sub)-genres represent a more code-oriented view. Finally, the particular way these (sub)genres are used in Postmodernism goes to negate all metanarratives. The first point has already been dealt with. The other three will be taken up separately in what follows.

Earlier, I indicated that the serious novel articulated the cultural codes or metanarratives justifying the humanist world view to itself. Obviously, concomitant to developments in the other systems making up the total cultural system at a given moment, various periods and/or movements stressed different codes: the Realists favored "objective" codes such as economics, law, religion, and class codes, the Naturalists emphasized "science." The Modernists preferred more "subjective" codes such as psychology to anchor their protagonists in their world. Moreover, with the Modernists allegiance to any metanarrative was already a provisional and temporary thing, rather than an unequivocal or permanent one (Fokkema and Ibsch 1984). In the last instance, all else failing, they put their faith in "high art" itself as the last metanarrative, the last bastion of the humanist world view, a move critically consecrated in the advent of the New Criticism and in Leavis's *Great Tradition*. It is this view and function of art in Modernism that Postmodernism attacks by singling out as the center of its literary system not "high art" but hitherto spurned popular (sub)genres. This phenomenon, which

Jameson (1983: 112) calls "the effacement ... of some key boundaries or separations, most notably the erosion of the older distinction between high culture and so-called mass or popular culture," has been observed not just in postmodern literature but likewise in postmodern art (Jencks 1977, Butler 1980, D'haen 1986a).

Borrowing a favorite term from Modernist criticism we could say that the popular (sub)genres surfacing in the center of the postmodern literary system are better (vaguely Eliotian) "objective correlatives" to the post-humanist world view than the serious novel. Throughout the period of dominance of the serious novel these (sub)genres existed as what Cawelti calls "formula stories." Formula stories primarily serve their audience's needs of escape and relaxation (Cawelti 1976: 8) by offering them "satisfaction and a basic emotional security in a familiar form" (Cawelti 1976: 9). As such, they embody or project "collective fantasies shared by large groups of people" (Cawelti 1976: 7). They "affirm existing interests and attitudes by presenting an imaginary world that is aligned with these interests and attitudes. ... By confirming existing definitions of the world, literary formulas help to maintain a culture's ongoing consensus about the nature of reality and morality. We assume therefore, that one aspect of the structure of a formula is this process of confirming some strongly held conventional view" (1976: 35). Obviously, Cawelti assigns more functions than just this one to formula stories. However, for the sake of my argument, this is the most interesting one. Moreover, even if also in other respects Cawelti sees formula stories as bearing on their culture, the function of creating consensus is for him the primary one: he cites it first of all, and all his other conclusions follow from this one. Formula stories, then, are doubly coded: *literary* codes conventionally express *cultural* codes.

To achieve these ends formula stories have highly exciting plots — suspense, sudden twists, highly charged emotions, particularly with regard to love and death — that resolve themselves in ways that uphold the established order. It is interesting here to draw a parallel with work being done on nineteenth-century popular genres such as the slave narrative or the melodrama in the vein of *Uncle Tom's Cabin*. There the ending likewise always upheld some form of established order even if that ending seems "bad" or "wrong" to twentieth-century sensibilities. A case in point is Tom's death scene in Harriet Beecher Stowe's celebrated novel as analysed by Jane Tompkins in her *Sensational Designs: The Cultural Work of American Fiction* (1985). In fact, then, it is the certainty that all will be right in the end that allows for the extravagance of the plot developments.

The setting of a formula story is an imaginary world that is slightly set aside from the "real" world, but that remains sufficiently close to it to be credible. Usually, a number of stereotypical settings reoccur. Each formula has its own typical set of characters. What is important is that the reader identify with the protagonist, as this ensures both his involvement in the fiction and his (at least temporary, i.e. while reading) allegiance to the views embodied.

In each of its instances, the serious novel shows us (a number of) characters that try to work out some *modus vivendi*, and sometimes *moriendi* within humanist culture. Thus, in each of its manifestations it offers us a (relatively) new experience and constantly invites us to compare the world of fiction to that of reality. The formula story in its repetitiveness offers us a familiar experience that invites comparison primarily with other works of the same formulaic genre. The formula's frame of reference, therefore, is primarily "generic" and not, as with the serious novel, "mimetic" (Cawelti's terms).

The move to the postmodern literary center stage of these formula stories, then, follows precisely from the fact that they so clearly betray their codedness. If man and his culture are code-determined entities, these stories admit as much also in the literary realm, rather than uphold the serious novel's fiction that some sort of compromise, some individual coming to terms is possible. Moreover, the generic frame of reference these formula stories posit tallies rather well with the Postmodernist idea of the world itself as story. From the point of view of deconstruction and post-structuralism — the critical complements to Postmodernism as New Criticism was to Modernism — it signals the world as "*texte.*" Thus, it expresses the postmodern distrust of language itself as a possible instrument for knowing "reality" (see Thiher 1984), even if only because of language's constant Derridian (1967) "différancing" processes.

If the very adoption of these formulaic genres by Postmodernists emphasizes these writers' awareness of the codedness of their cultural condition, at the same time the way the Postmodernists deal with these formula stories expresses their reaction to this *prise de conscience*. In effect, the Postmodernists turn the blatant codedness of these formulas upon itself in order to express their distrust/disbelief in all metanarratives: they play havoc with the formulaic conventions to upset, rather than uphold, the very idea that there could be such a thing as a tenable metanarrative, and to reveal literature's complicity in ideology building.

The typical western plot pits a hero — the good guy, whether he be a young cowhand such as the "Virginian" in Owen Wister's eponymous novel or an aging gunfighter such as Gary Cooper in *High Noon* — against a villain, with a number of subsidiary characters both looking on and having a stake in the action. Most prominent among these is the hero's sweetheart, usually either an Eastern schoolmarm or a heart-of-gold saloon lady or whore madam.

The conflict between the hero and the villain is not simply a personal one. The villain disturbs the established order in the world of the western: he is a gambler, a rustler, a bank robber, or a killer. In the lawless West, only few men (or women) dare stand up against him, as he is ruthless and quick on the draw. Moreover, there are always those who think to make a quick profit by him, or who plan to use him for their own purposes. The hero, on the contrary, often stands alone in his altruistic pursuit of justice or while carrying out what he considers his duty.

In the end, the hero succeeds, at the risk of his life, and often of his love, to reestablish order by resorting to the very violence the villain disturbs that order with. Usually, though, this also condems him to leave the very same society (village, town) he has defended and safeguarded: he rides off into the setting sun. In the more optimistic option, he gets both his sweetheart and a large(r) stake in his community. According to Cawelti (1976), the latter solution is typical of the earlier "romantic" type of western, such as *The Virginian*, and dominant — roughly — in the period 1900-1930s, whereas the-lone-rider-into-the-sunset-solution corresponds to the "classic" western of the late 1930s to 1950s. Each of these solutions represents a different relation of the individual to his culture and society concomitant to the periods in which these westerns were produced (written or filmed). However, the important thing is that in all cases the conventional order is reestablished.

All this takes place against a backdrop of majestic western landscapes that illustrate the magnitude of the principles pitted against one another involved: good versus evil, law and justice versus lawlessness, order versus anarchy. Needless to say, these principles are projections of the cultural codes or metanarratives mentioned earlier.

The typical strategy of the postmodern western is, precisely, to reveal the projective character of these principles by first invoking, and then negating the conventions evoking them.

As to geographical and temporal location and plot, Doctorow's *Welcome to Hard Times*, Brautigan's *The Hawkline Monster*, and Ferron's *De ballade van de beul* initially appeal to typical western conventions. All three novels take place around the turn of the century, in, respectively, the Dakota Territory, Eastern Oregon, and California. All three have opponents work their way through from an initial confrontation to a final duel. The first indication that *Welcome to Hard Times, The Hawkline Monster*, and *De ballade van de beul* are not traditional westerns is in the characters they parade. None of these novels has a traditional "hero."

Welcome to Hard Times has as its protagonist and narrator (this in itself is already unconventional, as the western is usually a third-person narrative) a fiftyish, rather bookish man called Blue. He is the self-appointed mayor of a fly-speck little settlement called, although we only find this out well into the novel, "Hard Times." And hard times they turn out to be when the villain rides into town: the Man from Bodie is a raving maniac, immensely strong and fast, who rapes, burns and plunders wherever he goes, without any one daring to oppose him. When the Man leaves, Hard Times is nothing but dying embers.

All the town's inhabitans are dead, or they have fled. Only Blue, Molly, one of the town whores, Jimmy, a little boy, and John Bear, an Indian medicine man, are left. Blue sets about building a dugout for Molly, Jimmy, and himself. When travelers come by Blue persuades them to stay. Slowly, the town is rebuilt: better, bigger than before. Blue again is addressed as "mayor." He settles to some sort of family life with Molly and Jimmy. The future looks bright enough. Then, the Man from Bodie returns.

If the Man from Bodie in *Welcome to Hard Times* shows a close enough resemblance to the typical western villain, the same cannot be said of Brautigan's Hawkline Monster, in the eponymous novel. Moreover, even as monsters go, this one is a highly unusual specimen: it consists of a particular kind of light, generated by "The Chemicals," the result of an eccentric professor's experiments. It can change things at will: it has changed the professor into an elephant foot umbrella stand, and it plays strange tricks upon the appearance and the thoughts of the two misses Hawkline, the professor's daughters. These daughters hire Cameron and Greer, two professional gunslingers, to help them get rid of the monster. Which they do by pouring a glass of whisky into the jar with The Chemicals during the final confrontation.

Cameron and Greer are hardly run-of-the-mill western heroes. They do not fight for justice or for any kind of ideal, and although they are professional killers, they are also highly sentimental, as when they decide to give up on killing a man when they see him amidst his happy family.

Perhaps the weirdest protagonist is Howard Hauser from Ferron's *De ballade van de beul*. He is a clothing store owner in San Ramon, a small California village. Already well advanced in age, he decides to take up the vacant post of hangman for the state of California. A clumsy man even at his best, Hauser fumbles his first execution. Butler, the hanged cowboy's friend, swears revenge. Throughout the book the focus is on Hauser as the protagonist. Yet Butler is portrayed as — and is even said to be — the more sympathetic figure, while Hauser emerges as a morose, pompous fool. It is clear that with Hauser, but likewise with Blue, there can be no question of reader-identification. Greer and Cameron, too, are presented in such an offhand manner; they are so obviously "characters" that again there can be no question of reader-identification. Instead, the reader is made to reflect on the difference between these characters and the typical western hero.

If the main characters, the hero and its opponent, in these three novels do not comply with typical western conventions, the same can be said of the other characters. In none of these novels do we find a clean spoken, god fearing, gentle and loving Eastern schoolmarm. In *Welcome to Hard Times* all the women are whores, and if one of them "converts," like Molly does, it is not to become a "good" woman, but rather because she is blinded by fear and revenge. In fact, Molly uses all her feminine skills to achieve her own ends. She tries to entice Blue first to take her away from Hard Times, and then to face Turner, the Bad Man from Bodie. She emotionally lays claim to Jimmy Fee and raises him to defend her from all men. Finally, she offers herself to Jenks, the newly appointed town sheriff, if he takes on Turner upon the latter's return to Hard Times.

In *The Hawkline Monster* we meet with not one, but two Eastern marms. Whatever they do, though, they certainly do not teach school, unless it be that of carnal love. The promiscuous misses Hawkline are a far cry from Wister's virginal miss Molly Wood. And in *De ballade van de beul* Hauser keeps a safe distance from all women, although there are hints that he may have once raped a girl in a neighboring village. At the time of the novel's action Emilou, the girl in question, has become the local hotel- and saloon-keeper. She has an affair with a professional gambler who turns out to be as much an inversion of the villain stereotype as Hauser is of the traditional hero: the gambler is an honest man, a faithful lover, and a man of principle.

Obviously, the character inversions taking place in these three novels likewise affect their plot developments. Whereas the traditional western obeys Tzvetan Todorov's tenet (1970: 171) that "tout récit est mouvement entre deux équilibres semblables mais non identiques," the postmodern western bluntly disobeys this same tenet. Or, if it does obey the tenet, the final equilibrium reached is a *reductio ad absurdum* of the original one. This is the case in *Welcome to Hard Times*. When the Man from Bodie returns, history (or story) repeats itself: again, women are raped, houses are burned, people are killed. This time Blue defends himself somewhat better than the previous time. However, he does not do so in the traditional western hero's fashion by outshooting the villain. Rather, he does it by tricking him into getting entangled in barbed wire. Even so, the result of Turner's second visit is identical, nay worse, than that of the first.

Blue takes Turner to Molly, to show her that he is now harmless. But Molly starts jabbing Turner with a knife, painfully revealing the hate-love relationship she has to him. Jimmy, horrified, kills both Turner and Molly, locked together, with one blast of his gun. Blue, who tried to stop him by muzzling the gun with his hand, is severely injured. Jimmy rides off: another crazed Bad Man from Bodie gone to haunt and torture the West. Blue is left to die. The equilibrium reached here can hardly be called the restoration or reestablishment of any kind of order. Rather, it is the denial of any final order that is asserted: what happened to Blue, and to Hard Times, is a mockery of justice, law, and all other values so conspicuously upheld in the traditional western.

If the final confrontation between hero and villain in *Welcome to Hard Times* does not follow the typical pattern, this applies even more so to *The Hawkline Monster* and *De ballade van de beul*. At the end of *De ballade van de beul* Hauser is actually longing for Butler to catch up with him, to put an end to a life he feels now to have been inauthentic and wasted. When Butler does catch up with Hauser, it is in Emilou's saloon. A shot rings out. Everybody ducks, except for Hauser, who thinks he feels the bullet entering his body. However, not Butler but Carradyne, a mysterious figure, almost a double of Hauser himself, whom Hauser has kept meeting throughout the book and who has played various tricks on him before, has fired the shot, shattering a whiskey bottle in front of Hauser. Hauser is unharmed. He begs Butler to shoot but nothing happens and he remains like this, afraid that the relieving shot will never come. Instead of with a return to order via the plot solution, we are here left with a non-solution, and hence with permanent disorder.

The duels in *Welcome to Hard Times* and *De ballade van de beul* invert some of the western clichés. The whisky in the jar episode of *The Hawkline Monster* mocks these clichés. Yet, in some sense, this duel leads to the most traditional solution. The villain (The Chemicals) is destroyed. Professor Hawkline has been changed back into his former self. The "heroes" have won and can now enjoy their spoils: the riches of the diamonds The Chemicals have turned into, and the favors of the misses Hawkline. However, *The Hawkline Monster* does not end with this solution. There follows another chapter narrating the further adventures of Greer, Cameron, the misses Hawkline, Professor Hawkline, and even the lake the Hawkline house has turned into after the destruction of The Chemicals caused it to burn down and the ice caves underneath it to melt. From this last chapter it appears that all that seemed stable at the time of the plot's resolution is sheer disorder in times to come. This temporary solution is thus shown up as sheer artifice, pure convention. In Wister's *The Virginian* the "coda" (Labov 1972, Pratt 1977) confirms the order reached in the plot solution and thereby upholds and underscores the conventional views articulated therein. In *The Hawkline Monster* the coda mocks the order adumbrated in the plot solution.

As in the traditional western, the postmodern western employs setting to express the mood of its characters, the wider import of their actions, and the importance of the issues at stake. To this end, the landscape of the traditional western impresses us with its spectacular majesty. The flatness and barrenness of the Dakota landscape in *Welcome to Hard Times* stands in sharp contrast to this traditional setting, just as Doctorow's characters and plot show up the emptiness of the views and values embodied by their paradigmatic counterparts. Brautigan has most of the action of *The Hawkline Monster* take place inside a gothic mansion plunked down in Eastern Oregon. Just as Brautigan's gunfighters are not "real" western heroes, his villain is not a true "villain," and his plot is not a true "western" plot, his setting is not a true western setting. In fact, we read *The Hawkline Monster* only as a western because it is set in the West (which is different from a "western" setting), because its characters are dressed like characters from a western, and — perhaps most of all — because the subtitle to the book claims it to be "a gothic *western*."

In other words, Brautigan exploits a number of extraneous parapher-
nalia to generate in his reader the expectation that he is going to read a true
western in order to be able to twist the conventions he has emphasized. In
the process, he is doing to all these conventions what his coda is doing to
the novel's "orderly" solution: he is showing them up *as* conventions and
nothing more. Of course, the fact that Brautigan chose to subtitle his novel
a *gothic* western already accounts for some of its peculiarities. However,
Brautigan deals fully as ironically and self-consciously with the gothic conventions as with those of the western.

The most extra-ordinary case of conventions being laid bare, though, is
Ferron's *Ballade van de beul*. In this novel, the landscape is all we expect it
to be in a western. Yet, it turns out that there we are truly facing convention as convention: the whole story of Howard Hauser Hangman turns out
to be a movie, starring the second-rate actor Howard Hauser. The landscape he moves against is not a setting, but a movie set inside a studio. In
fact, the plot involving Hauser as the hangman is framed by another plot
featuring Hauser as contemporary movie actor. We first become aware of
this framing device in the break from chapter one to chapter two. Chapter
one gave what we thought was a straightforward third-person narrative of
Hauser's decision to take the hangman job. The beginning of chapter two
shows us the actor Hauser being arrested for negligent driving. Further on
in the novel, though, we see an intrusive narrator discussing both the conventions of the western movie itself, and the possibility of writing a western
novel about a western movie. So we end up with a tree-layered structure,
each subsequent framing (Goffman 1974, D'haen 1983) story fulfilling a
metafictional role with regard to its framed story.

Each subsequent frame, then, also reveals the conventions by which
the other frames operate. The result is a fully self-conscious and self-reflexive novel which is as aware of its own role as projection as it is of that of the
traditional western, whether movie or novel. Moreover, in the final
metafictional layer, the narrator (presumably Ferron himself) makes clear
that all imaginative human constructs, in whatever media form, are projections: whether they be commercials propagating, and then exploiting, supposedly "American" ideals and values (e.g. Ferron 1980: 153), or "history"
(e.g. 202-203). They are scripts telling us what we want to see, or how our
society wants to see it and ourselves, and in this sense they are like western movie set landscapes. In fact, what Ferron is here metafictionally telling
us is a point he has also made in his other non-western novels, foremost

among them *Turkenvespers*, a novel freely situating identical characters and continuous actions in divergent historical periods, and "starring" Howard's "pseudo-father" Kaspar Hauser of (lately) postmodern Peter Handkian repute (see also Klinkowitz and Knowlton 1983: 112-115). It is a point similarly made by Doctorow's historical novels *Ragtime* and *Loon Lake*, and in Brautigan's *Trout Fishing in America*.

All three novels discussed, then, play on the character, plot, and setting conventions ruling the traditional western. All three, partly in similar, partly in different ways, invert these conventions. A number of other postmodern works, such as Thomas Berger's *Little Big Man*, the Canadian author Robert Kroetsch's *The Studhorse Man*, Tom Robbins's *Even Cowgirls Get the Blues*, Ishmael Reed's *Yellow Back Radio Broke-Down*, Donald Barthelme's "Daumier" (from *Sadness*) and "Porcupines at the University" (from *Amateurs*), William S. Burroughs' *The Place of Dead Roads*, Thomas McGuane's *Nobody's Angel*, Norman Mailer's *Why Are We in Vietnam*, John Hawkes's *The Beetle Leg*, a number of Sam Shepard's plays, and the Dutch novelist Willem Brakman's *Ansichten uit Amerika* likewise play (sometimes very freely) on (at least a number of) western conventions. (We can witness a similar phenomenon even with an author often taken to be a precursor of Postmodernism: Flann O'Brien in *At Swim-Two-Birds*.) With all of these works the result is a greater awareness in the reader of the grip conventions exercise over his expectations and how they are linked to the metanarratives justifying his culture to itself. Via the ways in which they thwart these expectations, these novels bring out the emptiness and the very conventionality of the conventions they started out by invoking. By extension, the metanarratives these conventions are inspired by and which they uphold are likewise revealed to be imaginative constructs: discourses projecting themselves in fictions, without any necessarily privileged relation to unknowable reality. They are revealed as their culture's "ways of world making" (Goodman 1978) rather than — as their culture would like to see them — eternal truths.

REFERENCES

Brautigan, Richard. 1974. *The Hawkline Monster*. London: Pan/Picador.
Butler, Christopher. 1980. *After the Wake: An Essay on the Contemporary Avant-Garde*. Oxford: Oxford University Press.

Cawelti, John G. 1976. *Adventure, Mystery, and Romance: Formula Stories as Art and Popular Culture*. Chicago and London: University of Chicago Press.

Derrida, Jacques. 1967. *L'Ecriture et la différence*. Paris: Seuil.

D'haen, Theo. 1983. *Text to Reader: A Communicative Approach to Fowles, Barth, Cortázar and Boon*. Amsterdam and Philadelphia: Benjamins.

D'haen, Theo. 1986a. "Postmodernism in American Fiction and Art," in Fokkema and Bertens 1986: 211-231.

D'haen, Theo, ed. 1986b. *Linguistics and the Study of Literature*. Amsterdam: Rodopi.

Doctorow, E.L. 1960. *Welcome to Hard Times*. New York: Bantam, 1981.

Even-Zohar, Itamar. 1979. "Polysystem Theory," *Poetics Today* 1, 1-2: 287-310.

Ferron, Louis. 1980. *De ballade van de beul*. Amsterdam: Bezige Bij.

Fokkema, Douwe and Hans Bertens, eds. 1986. *Approaching Postmodernism*. Amsterdam and Philadelphia: Benjamins.

Fokkema, Douwe and Elrud Ibsch. 1984. *Het Modernisme in de Europese Letterkunde*. Amsterdam: Arbeiderspers.

Foster, Hal, ed. 1983. *The Anti-Aesthetic: Essays on Postmodern Culture*. Port Townsend, Wash.: Bay Press.

Foucault, Michel. 1966. *Les Mots et les choses: une archéologie des sciences humaines*. Paris: Gallimard.

Goffman, Erving. 1974. *Frame Analysis: An Essay on the Organization of Experience*. Harmondsworth: Penguin.

Goodman, Nelson. 1978. *Ways of Worldmaking*. Harvester Studies in Philosophy 5. Hassocks, Sussex: Harvester Press.

Hassan, Ihab and Sally Hassan, eds. 1983. *Innovation/Renovation: New Perspectives on the Humanities*. Madison: University of Wisconsin Press.

Holquist, Michael. 1971. "Whodunit and Other Questions: Metaphysical Detective Stories in Post-War Fiction," *New Literary History* 3,1: 135-156.

Jakobson, Roman. 1978. "The Dominant," in Matejka and Pomorska 1978: 82-87.

Jameson, Fredric. 1983. "Postmodernism and Consumer Society," in Foster 1983: 111-126.

Jencks, Charles. 1977. *The Language of Post-Modern Architecture*. London: Academy Editions.

Klinkowitz, Jerome and James Knowlton. 1983. *Peter Handke and the Postmodern Transformation: The Goalie's Journey Home*. Columbia: University of Missouri Press.

Labov, William. 1972. *Language in the Inner City*. University Park: University of Pennsylviania Press.

Lefevere, André. 1986. "On the Processing of Texts, or: What Is Literature?" in D'haen 1986b: 218-244.

Lyotard, Jean-François. 1979. *La Condition postmoderne*. Paris: Minuit.

Matejka, Ladislav and Krystina Pomorska, eds. 1978. *Readings in Russian Poetics: Formalist and Structuralist Views*. Michigan Slavic Contributions 8. Ann Arbor: University of Michigan.

McHale, Brian. 1986. "Change of Dominant from Modernist to Postmodernist Writing," in Fokkema and Bertens 1986: 53-79.

Pratt, Mary L. 1977. *Toward a Speech Act Theory of Literary Discourse*. Bloomington: Indiana University Press.

Spanos, William V. 1972. "The Detective and the Boundary: Some Notes on the Postmodern Literary Imagination," *Boundary 2* 1,1: 147-168.

Tani, Stefano. 1984. *The Doomed Detective: The Contribution of the Detective Novel to Postmodern American and Italian Fiction*. Carbondale and Edwardsville: Southern Illinois University Press.

Thiher, Allen. 1984. *Words in Reflection: Modern Language Theory and Postmodern Fiction*. Chicago and London: University of Chicago Press.

Todorov, Tzvetan. 1970. *Introduction à la littérature fantastique*. Paris: Seuil.

Waugh, Patricia. 1984. *Metafiction: The Theory and Practice of Self-conscious Fiction*. London and New York: Methuen.

11

Reading One/Self
Samuel Beckett, Thomas Bernhard, Peter Handke, John Barth, Alain Robbe-Grillet

Alfred Hornung

In his contribution to the 1979 MLA workshop in San Francisco on "The Self in Postmodernist Fiction," John Barth traced the question of "authorial self-consciousness" all the way back to an Egyptian papyrus of circa 2000 B.C., in which the "I," the scribe Khakheperresenb, complains "that he has arrived upon the scene too late; that literature is already exhausted" (Barth 1984: 210). As stages in this long line from papyri to postmodern texts Barth lists Homer's *Odyssey*, Dante's *Divina Commedia,* Rabelais' *Pantagruel*, Cervantes' *Don Quixote*, the 18th-century novel, the romantic confessional novel, and the modern author-hero, in short: practically all literature of epic dimension. Barth's long and indiscriminate excursion into the history of self-conscious literature can be shortened considerably, if one tries to correlate the writing process with the reading process of a given text. Thus one could establish three periods in the development of prose writing which show us three possible interrelations between the authorial self and the reader: 1. in the premodern novel, the author's practice of addressing the reader in prefaces and inter-chapters in order to authenticate the story; 2. in the modern novel, the inscription of some aspects of the author into the text as an exemplary presentation of self-consciousness to be emulated by the reader; 3. in the postmodern novel, the pose of the authorial self as the reader of his own fiction and by implication of his own life.

Applying Paul Ricoeur's narratological categories, advanced in *Temps et récit*, to these three periods, one can see a line of development from the prefiguration of narrative structures in the premodern life-world via the configuration of a narrative thread in the modern text to the refiguration of possible narratives on the part of the reader in postmodernism. The transitions between the three stages reflect historical moments of crisis and change in which the novel tries to define or redefine its genre.

Examples of the premodern correlation of author and reader abound in the 18th and 19th centuries. This practice of reader address marks the transition from prose narrative to prose fiction. In modernism, Henry James's international career serves as the best example for the cultural crisis experienced in Europe and America at the turn of this century. His life and work reflect the transition from the author-reader cooperation to extreme forms of self-conscious literature which require authorial explanation to enable the reader to understand. Henry James's *Prefaces* (1907) for the New York edition of his tales represent such an attempt to clarify and explicate his own work. In this interpretive activity James becomes his own reader. He knows that this re-vision of his work turns into a form of re-writing which involves his whole personality (James 1934: 3-4). In reading and revising his work, Henry James expands its implicit potential of meaning and comprehends the series of prefaces as a story whose protagonist he is. In a logical consequence of this conception of reading, Henry James is led to write his three-part autobiography, begun in 1910 after the death of his brother William. The reading and revisions of past works as well as the writing of his autobiography as the reading and revision of his past life represent for him attempts to overcome personal crisis situations in art and life and to reconcile his unstable presence with his stable past in the configuration of one narrative self.

In contemporary literary practice, Henry James's consecutive stages of the critical reading of his art (converted into the theoretical configuration of his *Prefaces*) and the critical reading of his life (converted into the narrative configuration of his *Autobiography*) appear to be joined into one act of writing. While the modern writer stresses the configurative act of constructing a plot in the text, the contemporary postmodern writer stresses the refigurative act of the reader as one of many possible ways of making sense. The reading of earlier stages of art and life, which according to postmodern premises are inseparable, forms the basis for an innovative rewriting. Although it might appear as inconsistent with postmodern narrative art, it is precisely those practitioners of the experimental new fiction, both in Europe and the United States, who engage in these forms of writing based on reading oneself. Prominent examples are Christa Wolf, Thomas

Bernhard, Peter Handke, Bernhard Vesper, Fritz Zorn in the German language (cf. Schwab 1981; Frieden 1983), Nathalie Sarraute, Marguerite Duras, Julia Kristeva, Philippe Sollers, Claude Ollier, Alain Robbe-Grillet in the French language, Martin Amis, John Fowles, Simon Gray, Samuel Beckett, John Barth, Raymond Federman, William Gass, Ronald Sukenick in the English language. All of these writers seem to be faced with a crisis situation which consists of both personal predicaments and impasses of their fictional genre. These destabilized writers seek to overcome their life and art crises by turning back to earlier writings and hence to earlier stages of their lives in order to substantiate the only stability left to them: their own selves. Their writing thus represents the transformation of the process of reading both themselves and their selves. This act of refiguring a story from the fragments of one's art and life seems to be expressive of the latent wish of reading the unity of one self (cf. also Caramello 1983). Its implicit intention is to stay the inevitable end of life through the permanent life of narrative art.

In the following paper I will concentrate on recent works by major European and American writers, invariably classified as postmodern: Samuel Beckett, Thomas Bernhard, Peter Handke, John Barth, and Alain Robbe-Grillet. First, I will point out in each writer's life and art moments of crisis which, when taken together, add up to a cultural phenomenon in Europe and the United States. Second, I will redefine the process of reading oneself as the basis of postmodern writing which constitutes a form of dialogic imagination. Third, I will discuss the paradox of this narrative refiguration and emphasize the importance of illusory structures implicit in narrative language as a fictional antidote to death. I will complete this essay with some suggestions about the refigurative act to be performed by the reader of postmodern texts, and about the role of reader response theory in contemporary literature.

1. Crisis Situation in Art and Life

The phenomenon of mid-life crisis has been a major subject of psychological studies for many years. This field of research is concerned with an examination and analysis of a phase in human life which could be called a turning point, or in a more charged term, a moment of conversion. Researchers in the field confirm the basically biological conditions of an ascendant and a descendant phase in life. Poets and writers, in turn, have stressed such turning points in a person's life and tried to explore the psychological

factors that accompany such moments of change. Dante makes the dis-
orientation in his mid-life the initial theme of his *Divina Commedia*:

> Nel mezzo del cammin di nostra vita
> mi ritrovai per una selva oscura,
> ché la diretta via era smarrita (*Inferno*, 1. 1-3).

He seems to highlight unconsciously the psychological ramifications of what
eventually becomes a religious conversion. Tragedians use the peripety of a
plot structure to show the crisis as a decisive turning point in the development of their protagonists. Just as Dante sees the experience and thematization of a mid-life crisis as the "beginning of man facing death" (Wolf
1978: 3), the tragic characters begin to realize the inevitability of their fatal
end. From a psychoanalytic point of view, C.G. Jung de-emphasizes this
fear of death and concentrates on the phase of transition between the first
half and the second half of life. For Jung this represents a transition from
nature, i.e. the constantly changing biological factors of individual life, to
culture, i.e. the more permanent spiritual components of a transindividual
mind (Jung 1953: 124-125). In his words, this moment of crisis means "the
reversal of all ideals and values," and the transition constitutes in Wolf's
paraphrase of Jung "a rite of passage between the more externalized goals
of the first half of life, growing up, marriage, becoming a parent and house-
holder; and the more internalized goals of the second half of life, the
development of a kind of intuitive spirituality" (Jung 1953: 120-125). The
particular crisis results from the conflict between nature's laws of change
and culture's aspirations for permanence. The conflict is resolved by a
belief in the illusion of permanent art.

Although such moments of crisis are a universal feature of human
nature, the belief in the salutary effects of the illusory structures of art and
in the stabilizing effects of culture in general is specific to the writer. In contemporary postmodern fiction, the mid-life crisis coincides with a crisis of
the arts. This necessitates a twofold reorientation brought about by a look
backward. C.G. Jung explains:

> Conservative tendencies develop if all goes well; instead of looking for-
> ward one looks backward, for the most part involuntarily, and one begins
> to take account of the manner in which life has developed up to this point.
> Thus the real motivations are sought and real discoveries made. The criti-
> cal survey of himself and his fate permits a man to recognize his individual-
> ity, but this knowledge does not come to him easily. It is gained only
> through the severest shocks (Jung 1953: 120).

While mid-life and mid-art crises coincide chronologically in Thomas Bernhard's, Peter Handke's, and John Barth's careers, they appear to be spread out over a number of years in the literary developments of Samuel Beckett and Alain Robbe-Grillet. At a time when the media of the arts experience generic crises, when the genre of the novel is questioned and "the death of the novel" proclaimed, these writers announce a new change in the narrative art and mark the transition from fragmentation to the refiguration of a narrative through reading one/self.

In literature, Samuel Beckett, the postmodern ancestor, was the first to register the general crisis of culture which effected the transition from modern to postmodern literature. His separation from James Joyce in the 1930s also meant his break with the principles of modernism. His decision in 1937 to leave Ireland for good and to settle in Paris in order to become a writer must be regarded as the turning point in his life. Interestingly, this decision was brought about by a denial of modernistic configurations and a resort to a survey of his own early life revolving around the strong persona of his authoritarian mother, his abortive love to his cousin Peggy Sinclair in Kassel, and his plans to become a writer, thematized in the yet unpublished novel, *Dream of Fair to Middling Women* (1931-32), episodes of which were used, in a slightly revised version, in the collection of short stories, *More Pricks Than Kicks* (1934). And writing about his psychiatric treatment in London in the novel *Murphy* (1935) allowed him to opt for a career as a man of letters.

A second crisis situation in his life is equally resolved through the review of earlier episodes of his life. The autobiographical short stories ("The Expelled", "The Calmative", "The End", "First Love"), written in 1946, mark the transition to his mature creativity, a transition from a preoccupation with exterior manifestations of the human nature to the interior reflections of the human mind, as evidenced in his trilogy of novels, *Molloy, Malone Dies*, and *The Unnamable* (1959). In the play, *Krapp's Last Tape* (1959), Beckett seems to allude to this period of his life, by having his protagonist listen to episodes from a past which closely resembles his own, recorded on his 39th birthday, which coincides with the year of Beckett's life when he actually wrote the autobiographical short stories. A third crisis situation occurs in the seventies, when Beckett writes a number of short plays in which he is concerned with different versions of the self and the concomitant reduction of human character to a mere voice. With the autobiographical fiction *Company* (1980), Beckett presents a reading of his earlier life and art aimed at the refiguration of one life-story to be turned into art.

The mid-life and mid-art crisis in Thomas Bernhard's career is documented by the six-volume recollection of his childhood and adolescence from his birth in 1931 to 1950 and of his friendship with Wittgenstein's nephew Paul from 1967 to 1979. In the arrangement of the volumes he does not strictly follow the chronology of his life. The block of four consecutive life-stories, *Die Ursache: Eine Andeutung* (1975), *Der Keller: Eine Entziehung* (1976), *Der Atem: Eine Entscheidung* (1978), *Die Kälte: Eine Isolation* (1981) — which relate the war years in Salzburg of 1944-45, the unfit education received from educators at home and at school, Nazi fascism and Catholic religion in a boarding school (*Die Ursache*), his experience of the labor world among social outcasts after his decision to leave school (*Der Keller*), and his treatment in a hospital for tuberculosis patients and the insensitive behavior of doctors (*Der Atem*; *Die Kälte*) — is framed by his account of his childhood as an illegitimate and unwanted child who finds compassion and understanding with his grandfather, Johannes Freumbichler, a writer of regional renown (*Ein Kind*, 1982), and the account of his real life-crisis in 1967 when he had a tumor removed from his lungs. During the recovery from this near-death experience he befriends the fellow-patient Paul Wittgenstein treated for insanity (*Wittgensteins Neffe*, 1982). Bernhard's serious operation at the age of 36 seems to constitute his mid-life crisis, followed by a mid-art crisis which he overcomes by turning to the reading of his own life in the seventies. The first installment of his autobiography, written in 1975, comes after an impressive series of novels and plays which portrayed depressed and destructive characters mostly ending in suicide. Contrary to this deconstruction of human life, coupled with formal deconstructions, the message of the autobiographical texts is a decision for life (*Der Atem: Eine Entscheidung*) and the rediscovery of a narrative story-line to follow the life-line. Thus the mid-life crisis engenders a reading of earlier stages of his life and brings about a change in his narrative art.

While Thomas Bernhard's turning point in life and art originated in a serious illness, Peter Handke's reorientation in his mid-thirties was caused by ruptures in human relationships. His separation from his wife and his decision to raise his daughter as a single parent, about which he also writes in his fictions (*Der kurze Brief zum langen Abschied*, 1972, and *Die linkshändige Frau*, 1976), as well as his mother's suicide in 1971

(*Wunschloses Unglück*, 1972) bring about a change in his outlook on life and he begins to reflect on the fictional character of his art in mid-life. In the late seventies he starts to write journals and aphoristic accounts which run parallel to his fictional texts. Thus he publishes two books of journal entries, *Das Gewicht der Welt: Ein Journal (November 1975 - März 1977)* and *Die Geschichte des Bleistifts* (1982). Along with the text *Die Lehre der Sainte-Victoire* (1980), which comes close to a poetology of narrative art, these factual expositions comment on the novel *Langsame Heimkehr* (1979) and the autobiographical account *Kindergeschichte* (1981), which relates glimpses from his child's life and upbringing up to the age of ten. While *Langsame Heimkehr* and *Kindergeschichte* thematize aspects of an authorial self vicariously through fictional characters and his daughter, the corollary texts give the genesis and biographical background to each story and simultaneously sketch a narratological theory. One can infer that the autobiographical references to his life and the self-conscious reflection on his art will bring about a new form of writing.

Just as with Peter Handke, mid-life and mid-art crisis commingle in John Barth's case in form of a divorce and writer's block. Although Barth had used the form of fictional autobiography in his second novel, *The End of the Road* (1958), and had played with autobiographical pieces in *Lost in the Funhouse* (1968), with obvious references to his own career, he did not experience his personal and professional crisis until 1969, at the age of 39. In order to overcome both crises he decided to write about them by reading earlier parts of his life and art. This is when he started his narrative project *LETTERS: An Old Time Epistolary Novel By Seven Fictitious Drolls & Dreamers Each of Which Imagines Himself Factual*, eventually published in 1979. John Barth, who also appears as a character in the book, comments on this crisis in *LETTERS:* "... I put aside, in 1968, in Buffalo, a *Marylandiad* of my own in favor of the novel *LETTERS*, whereof Mensch's *Perseid* and Bray's *Bellerophoniad* were to be tales-within-tale. Then, in '69, '70, and '71, I put by *LETTERS*, in pursuit of new chimera called *Chimera*: serial novellas about Perseus, Bellerophon, and Scheherazade's younger sister" (Barth 1979: 49). In *Chimera*, which also originated in the author's crisis, the character of Genie figures as John Barth's textual self and clearly formulates the turning point in his life and art:

> He was a writer of tales — ... His own pen ... had just about run dry: ...
> the Genie's life was in disorder — but so far from harboring therefore a
> grudge against womankind, he was distractedly in love with a brace of new

mistresses, and only recently had been able to choose between them. His career, too, had reached a hiatus which he would have been pleased to call a turning-point if he could have espied any way to turn: he wished neither to repeat his past performances; he aspired to go beyond them toward a future they were not attuned to and, by some magic, at the same time go back to the original springs of narrative. ... he couldn't say how much of his difficulty might be owing to his own limitations, his age and stage and personal vicissitudes; how much to the general decline of letters in his time and place; and how much to the other crises with which his country ... was beset — crises as desperate and problematical ... and as inimical to the single-mindedness needed to compose great works of art or the serenity to apprehend them (Barth 1972: 17-18).

What emerges from the author's reference to his crisis is the realization that life and art are inextricably intertwined. This exemplification of the post-modern belief in the impossibility of distinguishing between art and reality, practiced in *Chimera*, is intensified in *LETTERS*. This aesthetic principle of postmodernism allows John Barth to voice his distaste for autobiographical romances and to use it as a narrative technique to emerge from his crisis: "For autobiographical 'fiction' I have only disdain; but what's involved here strikes me less as autobiography than as muddling of the distinction between Art and Life, a boundary as historically notorious as Mason and Dixon's Line" (Barth 1979: 51-52).

Alain Robbe-Grillet, the first writer totally committed to the practice and theory of the *nouveau roman*, also recognizes the shifting boundaries between life and art in his recent autobiographical enterprise, *Le Miroir qui revient* (1984). Although one cannot perceive a crisis in Robbe-Grillet's life as the origin of this fiction, and would, indeed be hard put to call it a mid-life crisis referring to a writer past the age of 60, a crisis of his art is easily recognizable in this autobiographical text. The fact that this work was started in the seventies, such as the other autobiographical fictions under discussion here, allows us to establish a pattern common to postmodern European and American writers of fiction. All of these writers realize the crisis of their art, in which their lives are intricately bound up, and try to overcome it by turning to earlier phases of their art and life. This autobiographical turn also marks a transition to a new form of narrative art and represents an attempt at the redefinition of the genre. Thus he addresses the question "qu'est-ce qu'un roman aujourd'hui?", and wonders whether Roland Barthes could be called "un romancier" (Robbe-Grillet 1984: 69). Such an expansion of the concept of fiction would allow it to take the place of philosophy: "La fiction romanesque, c'est déjà comme le devenir-monde de la philosophie" (ibid.). From the perspective of this crisis of fictional art he recognizes that his former program of the *nouveau roman* seems "avoir fait [son] temps: [les techniques] ont perdu en quelques années ce qu'elles pouvaient avoir de scandaleux, de corrosif, donc de révolutionnaire...," in other words, they have been coopted by the ruling ideology and have turned into ideology themselves (11 et passim). His former covert intention has now become his overt practice when he praises the advantages of narration as a means of spanning life and art.

> ... j'éprouve aujourd'hui un certain plaisir à utiliser la forme traditionelle de l'autobiographie: cette facilité dont parle Stendhal dans ses *Souvenirs d'égotisme*, comparée à la résistance du matériau qui caractérise toute création. Et ce plaisir douteux m'intéresse dans la mesure où, d'une part, il me confirme que je me serais mis à écrire des romans pour exorciser ces fantômes dont je ne venais pas à bout, et me fait d'autre part découvrir que le biais de la fiction est, en fin de compte, beaucoup plus *personnel* que la prétendue sincérité de l'aveu (Robbe-Grillet 1984: 16-17).

Suddenly Robbe-Grillet seems to discover that all of his work has been about himself: "Je n'ai jamais parlé d'autre chose que de moi" (10).

2. *Reading as the Basis of Writing; or, The Dialogic Imagination*

The resort to autobiographical narration at a time of crisis in life and art, the falling back on oneself and one's own resources, indicate a moment of transition and reorganization. Past experiences, their processing in the mind and their transformation into narrative art seemingly function as elements of stability in an unstable situation of the present. Hence the reading of the past becomes the prerequisite to achieve such stability in the present. Reading, which next to the general meanings of "to consider, interpret, discern" and "to make out or discover the meaning or significance of" is historically also used in the sense of "considering or explaining something obscure or mysterious" and "having or exercising control over something" (*OED* 1961: VIII, 193), is here understood as an act of interpretation for the purpose of discovering meaning and of gaining control over the twofold crisis situation. It is, therefore, not surprising that contemporary critics of literature in general (de Man 1979) or of autobiography in particular (Gunn 1982) stress the primacy of reading and maintain that the "passage from 'life' to writing corresponds to an act of reading..." (de Man 1979: 57). This correlation of reading and writing could be seen as a form of dialogue

between two versions of the authorial self. In contemporary literary practice, the two activities of reading and writing appear as interdependent,
with the overarching mental faculty of imagination mediating between
them. Given the precarious role of a deconstructed subject in the postmodern world, one could use the concept of the "dialogic imagination"
derived from Bakhtin's work (1981) to describe the interdependence of
reading and writing as the primary manifestation of a postmodern author in
the state of transition. Reading and writing as human activities in search of
control at a time of crisis would then correspond with Gabriele Schwab's
interpretation of Bakhtin's dialogic imagination in its dual role of stabilization and subversion of the boundaries of the individual: "Thus the dialectic
of stabilization and subversion no longer appears in the guise of opposing
functions, but rather as one of the superior constitutive functions of decentered subjectivity" (Schwab 1984: 463). This function of the dialogic imagination seems to be at the basis of all contemporary writers discussed here.

Most of Samuel Beckett's works present some form of a decentered or
deconstructed subjectivity. His experimentations with several versions of
one self and the reduction of the self to one or several voices have been his
central concern for many years. The technical device of a tape recorder
used in *Krapp's Last Tape* to distinguish between two versions of the self
has changed to dramatized dialogues of several voices of one self in the
autobiographical play, *That Time*, performed in 1976, which, in turn,
appears as a dramatized precursor to the autobiographical narrative *Company*. This prose narrative opens with the following proposition: "To one
on his back in the dark a voice tells of a past. With occasional allusion to a
present and more rarely to a future as for example, You will end as you
now are. And in another dark or in the same another devising it all for company" (Beckett 1980: 7-8). The authorial and hence autobiographical self
consists here of dialogues between the voice, the person on his back, and
the deviser of the fiction. The three persons figure as the grammatical pronouns I, you, and he in the text: "Use of the second person marks the
voice. That of the third that cankerous other. Could he speak to and of
whom the voice speaks there would be a first. But he cannot. He shall not.
You cannot. You shall not" (8). While the voice creates company between
itself and the listener and thus dispels the loneliness by recollecting glimpses of the past, the actual protagonist is displaced or decentered. Rarely
does this first person "I" appear in the text (16, 21, 24, 34, 61). Yet in the
same sense in which the person on the back listens to the Voice, Beckett

reads events of his past life: his birth on Good Friday, the day Christ died; episodes from his childhood and youth and his relationship with his father and mother; glimpses of his love affair with his cousin Peggy Sinclair; his juvenile guilt feelings for having caused the death of a hedgehog. Reading in the form of listening is the attempt described above to interpret these events, discover their meaning and gain control over them. The actual control takes the form of writing. In the same sense in which the deviser uses the dialogue between voice and listener as the basis of his fiction, Beckett makes the reading of his past life and art the basis of his writing. So the dialogic imagination works on several levels in *Company* and transcends closed circles of communication, or overcomes close readings through writing. Both activities, speaking and listening as well as reading and writing, are basic human manifestations and fulfil the vital need of reaffirming one's existence.

Thomas Bernhard's autobiographical texts represent an almost perfect example of what Bakhtin calls an internal dialogue between an earlier and a later self whose communicational relation is a temporal one (Bakhtin 1981: 427; Lotman 1977: 9). This temporal gap between the past experiential self and the present authorial self, classically rendered in the text as the grammatical distinctions between the "he then" and the "I now," is accepted as the methodological necessity to achieve the psychological goal of the reconciliation with the past in the present. Bernhard's conciliatory attitude toward his life develops during his long stay in the sanatorium where he comes close to death and re-emerges with an indefatigable will to live. Although his own life-story resembles in many ways the sordid miseries of his fictional characters, he is different insofar as he has a will of his own and can make his own decision for life: "Ich wollte *leben*, alles andere bedeutete nichts. Leben, und zwar *mein* Leben leben, *wie und solange ich es will.* ... Von zwei möglichen Wegen hatte ich mich in dieser Nacht in dem entscheidenden Augenblick für den des Lebens entschieden" (Bernhard 1978: 20). In the same sense in which this decision to live is occasioned by the direct experience of the death of his fellow patients in the "Sterbezimmer," his career as a writer is initiated by his grandfather's death; it begins with the discovery of reading literature and the discovery of his own poetic vein. Both serve therapeutic aims and reaffirm his existence (Bernhard 1978: 140, 152-153). In "Grosser Hunger, unbegreiflicher Hunger" (1954), an early autobiographical sketch for an anthology of contemporary writers, Bernhard states bluntly: "In der Lungenheilstätte Grafenhof

begann ich, immer den Tod vor Augen, zu schreiben. Daran wurde ich vielleicht wiederhergestellt" (Dittmar 1981: 13). The writing of poems, even
though he realizes that they are without literary value, are the most important thing for the recovering 18-year old man, for they stand for his life:
"...ich existierte nur, wenn ich schrieb..." (Bernhard 1981: 36). The actual
turn to the autobiographical rendition of his own life, to the difficult task of
reading and describing oneself (Bernhard 1975: 126-127), comes only after
his operation for cancer of the lungs in 1967 which brings about a change in
his attitude to life and writing. Through the experience of his long illness,
he has reconciled himself with Kierkegaard's knowledge of our sickness
unto death (Jurgensen 1981: 83) and accepts the fact "dass unser
Lebensprozess in Wahrheit nichts anderes ist als ein Krankheitsprozess..."
(Bernhard 1973; Dittmar 1981: 153). Once he starts reading the case story
of his own life, the despair and destructive failure of his fictional characters
give way to the qualified hope for the continuation of his existence and the
therapeutic value of his turn to himself. While these recollections can be
seen as "Protokolle verzweifelter Überlebenslust" (Rolf Michaelis in
Dittmar 1981: 228), they can also be seen as a new direction in his writing,
an emancipation from his fiction in favor of the genre of autobiography
(Jochen Hieber in Dittmar 1981: 202). Thus the reading and the writing
about the self represent both a biological and an artistic process of healing.
The desire for a new life is also the desire for a new, an autobiographical
art. Both attempt to stay the inevitability of death.

Peter Handke's turn, in his most recent writings, to a more mythic and
hence more harmonizing attitude toward life, which has been severely
criticized as artistic failures (Durzak 1982: 146-169), does not conceal the
fact that his recent autobiographical accounts continue to be motivated by
the knowledge of an inevitable death. Yet, just as in Thomas Bernhard, the
author has moved away from a thematic preoccupation with the problem of
death: "Und werde andrerseits nie vom Glück schreiben, geboren zu sein,
oder vom Trost in einem besseren Jenseits: das Sterbenmüssen wird immer
das mich Leitende, doch hoffentlich nie mehr mein Hauptgegenstand sein"
(Handke 1980: 21). The inclusion of the author into the text automatically
changes the nature of the representation. His mid-life crisis in the early
seventies, compounded by the suicide of his beloved mother in 1971, bring
about a change visible in the coexistence of two forms of the prose narrative. The immediate reactions to these two crises in the fictionalization of
his separation in *Der kurze Brief zum langen Abschied* and the compassion-

ate memoir of his mother as an expression of his mourning in *Wunschloses Unglück*, both published in 1972, could be seen as attempts — in Bakhtin's words — "to faithfully reflect reality, to manage reality and to transpose it" (Bakhtin 1981: 412), equivalent to the control function of reading defined above. What results are two types of narrative which respectively represent "a novel that tests literary discourse" and a biographical text in which the "literary, novelistic discourse [is] being tested by life, by reality" (Bakhtin 1981: 412). Peter Handke's recent literary products appear to be a further development in this autobiographical turn and match the two types, distinguished by Bakhtin, for the testing of novelistic discourse: "The first type concentrates the critique and trial of literary discourse around a hero — a 'literary man,' who looks at life through the eyes of literature and who tries to live 'according to literature,'" e.g. *Don Quixote* and *Madame Bovary*. "The second type of testing introduces an author who is in the process of writing the novel (a 'laying bare of the device,' in the terminology of the Formalists), not however in the capacity of a character, but rather as the real author of the given work," e.g. *Tristram Shandy* (1981: 413). Starting with the aphoristic journal, *Das Gewicht der Welt* (1977), Handke's testing of the novelistic discourse from the point of view of the author becomes a constant concern (cf. Frieden 1983: 172-184). The authorial self that emerges from the journal presents itself in the form of a dialogue between the practitioner and the theoretician of the writing tested by the reality of his life. Thus the journal serves both a psychological and an artistic purpose as an expression of an identity crisis (Jurgensen 1979: 188) and as an experience of freedom from literary traditions. Handke records this "Erlebnis der Befreiung von gegebenen literarischen Formen und zugleich der Freiheit in einer mir bis dahin unbekannten literarischen Möglichkeit" (Handke 1977: 5). Handke continues this running commentary on his art and life with the alternation between novelistic practice and narrative theory, which results from his reading and writing of the self — the basis of his dialogic imagination —, with *Langsame Heimkehr* (1979) and *Die Lehre der Sainte-Victoire* (1980) and the pair *Kindergeschichte* (1981) and *Die Geschichte des Bleistifts* (1982). In *Die Lehre der Sainte-Victoire* Handke tries to explore Paul Cézanne's predilection, in his mature work, for the range of mountains in the Provence, called Sainte-Victoire. By hiking up the mountain on different trails and at different times he discovers Cézanne's art of painting and simultaneously wins clarity about his own art of writing by going back to earlier stages of his life and literature. At the same time it provides the

genesis and a comment on the novel *Langsame Heimkehr* in which the
authorial self seems to be split into the corollary pair of Sorger and Laufer.
This fictional split is overcome in the autobiographical text in which the
combination of reading and writing, i.e. the dialogic imagination allows the
author to arrive at "ein Bild der Einheit zwischen meiner ältesten Ver-
gangenheit und der Gegenwart" (Handke 1980: 11). This psychological
unity of the self is Handke's "Lust auf das Eine in Allem" which realizes
itself in the coherence of the narrative text: "Ich wusste ja: Der Zusam-
menhang ist möglich. Jeder einzelne Augenblick meines Lebens geht mit
jedem anderen zusammen — ohne Hilfsglieder. Es existiert eine unmittel-
bare Verbindung; ich muss sie nur freiphantasieren" (100). The dialogue
between the reading of the past and the writing in the present becomes a
coherent whole by way of the author's imagination. Handke expresses this
poetological principle by casting it in an analogy with his friend's design of
a dress:

> "Bei der Anfertigung eines Kleids muss jede bereits benutzte Form für die
> Weiterarbeit im Gedächtnis bleiben. Ich darf sie aber nicht innerlich
> zitieren müssen, ich muss sofort die weiterführende, endgültige Farbe
> sehen. Es gibt in jedem Fall nur eine richtige, und die Form bestimmt die
> Masse der Farbe und muss das Problem des Übergangs lösen.
> "Der Übergang muss für mich klar trennend *und* ineinander sein"
> (Handke 1980: 119).

Handke's autobiographical account *Kindergeschichte* is such a text in which
the reading of his past life with his daughter forms the basis for creating in
the present. The aphoristic companion piece, *Die Geschichte des Bleistifts*
(1982), substantiates the poetological principle of a dialogical imagination
between past and present, between reading and writing as a form of gaining
control through self-interpretation and as an expression for a transitional
concept of art. Bakhtin calls these forms of changes "the process of re-
accentuation" (1981: 419-421), in which "every age re-accentuates in its
own way the works of its most immediate past" (421). This general recognition of the dynamic quality of a work of art is here applied to the life and
work of an individual writer as exemplarily expressed by Handke: "Jeder
wird, um weiterdenken zu können, die alten, in anderen Zeiten wohlbe-
schriebenen Lebensumstände für sich neu — schreibend oder lesend —
festhalten müssen (wiederholen müssen)" (Handke 1982: 26). Reading and
writing in this definition of a dialogic, imaginative re-accentuation is not a
mere repetition of some given facts, but the discovery of hidden qualities

which exist, but are unknown. The consecutive stages of reading and writing will bring them to the surface: "Eine Empfindung von Wirklichkeit habe ich ... im wiederholenden Wiedersehen. Schreiben heisst, sich zu verbergen *und* sich zu zeigen, usw., usw., bis man *ist*" (166).

Handke's reading and writing, which expresses itself in the corollary publication of works in theory on and practice of autobiographical fiction, seems to be merged into one text in Alain Robbe-Grillet's *Le Miroir qui revient*. In a slight modification of Bakhtin's term for the second type of novel in which the testing of the novelistic discourse by life "introduces an author who is in the process of writing" (Bakhtin 1981: 413), one could call this text a testing of the autobiographial discourse and hence "an autobiographical fiction about autobiographical fiction." For next to almost random episodes from the author's life, *Le Miroir qui revient* consists of discussions of the nature of the *nouveau roman* and its sequel. Hence this text necessarily represents Robbe-Grillet's reading of his past life and art as well as the tradition of literary predecessors, e.g. Flaubert, Sartre, Camus, and contemporary literary critics. While this internal dialogue seems to be the author's reaction to his fear of loneliness and his angst of his interior ghosts, it also appears as a defense of his fragmentary way of writing. Reading himself he realizes that his writing has to be directed against himself because reality defies the harmony which the human mind seeks:

> J'écris d'abord contre moi-même, nous l'avons vu, donc contre le public aussi. Faire mieux comprendre quoi? Du moment que je poursuis une énigme, qui m'apparaît déjà comme un manque dans ma propre continuité signifiante, comment serait-il envisageable d'en faire un récit plein, sans faille? Que pourrais-je traduire 'avec simplicité' d'un rapport si paradoxal au monde et à mon être, d'un rapport où tout est double, contradictoire et fuyant? (Robbe-Grillet 1984: 40-41)

This turning against himself is, however, the methodological prerequisite for reading oneself, for self-discovery and control. It is technically cast in the image of the mirror which forms the titel of the book: "le miroir qui revient." What comes back are images of the past, impressions which need to be analyzed in form of an active interchange between the specular image and the person in front of the mirror. Thus the mirror serves as a visible image of Robbe-Grillet's dialogic imagination. "Et ce livre-ci, à son tour, qui semble s'adresser nommément au lecteur, ou même au critique, je ne suis pas si sûr de ne pas être, comme d'habitude, l'unique cible. On crée toujours pour soi..." (Robbe-Grillet 1984: 184). The dialogic imagination plays between the outside world and the subjective interior world of spectres. The impossibility of doing justice to both areas, Robbe-Grillet maintains, arises from the nature of our language. As an expression of consciousness, language works according to rules of logic, but at the same time it is this "conscience claire ... qui se plaint du non-sens et du manque" (41). While reading in its interpretive effort at discovery and control tends in its sense-making attempt to find coherences and harmony, as seen with Handke, writing in its fragmentary form represents for Robbe-Grillet a way to break up the closed circle of self-referentiality and self-reading. The closure of reading is thus overcome through the open process of writing as a reflection of the continuity of life.

John Barth's magisterial work *LETTERS* pursues a similar effort of making the past available for the continuation of life and the progress of art. The subsequent stages of reading and writing, which in Handke expressed themselves as theory on and practice of self-conscious literature published in separate works, and which in Robbe-Grillet were joined into one autobiographical text, appear as the summation of his life and art wrought into a grand fictional design. The letters written to and read by fictional characters of his earlier works and himself as their author create an intertextual network in an effort to overcome the crisis of the narrative, expressed in the seminal essay, "The Literature of Exhaustion" (Barth 1967). Starting from Borges' assumption that no originality is possible anymore, Barth defines the role of the postmodern writers as "more or less faithful amanuenses of the human spirit" (Barth 1979: 656). Yet his idea of repetition is not a mere reading or re-reading of his life and work, but a transcendence through writing. The novel *LETTERS* performs this task by resorting to the principle of the dialogic imagination. Todd Andrews and Ambrose Mensch, characters from earlier novels, attempt to recycle their lives; for these characters recycling is connected with the mythic and dramatic concept of re-enacting the past, bound up in the larger framework of re-enacting America's history in form of revolution and the fictional design of creative reading and writing. Although John Barth expresses his dislike for his characters' wish for recycling and their attempt to possibly recover earlier stages of their lives, he recognizes this phenomenon as an expression of mid-life crisis: "(a sure sign, such recycling, that an author approaches 40)" (654), and actually grants such a form of reorientation in mid-life. In one of his letters to Ambrose Mensch he shows his understanding for his droll's position (which is also his own as the creator of this fiction): "At least I understand, to the heart, your impulse at the midpoint of your life to 'empty yourself' before commencing its second half. Surely that's what midpoints and the Axis Mundi are all about" (656).

Barth's expression for this form of creative recycling is "reorchestration." It seems to be an innovative merger of the Bakhtinian terms of "orchestration" and "re-accentuation," in which the fictional text resembles the multi-voice consonance of a musical score and the innovative re-creation of the past in the light of the present. While Barth calls his earlier tales, particularly those of *Lost in the Funhouse* (1968), "a little reorchestration of the oral narrative tradition," he is "inclined now to make the great leap forward again to Print: more particularly, to reorchestrate some early conventions of the Novel," such as the epistolary one (654). The theoretical formulation and the practical demonstration of the transitional state of (Barth's) narrative art, merged here in one fictional design, is a supreme expression of the principle of the dialogic imagination, which is indispensable for John Barth: "Never mind what your predecessors have come up with, and never mind that in a sense this 'dialogue' is a monologue; that we capital-*A* Authors are ultimately, ineluctably, and forever talking to ourselves. If our correspondence is after all a fiction, we like, we *need* that fiction: it makes our job less lonely" (655).

John Barth's reading of his life and art as the basis of re-creative writing shares with the other writers discussed here a psychological and an artistic component. On the one hand Barth needs the company of his drolls and dreamers, like Beckett, in order to establish a dialogue with them. On the other hand this internal dialogue is an ongoing process of interpretation and discovery through reading complemented by an aesthetic control through writing. Earlier models of fiction yield new meanings when seen from a temporal distance, as Barth states in an interview:

> Particularly since I've been in my thirties and forties, I really do try to see what it is I've been up to. Especially when I'm thinking of what I want to do next, I like to look back... I try to seek out patterns — the thematic and structural directions, the personality of the voices, other such things — in the books leading up to where I am at the moment. Sometimes, ten years after you've finished a piece, you can see the patterns and suggestions more clearly; perhaps you were not very aware of them or were only half-intuitively groping for their formulation (Bellamy 1972: 5).

3. *The Paradox of Narrative Refiguration*

The writer's attempt at the refiguration of a coherent story from incoherent episodes of life and elements of art in the act of writing is both marked and marred by the multitude of stories to which life and art lend themselves. For the authorial intention of reading oneself and writing one self is constantly denied by the fluidity of life. Although life and art have become inseparable and textually one, the ultimately inevitable randomness of life and the impossibility of language to represent it in its complexity thwart all artistic endeavors which appear reductive.

One of the central features of Samuel Beckett's art is that of reduction. It is visible in his autobiographical text *Company* in the reduction of human life to three voices marked by grammatical pronouns, the reduction of human company to loneliness, of dialogue to inaudible monologue. As before, a psychological and an artistic aspect are at the basis of this reductive principle. It is encapsulated in the last word of the text: "Alone" (Beckett 1980: 63). Unity can be attained when the "words are coming to an end" (62) in the form of an all-one-ness, however at the expense of physical loneliness and artistic closure. Ihab Hassan puts this paradox involved in Beckett's life- and art-writing into the succinct formula of "a silence that sings" (Hassan 1982: 211). While the closure of art imparts permanence, the narrative refiguration of life cannot stay the inevitability of death. Yet, even though death proves to be "the veto of the imagination" (Renza 1977), its certainty simultaneously activates it. So he nurtures the illusion of prolonging life through the coherence of a narrative and draws consolation and confirmation from it, stated repeatedly in the text: "... I know this doomed to fail and yet persist" (Beckett 1980: 61), or "Devising figments to temper his nothingness..." (46).

Thomas Bernhard's near-death experience during his stays in sanatoriums looms behind his unending attempts at the narrative refiguration of his life and the discovery of art. The provocative, but honest opening of his speech of acceptance of the Austrian State Prize for literature in 1968 expresses the paradox involved in the writing of life-stories and puts everything in perspective: "Es ist nichts zu loben, nichts zu verdammen, nichts anzuklagen, aber es ist vieles *lächerlich*, wenn man an den Tod denkt" (Dittmar 1981: 98). Since immortality and perfection are impossible to achieve in human life, the writer uses the illusion which automatically enters into the narrative representation of lived life to reconcile himself with the paradox of life through art.

Die Vollkommenheit ist für nichts möglich, geschweige denn für Geschriebenes und schon gar nicht für Notizen wie diese, die aus Tausenden und Abertausenden von Möglichkeitsfetzen von Erinnerung zusammengesetzt sind. Hier sind Bruchstücke mitgeteilt, aus welchen sich, wenn der Leser gewillt ist, ohne Weiteres ein Ganzes zusammensetzen lässt (Bernhard 1978: 87).

In the attempt to inscribe recollected episodes into narrative language, imagination inevitably intervenes (cf. Schwab 1981: 103). The mythopoeic quality of representation falsifies the experiential quality of the original event: "Die Wahrheit, denke ich, kennt nur der Betroffene, will er sie mitteilen, wird er automatisch zum Lügner. ... Das Gedächtnis hält sich genau an die Vorkommnisse und hält sich an die genaue Chronologie, aber was herauskommt, ist etwas ganz anderes, als es tatsächlich gewesen ist" (Bernhard 1976: 42-43). This allows or forces the writer to live two forms of life, a real and an imagined one which in their coexistence constitute the dynamic quality of life which both defies and desires unity and closure.

Peter Handke thematizes the paradox of narrative refiguration in his texts on the theory of reading life and writing fiction. At the end of his journal, *Das Gewicht der Welt*, Handke deplores the loss of the infantile unity between thinking and inscription in language: "Die im Lauf der Zeit verlorene Verbindung mit meiner schreibenden Hand (als Kind doch eine selbstverständliche Einheit zwischen den durch mich entstehenden Buchstaben und mir)" (Handke 1977: 324), and projects mythic forms of writing, possible in the epic genre, to make up for the loss (321). In *Die Lehre der Sainte-Victoire* he actually evokes such propitious moments in images which have been called *"Nunc stans"* (Handke 1980: 9). These images of the 'standing now' provide a unity between the past and the present for the self (11). The narrative equivalent of these short "Beseligungsmoment[e]" (9) is a coherent story which, however, proves to be impossible. So the purpose behind Handke's wish "eine lange, zusammenhängende Geschichte zu schreiben" is "wieder einmal die Möglichkeit des Versagens zu erleben" (Handke 1982: 15). Yet, this paradoxical enterprise is not superfluous, for, despite all superficial illusions, it is in this process of writing and narrating that the author generates new energy and refuels life: "... meine Herkunft aus der Herkunftslosigkeit wird mich für immer davon abhalten, einen 'Text,' eine 'Story,' ein 'Sittenbild,' eine 'Widerspiegelung,' ja sogar ein 'Gedicht' zu schreiben, aber was sonst? — Eine die Leere in Energie umwandelnde und so erhaltende Erzählung" (16).

Alain Robbe-Grillet shares this belief in energy generated by reading and writing. The gain in energy compensates for the impossibility to achieve any form of harmonization. While Handke cherishes the idea of a unifying illusion in the full awareness of its eventual failure, Robbe-Grillet reproduces in his text the aleatory structure of reality and acknowledges it as such:

> Tout cela c'est du réel, c'est à dire du fragmentaire, du fuyant, de l'inutile, si accidentel même et si particulier que tout événement y apparaît à chaque instant comme gratuit, et toute existence en fin de compte comme privée de la moindre signification unificatrice. ... le réel est discontinu, formé d'éléments juxtaposés sans raison dont chacun est unique, d'autant plus difficiles à saisir qu'ils surgissent de façon sans cesse imprévue, hors de propos, aléatoire (Robbe-Grillet 1984: 208).

Robbe-Grillet's insistence on the unpredictable course of life and the chaotic conception of reality change, however, when he tries to account for the one fixed reality in life which is death which, in turn, determines the meaning of the self (Wyschogrod 1985). Here the illusory function of narration re-emerges: "Construire un récit, ce serait alors — de façon plus ou moins consciente — prétendre lutter contre elle [la mort]" (Robbe-Grillet 1984: 27). If, as Robbe-Grillet argues, "le réel commence juste au moment où le sens vacille" (212), then it is the thought of death which reinstates the task of making sense, of filling in the gaps and of constructing a story out of an aleatory life. "N'est-ce pas là, précisément, la métaphore du travail d'un romancier moderne (Flaubert, c'est moi!) sur la trame trouée du réel, l'écriture comme ensuite la lecture allant de manque en manque pour constituer le récit?" (213). This narration, result of and material for reading, flawed as it may be, represents the real playfield for the experimental writer as well as for his readers and makes them free: "La liberté de l'écrivain (c'est-à-dire celle de l'homme) ne réside que dans l'infinie complexité des combinaisons possibles" (220).

John Barth uses this freedom to the utmost in *LETTERS* which is the product of the infinite possibilities of a dialogic imagination. This freedom is limited only by the certainty of death, which takes — in Barth's scientific metaphor — the form of the second law of thermodynamics, i.e. entropy. This inevitable process of the degeneration of a system can, however, be counterbalanced by the dramaturgy of life in form of a plot (Hoffmann 1985: 275-276). At the end of *LETTERS* Barth proclaims: "Entropy may be where it's all headed, but it isn't where it is; dramaturgy ... is negentropic, as are the stories of our lives" (Barth 1979: 768). In order to incorporate both art and life, plot and dramaturgy (which Barth seems to use interchangeably) need to take on a new meaning which combines the unity of art with the disunity of life. Barth promises such a unifying structure accompanied by the process of structurization early on in *LETTERS*: "Their [*seven fictitious drolls & dreamers*] several narratives will become one; like waves of a rising tide, the plot will surge forward, recede, surge farther forward, recede less far, et cetera to its climax and dénouement" (49). The literary practice eventually yields the following definition of plot or dramaturgy, formulated at the end of *LETTERS*: "... the incremental perturbation of an unstable homeostatic system and its catastrophic restoration to a complexified equilibrium" (767; LeClair/McCaffery 1983: 14). The simultaneity of a search for and realization of control in fleeting moments of "complexified equilibrium" is achieved through the process of reading and writing one/self. Both reading and writing represent ways of replenishing former texts and of generating creative energy. Barth's definition and practice of plot as a dramaturgy of life indicate that his readings and rewritings transcend mere repetitions ("Echo, yes; repeat, no." [768]) and aspire to eternal aesthetic values. "Escalation of echoing cycles into ascending spirals = *estellation*: the apotheosis of stories into stars" (ibid.). This transcendence of life through art replenishes Henry James's belief that "it is art that *makes* life" (Miller 1972: 91), for it is also life that makes art, as contemporary readings and writings of one/self show (cf. Caramello 1983: 63). When the boundaries between life and art disappear, the spiraling ascent to estellation can set in. So Barth's way out of the paradox of transcending finite life through the astral ascent of art is to seek illumination, for he knows that solution is not possible (Barth 1979: 768).

The reader of the postmodern texts discussed here is invited to continue the process set in motion by the author. In this sense he concretizes in Iser's terminology (1974: 274) the play of the dialogic imagination between reading and writing one/self. The dialogic interaction between the writer's text and the reader's self will yield on the part of the reader a form of unity and identity which "represent quite abstract principles drawn from the experience of *text* or *self*" (Holland 1980: 122). Just as in the case of the writer, so do the psychology of experience and the practice of reading interact in the reader. As a co-author of the text, the reader duplicates the writer's interpretation of experience and his control over it in the text. Thus a hermeneutics and a poetics of experience merge in the reader's mind (cf. Gunn 1982). The hermeneutic and poetic activities are embedded in a cultural context in which the reading self appears both as an interpreter and as an interpretation (cf. Michaels 1980: 199). It is hoped that the energy generated from the reading of postmodern texts will allow us to use the described "dual-meaning structure[s]" to turn "the intrasubjective dialogicity between the polarized modes of being into intersubjective communication" (Schwab 1984: 463), to make the necessary changes and transitions to enable us to go on.

REFERENCES

Bakhtin, Mikhail M. 1981. *The Dialogic Imagination: Four Essays by M.M. Bakhtin*, ed. Michael Holquist, trans. Caryl Emerson and Michael Holquist. Austin: University of Texas Press.

Barth, John. 1967. "The Literature of Exhaustion," reprinted in Bradbury 1977: 70-83.

-----. 1972. *Chimera*. New York: Fawcett.

-----. 1979. *LETTERS*. New York: Putnam.

-----. 1984. *The Friday Book: Essays and Other Nonfiction*. New York: Putnam.

Beckett, Samuel. 1980. *Company*. New York: Grove Press.

Bellamy, J.D. 1972. "'Algebra and Fire': An Interview with John Barth," *Falcon* 4: 5-15.

Bernhard, Thomas. 1975. *Die Ursache: Eine Andeutung*. Salzburg: Residenz Verlag.

-----. 1976. *Der Keller: Eine Entziehung*. Salzburg: Residenz Verlag.

-----. 1978. *Der Atem: Eine Entscheidung*. Salzburg: Residenz Verlag.

-----. 1981. *Die Kälte: Eine Isolation*. Salzburg: Residenz Verlag.

Bradbury, Malcolm, ed. 1977. *The Novel Today: Contemporary Writers on Modern Fiction*. Glasgow: Fontana.

Caramello, Charles. 1983. *Silverless Mirrors: Book, Self & Postmodern American Fiction*. Tallahassee: University Presses of Florida.

Dittmar, Jens. 1981. *Thomas Bernhard Werkgeschichte*. Frankfurt: Suhrkamp.

Durzak, Manfred. 1982. *Peter Handke und die deutsche Gegenwartsliteratur: Narziss auf Abwegen*. Stuttgart: Kohlhammer.

Frieden, Sandra. 1983. *Autobiography: Self into Form; German-Language Autobiographical Writings of the 1970's*. Frankfurt: Peter Lang.

Gunn, Janet Varner. 1982. *Autobiography: Toward a Poetics of Experience*. Philadelphia: University of Pennsylvania Press.

Handke, Peter. 1977. *Das Gewicht der Welt: Ein Journal (November 1975 - März 1977)*. Salzburg: Residenz Verlag.

-----. 1980. *Die Lehre der Sainte-Victoire*. Frankfurt: Suhrkamp.

-----. 1981. *Kindergeschichte*. Frankfurt: Suhrkamp.

-----. 1982. *Die Geschichte des Bleistifts*. Salzburg: Residenz Verlag.

Hassan, Ihab. 1982. *The Dismemberment of Orpheus: Toward a Postmodern Literature*. 2nd ed., Madison: The University of Wisconsin Press. First ed. 1971.

Hoffmann, Gerhard. 1985. "Comedy and Parody in John Barth's Fiction," *Amerikastudien* 30: 235-278.

Holland, Norman. 1980. "Unity Identity Text Self," in Tompkins 1980: 118-133. Rpt. from *PMLA* 90 (1975): 813-822.

Iser, Wolfgang. 1974. *The Implied Reader: Patterns of Communication in Prose Fiction from Bunyan to Beckett*. Baltimore: Johns Hopkins University Press.

James, Henry. 1934. *The Art of the Novel: Critical Prefaces*, ed. Richard P. Blackmur. Rpt. New York: Charles Scribner's Sons 1962.

-----. 1968. *Autobiography*, ed. Frederick W. Dupee. New York: Criterion Books.

Jung, C.G. 1953. *Psychological Reflections: An Anthology of the Writings of C.G. Jung*, ed. Jolande Jacobi. New York: Pantheon Books.

Jurgensen, Manfred, ed. 1979. *Handke: Ansätze - Analysen - Anmerkungen* Bern: Francke.

-----, ed. 1981. *Bernhard: Annäherungen*. Bern: Francke.

LeClair, Tom and Larry McCaffery, eds. 1983. *Anything Can Happen: Interviews with Contemporary American Novelists*. Urbana: University of Illinois Press.

Lotman, Jurij. 1977. *The Structure of the Artistic Text*, trans. R. Vroon. Ann Arbor: Department of Slavic Languages and Literatures, University of Michigan.

Man, Paul de. 1979. *Allegories of Reading: Figural Language in Rousseau, Nietzsche, Rilke, and Proust*. New Haven: Yale University Press.

Michaels, Walter Benn. 1980. "The Interpreter's Self: Peirce on the Cartesian 'Subject,'" in Tompkins 1980: 185-200. Rpt. from *Georgia Review*

31 (1977): 383-402.

Miller, James E., ed. 1972. *Theory of Fiction: Henry James*. Lincoln: University of Nebraska Press.

Renza, Louis A. 1977. "The Veto of the Imagination: A Theory of Autobiography," *New Literary History* 9: 1-26.

Ricoeur, Paul. 1983. *Temps et récit*. Paris: Seuil.

-----. 1984. *Time and Narrative*, trans. Kathleen McLaughlin and David Pellauer. Chicago: University of Chicago Press. Translation of Ricoeur 1983.

Robbe-Grillet, Alain. 1984. *Le Miroir qui revient*. Paris: Minuit.

Schwab, Gabriele. 1984. "Genesis of the Subject, Imaginary Functions, and Poetic Language," *New Literary History* 15: 453-474.

Schwab, Sylvia. 1981. *Autobiographik und Lebenserfahrung: Versuch einer Typologie deutschsprachiger autobiographischer Schriften zwischen 1965 und 1975*. Würzburg: Königshausen und Neumann.

Tompkins, Jane P., ed. 1980. *Reader-Response Criticism: From Formalism to Post-Structuralism*. Baltimore: Johns Hopkins University Press.

Wolf, Howling. 1978. *Conversion: Essays in Dialectical Criticism*. New York: Black Sun Press.

Wyschogrod, Edith. 1985. *Spirit in Ashes: Hegel, Heidegger, and Man-Made Mass Death*. New Heaven: Yale University Press.

12

Michel Leiris' Autobiography *La Règle du jeu* and Postmodernism

Olav Severijnen

> "Il faudrait pour ce que j'ai à dire inventer un lan-
> gage aussi nouveau que mon projet."
> Jean-Jacques Rousseau, *Les Confessions*

1. *Introduction*

Michel Leiris wrote his first autobiography, *L'Age d'homme* (1939), between 1930 and 1935. In it we can find a converging presence of Modernist features on the semantic, syntactic, and pragmatic levels. As far as these characteristics are relevant for explaining the difference between *L'Age* and *La Règle du jeu* they will be briefly discussed here.

In his essay "De la littérature considérée comme une tauromachie," which he added to the first post-war impression of *L'Age* in 1946, Leiris announced his intention: "Faire un livre qui soit un acte" (Leiris 1973: 14). He endeavors to capture the truth and to avoid aesthetics; his ideal autobiography would be "la négation d'un roman" (15). The contradiction between this essay and the autobiography itself is indicative of the transition from Modernism to Postmodernism. In the 1946 essay, which shows the influence of existentialist thought and ideas about committed writing, Leiris condemns exactly the kind of writing of the earlier *L'Age* without quite seeming to be aware of it.

Macrostructurally, *L'Age* is based on a restricted number of metaphors which organize the material and which — on a higher level — are metonymically related. Leiris, however, has to acknowledge that his mode of writing is characterized by "un certain arbitraire" (Leiris 1973: 134) and that his thematic approach can be unmasked as "un simple procédé de composition esthétique" (128). These doubts about content and method, hinted at in metalingual comments, do not dissuade him from his project; nor do they result in failure to complete the text. Although the metaphorical method is responsible for a high degree of fragmentation, the coherence between the clusters of metaphors remains intact and this is due to the presence of a (hypothetical) teleology in L'Age.

As a result of the pressure of interiorization, very little attention is paid to the historical context of the autobiographer; consequently, the role of the autobiographer-narrator dominates at the cost of the autobiographer-protagonist. The past is emphatically viewed from the present and narrative experiments draw the reader's attention to the process of writing the text. L'Age appears to be a self-enclosed, solipsistic text. This is also due to the overall structure of the work: the first part (chapters 0-6) is ordered themat-ically, the second chronologically (chapters 7 and 8). The first part seems to be the account of a quest, but is in fact the opposite: Leiris transforms his beginning into his end by presenting the metaphorical and archetypal fig-ures of Lucrèce and Judith as the outcome of his search. Such a consolida-tion, which ends with the beginning, gives a hermetic character to this part of the autobiography. This unmistakably aesthetic process does not, of course, agree with Leiris' wish — as expressed in "De la littérature consi-dérée comme une tauromachie" — to avoid any aesthetic strategy.

La Règle du jeu[1] is, at least in the first three volumes, tautological and therefore more hermetic than L'Age. Not only on the semantic, but also on the syntactic level the end turns out to be the beginning, as will be elabo-rated below. While in L'Age Leiris' erotic development was the theme by means of which he sought to discover the workings of his consciousness, in La Règle it is language that takes over this role. This implies, for one thing, that in La Règle no autobiographical material is required, and that narra-tion itself can become the subject of the discourse (which again locks the text up in itself).

Fragmentation, which in L'Age did not prevent some degree of coher-ence because of Leiris' wish to produce new insights and meanings, acquires a different character in La Règle. In volume I, II and III (volume IV demands separate treatment) fragmentation is a result of Leiris' technique of interweaving various materials on different levels (phonetic, semantic, syntactic). This technique of interweaving allows no meaning that is *a priori* intended (as in *L'Age*), but has to generate meaning itself.

2. Permutation

According to Lodge (1977) and Fokkema (1984), the process of permutation can be considered an aspect of Postmodernist writing. Permutation appears in the device of "incorporating alternative narrative lines in the same text" (Lodge 1977: 230). Lodge does not differentiate between syntax and semantics. Besides being a syntactic or structural category, permutation is, however, also an aspect of the semantic principle of nonselection. Its starting-point is the wish not to exclude particular meanings and forms. As a result, the essence of *La Règle* is the overt preference for language, not over, but against silence. In this four-volume autobiography language does not function as a simple "jeu de mots," but as a "moyen de révélation" (I, 52). This means that Leiris returns to his earlier Surrealistic credo. Thus we understand that the beginning of the autobiography is not located at his physical birth, but at his birth-in-language. In the first chapter of *Biffures*, "...reusement!", the child Michel Leiris loses his personal power and control over language. *La Règle* can partly be considered as a quest by which Leiris tries to find back this magical state.

It may indeed be said that the device of permutation constitutes the essence of *La Règle*: the cycle is fundamentally nothing more than the endless process of the mingling of themes and their variations around a core that is the void, nothing, silence. The metaphors that Leiris himself chooses for his "jeu" justify this hypothesis: he splits up the title of the first volume of *La Règle* (i.e. *Biffures*) into "bifur" (synonymous with "bifurcation," forking) and "biffure" (synonymous with "biffage," erasure). His definition of "bifur" (I, 278-279) is at the same time an illustration of the meaning of the word (which demonstrates the narrow tie between syntax and semantics in Leiris' work), and amounts, in short,   to this: the term "bifur" emphasizes

> l'accent même de bifurquer, de dévier, comme fait le train qui modifie sa direction selon ce qui lui commande l'aiguille et comme fait la pensée, engagée quelquefois, par les rails du langage, dans on ne sait trop quoi de vertigineux ou d'aveuglant et entraînée dans un mouvement qui pourrait être baptisé tout aussi bien *biffure*, car on perçoit ici une equivoque, un loup sur lequel on revient, comme cela se produit dans le cas d'un lapsus (sitôt laché et sitôt raturé) à l'instant qu'on se dit "c'est ma langue qui a fourché," ma langue qui s'est fourvoyée, à une fourche de routes ou croisée de chemins (I, 279).

In this process of permutation the distinction between narration and metanarration is blurred. The ramifications are the result of a predilection for "juxtaposition ou de combinaison" (I, 277), for enumeration, for association, and for puns; their movement is directed to "la recherche de tracés anciens" (I, 284). Apart from this, there is also the process of correction, which entails "eliminations successives de valeurs illusoires" that are oriented towards "le futur puisqu'il s'agit de préparer les voies d'une transformation" (ibid.). This process of creation and destruction never comes to an end: Leiris' fear of "[l'] anéantissement" forces him à "ne vivre jamais qu'*en avant* de moi-même" (I, 246). Leiris captivates the future; for the autobiographical project this implies that the author keeps postponing to finish his writing by announcements of the next supplementary volume and by turning the search itself for "la règle du jeu" into an end instead of a means (so that the end cannot be defined anymore). In this way Leiris' "écriture" becomes a way of formulating questions that inhibits finding any answers.

Interweaving or permutation takes place on various levels. Focusing on one element (a theme, a word, a sound, a memory, an opposition, the narration itself, etc.) the game begins as an attempt to acquire knowledge about his personality. The first phase consists of a process of decomposition (the play with signifier and signified, the analysis of the different networks of the signified, the association with autobiographical data, etc.). This beginning threatens to collapse under the weight of the countless ramifications, which (note Leiris' "totalitarian" design) acquire a suggestion of coherence because of the interweaving that intersects at all levels of the text (phonetic, semantic, syntactic, discourse and metadiscourse). After this process of decomposition and analysis, the movement veers round and turns itself into a synthesizing process which tries to recapture the starting-point. The original contiguous associations are brought together in an all-embracing system that is a consolidation of the starting-point, which becomes questioned again in the next phase. This is the result of Leiris' hesitations about the possibilities of self-analysis in general and of his own method in particular.

James Leigh focuses on a perfect example of the technique of permutation. In one of the fragments Leigh analyses, Leiris presents a scene from the past, a family of travelling dancers. Leigh argues that the terms in which these four people are described acquire a life of their own: "The event weaves itself into all of the themes of the text as well as into the modes of transmission between them" (Leigh 1978: 741). He illustrates his statement convincingly. But, without saying so explicitly, Leigh hints at a twofold metonymic process: not only are the events described by means of words from their immediately contiguous contexts, but the metadiscourse also uses elements derived from the main discourse. The metonymy is in this case responsible for a strong proliferation of interaction between the various levels of narration.

Leiris' strategy of delay arises from two contradictory aims: on the one hand he wishes to postpone the end of the project, which he fears since it will cause his writing to be superseded by silence; on the other hand he wants to reach a certain target, i.e. to formulate "la règle d'or." Manoeuvering between these two desires Leiris' discourse develops a remarkable ambiguity: "Balancier entre l'innommable (la mort) et l'indicible (l'oracle et le secret), entre le vide fascinant et le trésor caché" (Lejeune 1975a: 279). In his endeavors to say what cannot be said and to find what cannot be found, Leiris will eventually lose the game, but as long as he can go on writing he won't.

The continuous interaction between part and whole, discourse and metadiscourse, together with the hermetic technique of de- and recomposition, makes of *La Règle* not only a self-enclosed text, but also a text that is able to generate itself and one that slips from one interior duplication into another. *La Règle* is centripetal (but where is its center?) and continuously turns away from the referential outside world. Morrissette's observation that in Postmodernism "the work becomes self-contained, if not self-productive" (Morrissette 1975: 259-260) can be applied not only to the semantic pole of *La Règle* (thus, according to Jeffrey Mehlman, the figure of Persephone generates *La Règle* on the semantic level), but also to the syntactic pole of the cycle. The following *mise en abyme* (a special form of interior duplication) may illustrate this. Just as *La Règle* is an account of a quest for something which does not exist in the referential outside world but only in the linguistic world of the text, Leiris looks in vain for various objects (for instance, a toy representing a "tambour-trompette") which have no existence outside the text. The *mise en abyme* does not merely concern the theme of the quest, as Leiris himself points out (I, 262), but asserts itself at the same time on the structural level: just as Leiris' desire to find "la règle d'or" loses itself in the endless, labyrinthine and textual network of *La Règle*, so the "objets du désir" disappear from the text without ever having been able to become more than nonreferential signifiers.

Leiris strains after a duplication of himself in and by *La Règle*, and the text duplicates (multiplies?) itself in its *mises en abyme*. Duplication is a result of the fear of death and of the wish for self-deconstruction. Leiris presents himself as a Narcissus who wants to jump towards his reflected image (the duplication) in the water as a last effort to escape logical and physical laws (I, 235). In the person of Leiris there exist at the same time a "besoin de négation" (I, 239) and a striving for artistic duplication. After *Fourbis* it will be evident that the two are incompatible. *Fibrilles* will give an account of this insight, which results from the annihilation of the ontological boundary between the autobiographical subject and the autobiographical object, a kind of "short-circuit" (Lodge 1977: 239). This identification will not produce the desired effect. But before this process of negation and annihilation will be described, first the other important technique employed in structuring the text of *La Règle* will be discussed: correction.

3. *Correction*

Correction in *La Règle* is implied by the second meaning of "biffures": the "biffage." As a Postmodernist device, correction is perhaps more important than permutation (cf. Ibsch in Fokkema and Bertens 1986: 119-133). Correction results from an increased distrust of the knowability of the "I" or "self" (i.e. the autobiographical subject) and of reality. While during Modernism hypotheses about both the inner and the outer worlds were still possible, in Postmodernism we see a downward spiral movement of hypotheses and refutations, which can only end in silence. This has special consequences for autobiography, for precisely in this genre the ontological boundary between literature and reality, between text and author, is crucial.

Leiris' mode of writing is characterized by "détours, retours, ratures, biffures, bifurcations diverses" (I, 78). These features can be found in long stretches of metalingual comments on his method and the attainability of his aim. His sentences, which are often long and tentative and make elaborate detours in order to reach some revelation, are eventually lost in modifications and self-reflexive considerations. Before the end of a sentence or of an argument is reached, it has already been relativized. And when Leiris decides to "examiner un peu près la structure de mes phrases," he has to acknowledge that his sentences are nothing but:

> formations parisitaires qui prolifèrent dans tout ce que j'écris, masquant la

> pensée authentique plutôt qu'ils ne l'aident à se traduire avec plus de pré-
> cision et se révélant tout compte fait comme une série d'écrans, qui s'inter-
> posent entre mes idées et moi, les estompent, les étouffent sous le poids
> d'une trop grande masse verbale, finissent par me les rendre étrangères ou
> les dissoudre complètement (I, 84).

This self-criticism leads to a continuous process of corrections. Although Leiris was already worried by the question of the attainability of his ideal in *Biffures*, it is only in *Fibrilles* that he realizes that the downward spiral cannot be stopped. The corrections in this volume reach further than in *Biffures* and *Fourbis*; not only does he discover that the frequent "délais" and "biffures" make his autobiography less authentic (III, 233), but he also gives up the fight against the annihilating power of time (III, 229) and acknowledges the "échec" of his entire project (III, 230). At this stage his "jeu" runs the risk of being replaced by the "négativité de l'absolu silence" (III, 255). Ihab Hassan describes this situation aptly: "The negative, acting through art, language, and consciousness, shapes the boundary state I call silence. In practice, this is a state men may approach without ever reaching" (Hassan 1971: 14). However, the situation appears even more complicated when we have a closer look at the extent of the "échec."

In traditional, pre-Modernist autobiographies there is a clear distinction between autobiographer-narrator and autobiographical protagonist. This distinction is largely maintained in Modernism, and therefore also in *L'Age*, but Leiris announces its destruction in his essay "De la littérature considérée comme une tauromachie," and at the ending of *Biffures* the distinction has disappeared. At that point we note a change in the aim of writing (which allows us to speak of a "biffage" on the pragmatic level too). The identification of autobiographical subject and object invalidates the original, object-oriented intention (i.e. to acquire insight into the personal past) and is replaced by a new, subject-oriented intention (i.e. to acquire insight in the personal presence and future). At this moment chronology disappears from *La Règle*. Attention is now focused on new fields of interest: the concentration on writing itself and on the autobiographical present, as well as the question of what lies beyond (or after) the autobiographical activity. For the first time in the history of autobiography, not the past, but the future becomes the center of narration.

The identification of author and protagonist is the consequence of Leiris' decision to give up his "détachement" (I, 288); this is his penultimate refutation: he considers his "jeu" to be unjustifiably uncommitted. Because

of this "biffage" he discovers that his project will come to an unintended
end and he feels the menace of silence becoming manifest. However, to be
silent is better than to tell stories without any commitment. At this moment
the most important turning-point in *La Règle* is reached: "Mais 'silence'
étant pour moi presque le synonyme de 'mort' ..., je ne puis me résoudre à
me taire" (I, 294). Because Leiris has identified himself with his text (i.e.
his textual "self"), the final silence would imply both the end of his project
and the end of his life. Leiris then opts for the following solution:

> parler à tort et à travers, ce qui doit me permettre en tout cas de rompre
> le cercle enchanté dans lequel m'ont fermé la raison raisonnante, le dis-
> cours discoureur, l'écriture écrivante (I, 294).

This choice demands from him a leap across silence, the void and death, in
order to realize the endless delay of the last word and to postpone the
definitive correction of life itself. The leap is based on hesitations and origi-
nates from negativity: "prendre pour planche de salut une planche dont je
sais pertinemment que c'est une planche pourrie" (ibid.). In *Biffures* Leiris'
choice between the jump into "le lac dont les eaux dormantes m'attirent,
seul moyen d'échapper à une contemplation stérile de Narcisse" (I, 106)
and the leap across the deathlike silence is decided in favor of the second
possibility. This is the leap "to the other side of silence" (Hassan 1975: 53)
into the realm of "alittérature" (Mauriac 1969: 83).

In *Fibrilles*, however, Leiris gives the account of the definitive "biffage": the end of the project has indeed coincided with the (unsuccessful)
end of its maker. But just as Leiris' attempt at suicide was abortive, so *La
Règle* is not brought to silence either: *Frêle Bruit* forms, as its title indicates,
the last stage before definitive silence.

In *Biffures* and *Fourbis* the quest for the referent of "la règle d'or" is
still going on. Leiris searches for an aesthetic rule and an ethical rule which
coincide. This search for an *ars scribendi* and an *ars vivendi* — "j'ai voulu
me construire une poétique et une éthique imbriquées l'une dans l'autre et
capables, sans divergences, de me guider en tous domaines" (III, 245) —
produces only a series of interdictions, which is a "succès négatif" (III,
247). But even this series of seven rules is not exempt from the destructive
influence of correction. Leiris acquires the insight that this destructive tendency in his way of writing is necessarily part of what he considers to be literature ("poésie," which includes *La Règle*): "La négation va de pair avec
la poursuite de la poésie, puisque celle-ci vise à rompre — soit à nier — de
limites" (III, 254). This view of literature shows a strong resemblance to

Postmodernist poetics.

Taking account of the fact that Leiris has never condemned his Surrealist past, his views professed in that period suggest a similar conclusion. In the 1920s, Leiris wrote:

> En disséquant les mots que nous aimons, sans nous soucier de suivre ni l'étymologie, ni la signification admise, nous découvrons leurs vertus les plus cachées et les ramifications secrètes qui se propagent à travers tout le langage, canalysées par les associations de sons, de formes et d'idées. Alors le langage se transforme en oracle et nous avons là (si ténu qu'il soit) un fil pour nous guider, dans le Babel de notre esprit (quoted by Nadeau 1963: 31-32).

As long as Surrealism is not considered as a constituent of Modernism but rather as a precursor of Postmodernism (which makes Neosurrealism part of Postmodernism), it is legitimate to quote this fragment in support of the present argument. Because in *La Règle* Leiris uses language as a means to obtain insight in his own person and also because he uses the devices of decomposition and recomposition, we may conclude that the deconstructive poetics of Leiris is akin to the Neosurrealist aspect of Postmodernism (cf. Hassan 1975: 58). The Surrealists tried to attain the impossible: starting from nothingness, "including the ritual murder of language" (Hassan 1971a: 79), they wanted to describe the subconscious. The Surrealists also tried to destroy the distinction between art and reality, and when they felt this was realized they turned the process of destruction against Surrealism itself: "Suicide, symbolic or actual, becomes the consummation of the avant-garde" (ibid.). Death and silence coincide after this last and definitive destruction, as is the case in *Fibrilles*.

The last phase before silence is the phase of self-conscious writing and the final part of *Biffures*, certain parts of *Fourbis* and especially the final part of *Fibrilles* are characterized by a great deal of self-consciousness. Hesitations stifle the discourse to a narcissistic reflection about its own genesis. Alter's statement that self-reflexion is nothing else but "a long meditation on death" (Alter 1975: 229) is certainly applicable to *La Règle*. The text is entirely self-enclosed, it maintains itself by autogenesis against chaos and silence, and it can only realize its full meaning in the end when the rule of the game has been found. With every new correction, however, this becomes less possible and is the final erasure drawn nearer.

Frêle Bruit, the last volume of *La Règle*, is announced in *Fourbis* (II, 234) and *Fibrilles* (III, 292) as "Fibules" and is intended to contain Leiris' "aperçus éparpillés" (III, 292). Indeed, the book is built out of a great number of small fragments and of some longer essay-like parts. Leiris partly reformulates the rules of his game: the structure of *Frêle Bruit* will be determined by Leiris' physical and psychological decline. The much abused metaphor of increasing entropy is therefore appropriate to this case. Roland Simon articulates clearly this Orphic character of *La Règle*:

> le texte de *La Règle du jeu* est *écrit et lu à la fois*, d'une lecture intérieure qui est donc elle-même écriture, à l'image de l'infini de la boîte de cacao de *L'Age d'homme*, mais cette fois, elle n'est plus implosive mais explosive, ne tend pas à la réduction mais à l'expansion, débouchant toujours sur "quelque chose d'autre à dire," au lieu d'être une "voix" qui résume, c'est une voix qui développe, voix de l'éclatement de la personne, de sa dispersion (Simon 1984: 136).

In this last volume of *La Règle* even the "biffures"-strategies of permutation and correction are replaced by a discontinuous compilation of fragments around the circle-shaped void: "Si, boucle bouclée, nous devons retourner au néant d'où nous étions partis, n'est-ce pas un zéro — serpent se mordant la queue ou chemin de fer circulaire — qui résume toute la vie?" (IV, 59). No hypothesis about reality or the autobiographical subject (the "self") is possible, which inhibits autobiographical discernment. If the fact that language only functions as a medium to formulate hesitations and problems is taken into consideration, it is understandable that at this stage the "phrase" is replaced by the "antiphrase": "c'est le négatif qui engendre le positif" (IV, 356). The autobiographer admits his "échec" on all fronts. His fear is confirmed: "*Le projet, infléchi jusqu'à boucler la boucle, n'est plus que projet de projet*" (IV, 204).[2]

It may be clarifying at this point to compare *Frêle Bruit* with another autobiography, which shows certain similarities: Roland Barthes' *Roland Barthes par Roland Barthes* (1975). In contrast to that of Leiris, Barthes' option for fragmentation is a positive one. He cherishes the illusion "qu'en brisant mon discours, je cesse de discourir imaginairement sur moi-même, j'atténue le risque de transcendance" (Barthes 1975a: 99). Leiris, on the other hand, strives after such a "transcendance" and for him "la poésie" is the only medium to reach that aim. Leiris locks himself in his autobiography (IV, 181), and only in a few cases (e.g. the fragments in the third person) he is able to dissociate from his textual "self." For Barthes, there is no question of the danger of blurring autobiographical levels, because for him the autobiographical subject does not possess any referent; neither does the "je" ever leave the level of the signifier (Barthes 1975a: 60). Elsewhere Barthes even comes to the following conclusion: "Barthes n'a pu dire qu'une chose: qu'il est le seul à ne pouvoir parler vraiment de lui. Tel est le sens, 'décevant,' de son livre" (Barthes 1975b: 5).

4. *Conclusion*

Of course it is not legitimate to account for changes in the generic code of autobiography under the influence of Postmodernism by referring only to *La Règle du jeu*. The study of other autobiographical texts, of marginal genres — like the diary and "autofiction" (Lejeune 1983: 430) — and of other possible approaches will have to be undertaken before the changing appearances and functions of autobiography in literary history can be established. However, in presenting some generalizing observations I will stay close to the work of Michel Leiris.

On the syntactic level the Modernist hypothetical way of narration is replaced by a mode that generates only provisional meaning or denies even that possibility. Leiris may not entirely give up referentiality (which seems to be altogether impossible in the genre of autobiography), but refuses to establish any definite meaning in the final volume, *Frêle Bruit*. The shift from the principle of nonselection to those of correction and refutation can, however, already be found in the first volume, *Biffures*.

Discarding chronology and especially closing the gap between autobiographer-narrator and autobiographical protagonist have put an end to the possibilities of dissociation and of detachment which are still present in Modernist autobiographies. The autobiographer no longer writes about his former personality, but about his autobiographical situation during the writing of the text (without slipping into writing a diary). Only by means of language is it possible to formulate the "loss of subjectivity" (Hoffmann *et al.* 1977: 20) as a problem. Language functions as a medium to create a new (ontological) center which may never transcend the stage of a nonreferential signifier, like Leiris' "la règle d'or" or "tambour-trompette", or Barthes' "je." Self-reflexion, self-consciousness and *mise en abyme* foreground this non- or auto-referentiality.

A reference to the autobiography of Roland Barthes is again helpful to support my conclusions. Barthes tries to make clear that he does not write an autobiography of himself: "Je ne dis pas: 'je vais me décrire', mais: 'J'écris un texte et je l'appelle R.B.'" (Barthes 1975a: 60). Roland Barthes deconstructs Roland Barthes and the result is an alphabetically arranged series of fragments — "un ordre immotivé" (150) — which are not permitted to be connected with each other: "l'important, c'est que ces petits réseaux ne soient pas raccordés, c'est qu'ils ne glissent pas à un seul et grand réseau qui serait la structure du livre, son sens" (151). Like Leiris, Barthes holds that the text is both beginning and end of the autobiographical activity, and Leiris as well as Barthes could have written that no "dernier mot" exists but only "texte sur texte" (124). An essential distinction between Leiris and Barthes, however, is that the ontological gap between author and text is destroyed in *La Règle* but that in *Roland Barthes par Roland Barthes* the boundary does not only continue to exist, but has even become impossible to cross. And this makes irony and dissociation possible again.

The concentration on language and on the (im-)possibilities of describing the "self" or the emptiness which is called the "self" gives rise to an autobiographical discourse in which metalingual comment predominates. The predominance of self-consciousness makes autobiography into "anti-autobiography" (Brée 1978: 9).

Because the meaning of the text is no longer defined by the autobiographer and the text has to generate its own meaning, the task of the reader has grown in importance. Whereas the Modernist autobiography was closed within itself and kept the reader at a distance, with Postmodernism the reader seems to acquire some room for his or her own contribution. Michel Leiris allows his readers a considerable amount of freedom in constituting possible meanings of his text — "laisser au lecteur le soin de déterminer à quoi menait mon trajet" (III, 287).

Identity or the autobiographical "self" are negative concepts and can only be constituted, if at all, by the act of writing and by language, and not by something else. The changes on the pragmatic level, like the contribution of the reader, the changed intentions of the autobiographer and the blurring of the boundaries of the genre — the subtitle of Claude Roy's *Moi, Je* (1969) reads "essai d'autobiographie," the first sentence of *Roland Barthes par Roland Barthes* runs "tout ceci doit être considéré comme dit par un personnage de roman" (frontispiece) — are not brought out demonstratively, as was the case with Modernism. In Modernism the restrictions of the genre, such as the "rule" of truthfulness or the "rule" of the threefold identity of author, narrator and protagonist, were *explicitly* doubted (cf. Lejeune 1975a: 15; Bruss 1976: 10-11).

The selection of the semantic material is always a result of the pragmatic situation. When writing becomes a means for creating a new self against the threat of desintegration, the semantic world will be marked by such an intention. When we also take into account that autobiography can be meant to be at the same time a work of art and an act of commitment, as is the case with *La Règle*, the semantic material will be ambiguous and possess Modernist and Postmodernist characteristics at the same time.

The tentative mode of Leiris' discourse results mainly from the fact that he has no *a priori* idea of what he is looking for nor of what the work will look like. No rules exist any longer, in contrast to Modernism, which still offered some provisional certainty or made it possible for the autobiographer to express what was experienced as inexpressible. To *La Règle* applies what Lyotard writes about the sublime or the unpresentable: "Those rules and categories [i.e. the rules and categories which make the presentation of the unpresentable possible] are what the work of art itself is looking for" (Lyotard 1983: 341). Leiris writes his autobiography without rules but hopes to find them, a quest symbolized in the search for "la règle d'or" during the act of writing. Because his rules concern ethical and aesthetic categories at the same time, Leiris runs both a personal and an artistic risk, which I believe is a distinguishing feature of Postmodernist autobiographical writing. Autobiography is no longer allowed to be only a gratuitous act, but on the other hand the aesthetic claim cannot be denied. To discover this, Leiris has to go as far as the boundaries of the genre, where he will find that these boundaries "converge in the very act of writing" (Sprinker 1980: 342).

NOTES

1. *La Règle du jeu* (henceforth to be called *La Règle*) consists of *Biffures* (1948), *Fourbis* (1955), *Fibrilles* (1967) and *Frêle Bruit* (1976). Roman numerals refer to the volumes (I — IV) and Arabic numerals refer to the pages of the volume.

2. The "échec" of his project is confirmed by Leiris himself in his most recent publication: "les jeux de mots [sont] incapables de changer la vie et d'abolir la mort" (Leiris 1985: 157). The first can be considered to have been the aim of *L'Age d'homme*, the second the aim of *La Règle du jeu*. Sturrock partly explains this failure when he states that "language is never the possession of any individual, so that to employ it is to be alienated from the self" (Sturrock 1977: 58). On a more general level Elbaz points out that autobiography, like fiction, only can be a ceaseless beginning, because consciousness does not allow for any completion and because the notion of selfhood is nothing but an ideological mystification (Elbaz 1983: 197).

REFERENCES

Alter, Robert. 1975. "The Self-conscious Moment: Reflections on the Aftermath of Modernism," *Triquarterly* 33: 209-230.

Barthes, Roland. 1975a. *Roland Barthes par Roland Barthes*. Paris: Seuil.

-----. 1975b. "Barthes puissance trois," *Le Quinzaine littéraire* 205: 3-5.

Brée, Germaine. 1978. *Narcissus Absconditus: The Problematic Art of Autobiography in Contemporary France*. Oxford: Clarendon Press.

Bruss, Elisabeth W. 1976. *Autobiographical Acts: The Changing Situation of a Literary Genre*. Baltimore: Johns Hopkins University Press.

Elbaz, Robert. 1983. "Autobiography, Ideology and Genre Theory," *Orbis Litterarum* 38: 187-204.

Fokkema, Douwe W. 1984. *Literary History, Modernism, and Postmodernism*. Amsterdam and Philadelphia: Benjamins.

Fokkema, Douwe and Hans Bertens, eds. 1986. *Approaching Postmodernism: Papers Presented at a Workshop on Postmodernism, 21-23 September 1984, University of Utrecht*. Amsterdam and Philadelphia: Benjamins.

Hassan, Ihab. 1971a. *The Dismemberment of Orpheus: Toward a Postmodern Literature*. New York: Oxford University Press.

-----. 1975. *Paracriticisms: Seven Speculations of the Times*. Urbana: University of Illinois Press.

Hassan, Ihab and Sally Hassan, eds. 1983. *Innovation/Renovation: New Perspectives on the Humanities*. Madison: University of Wisconsin Press.

Hoffmann, Gerhard, Alfred Hornung and Rüdiger Kunow. 1977. "'Modern', 'Postmodern' and 'Contemporary' as Criteria for the Analysis of 20th Century Literature," *Amerikastudien* 22: 19-46.

Leigh, James. 1978. "The Figure of Autobiography," *Modern Language Notes* 93: 733-749.

Leiris, Michel. 1948. *La Règle du jeu*, I: *Biffures*. Paris: Gallimard.

-----. 1955. *La Règle du jeu*, II: *Fourbis*. Paris: Gallimard.

-----. 1967. *La Règle du jeu*, III: *Fibrilles*. Paris: Gallimard.

-----. 1973. *L'Age d'homme, précédé de De la littérature considérée comme une tauromachie*. Paris: Gallimard. Earlier editions in 1939 and 1946.

-----. 1976. *La Règle du jeu*, IV: *Frêle Bruit*. Paris: Gallimard.

-----. 1985. *Langage tangage ou ce que les mots me disent*. Paris: Gallimard.

Lejeune, Philippe. 1975a. *Le Pacte autobiographique* Paris: Seuil.

-----. 1975b. *Lire Leiris: Autobiographie et langage*. Paris: Klincksieck.

-----. 1983. "Le Pacte autobiographique (bis)," *Poétique* 14: 416-434.

Lodge, David. 1977. *The Modes of Modern Writing: Metaphor, Metonymy, and the Typology of Modern Literature.* London: Arnold.

Lyotard, Jean-François. 1983. "Answering the Question: What is Postmodernism?" in Hassan and Hassan 1983: 329-341.

Mauriac, Claude. 1969. *L'Alittérature contemporaine.* Paris: Albin Michel. First edition 1958.

Mehlman, Jeffrey. 1974. *A Structural Study of Autobiography: Proust, Leiris, Sartre, Lévi-Strauss.* Ithaca and London: Cornell University Press.

Morrissette, Bruce. 1975. "Post-Modern Generative Fiction: Novel and Film," *Critical Inquiry* 2: 253-262.

Nadeau, Maurice. 1963. *Michel Leiris et la quadrature du cercle.* Paris: Julliard.

Olney, James, ed. 1980. *Autobiography: Essays Theoretical and Critical.* Princeton: Princeton University Press.

Simon, Roland H. 1984. *Orphée Médusé: Autobiographies de Michel Leiris.* Lausanne: L'Age d'homme.

Sprinker, Michael. 1980. "Fictions of the Self: The End of Autobiography," in Olney 1980: 321-342.

Sturrock, John. 1977. "The New Model Autobiographer," *New Literary History* 9: 51-63.

13

Narrative Discourse in Postmodernist Texts: The Conventions of the Novel and the Multiplication of Narrative Instances

Ulla Musarra

In the Postmodernist novel, the general features of "fragmentation", "discontinuity" and "nonselection" (Fokkema 1986: 85) appear more concretely in certain devices of narrative organization such as duplication and multiplication. At the level of the "story" we may distinguish various operations of duplication and multiplication of action, character and narrated world; at the level of narrative discourse we see the duplication and multiplication of the writing process and the splitting up of the narrative subject into various narrative instances.

In many Postmodernist texts, the multiplication of narrative instances — which will be our main topic — is combined with the exploration of some of the most celebrated conventions of the (early, in part eighteenth-century) tradition of the novel: the convention of "le manuscrit trouvé," and further the conventions of the epistolary novel, the diary, the novel of recollection, and the frame-story. It is in conformity with these conventions that the narrative instances may represent not only narrators and narratees, but also — in a sometimes "nonselective" manner — authors, editors, commentators, translators, copyists and readers.

Of course, the device of multiplication may be represented more or less frequently and applied with different degrees of intensity. In the novels of some of the French *nouveaux romanciers* such as Alain Robbe-Grillet, Philippe Sollers and Michel Butor, who may be conceived of as belonging to the first Postmodernist generation (cf. Fokkema 1984: 39), the device is applied in a different and sometimes less spectacular way than, for instance,

in Borges, Cortázar, Nabokov, Barth, and some congenial European writers such as Raymond Queneau, Italo Calvino and the Danish writer Svend
Aage Madsen. In Michel Butor the device is related to the problematic
nature of the writing process. In Sollers and Robbe-Grillet the same may
occur, but here the device is often combined with the duplication and multiplication of action, narrated world and characters. In most *nouveaux
romanciers* and in the representatives of the *nouveau* Nouveau Roman
(Morrissette 1975: 256-257), as well as in some of the texts of Calvino and
Madsen, the device of multiplication forms part of the process of self-generation.

   The strategies followed by the various writers may present numerous
differences and variations, but some common features can be distinguished.
In order to stress these features I shall base my analysis on a simple narratological model, the model of narrative levels introduced by Gérard
Genette and others (Genette 1972, Bal 1977, Rimmon-Kenan 1983) and
limit myself to a few predominant multiplying operations: first the multiplication of the extradiegetic instances, second the multiplication of the
intradiegetic and hypodiegetic ones. In the first case the operation takes
place on the extradiegetic level: the novel seems to extend its outer frame.
In the second case the multiplication concerns the intra- and hypodiegetic
levels: the novel seems to expand toward its own center. In some novels the
two procedures are combined and supplement each other. In many cases,
however, it will be extremely difficult to distinguish the extradiegetic level
from the intra- and hypodiegetic ones. In the Postmodernist novel the bor-
derlines between the various narrative levels, between frame and narrated
story and between the story and "the story in the story", are often obliter-
ated.

The extradiegetic level

The extension of the outer frame of the novel is achieved by the frequent
appearance of the extradiegetic narrator and other extradiegetic instances.
The "self-conscious" return to the pre-modernist literary tradition, which
according to John Barth (1980: 70) is characteristic of Postmodernist narrative, implies a renovation of traditional narrative discourse. In some cases
this leads to the reintroduction of the personalized authorial third-person
narrator after his withdrawal at the end of the nineteenth century and during the Modernist period, or in Genette's terms, the reintroduction of the

extradiegetic narrator. *The Sot-Weed Factor* (1960) by John Barth is representative of this mode, but adds a dimension of parody. The excessively circumstantial chapter titles reflect the traditional authorial comment in a parodical way. In Postmodernist fiction, however, the authorial narrative situation often proves to be illusive. This is the case in *Our Ancestors* (*I nostri antenati*, 1960), one of the early texts of Calvino in which various Postmodernist characteristics may be discerned. Halfway the text, the story of Agilulfo, the "not-existing knight," turns out to have been told not by an extradiegetic anonymous narrator but by the nun Teodora. At the end of the text Teodora reveals her real identity. As the fighter Bradamante she belongs to the army of Charlemagne and has therefore been a witness to the narrated action. From an extradiegetic (and heterodiegetic) narrative situation the text moves toward an intradiegetic (and homodiegetic) one. A similar process takes place in *Hundred Years of Solitude* (*Cien años de soledad*, 1967) by García Márquez. The extradiegetic narrative voice depends entirely on the activity of the intradiegetic focalizers. This is illustrated by the curious combinations of authorial anticipations and protracted figural flash-backs. At the end of the novel the narrating voice is most surprisingly revealed as a voice which belongs not to an extradiegetic but to an intradiegetic instance, the gipsy Melquíades. In Thomas Pynchon's *V* (1963), which may be mentioned in the same context, there are numerous shifts from the extradiegetic to the intradiegetic level. In spite of an initial extradiegetic narrative situation the story seems to have been focalized, organized and partly written down by the character Stencil.

The return of what at first sight may seem to be the voice of a traditional extradiegetic narrator forms one aspect of the extradiegetic frame. Another aspect is constituted by the intrusion of the real author into the novel. As a result, the hierarchical order, which in traditional narrative characterizes the relation between author and narrator or between author and character, may be subverted. Moreover, the borderline between fiction and nonfiction is transgressed. This may occur in prefaces or postfaces, which form part of the extradiegetic frame. In *Giles Goat-Boy* (1966) by John Barth, for instance, two of the fictional prefaces and postfaces are signed by the real author. In the same novel the fictional editors allude to the real author, J.B., who in this way becomes part of the fiction. In *Les Oeuvres complètes de Sally Mara* by Queneau, which in their definite version have been edited in 1962, this procedure takes a rather extreme form. In the preface, Sally Mara, the "auteur prétendu imaginaire," alludes to the

real author, the "auteur soi-disant réel," as "un certain Queneau . . . ,
attaché à la maison Gallimard" (Queneau 1962: 5-6). In various texts this
type of shift from fiction to nonfiction is not confined to prefaces or postfaces, but takes place also in the novel itself. In this way elements of the
extradiegetic frame emerge within the diegesis. The device is applied again
and again by John Barth. In "Life-Story" (in *Lost in the Funhouse*, 1968)
the writer, "he," alludes to his "author" B. In "Dunyazadiad" (*Chimera*,
1972) the author John Barth makes his appearance as a fictional character,
a sort of *deus ex machina*, among the other fictional characters. In *Sabbatical* the two narrators, Susan and Fenwick, incidentally entrust the narration
to the "author": "Practical Susan says I say leave it to the author" (Barth
1982: 206). In *Letters* (1979) finally, Barth himself is one of the seven letter-
writers and figures thus as a character or better as a first-person narrator of
the same status as the other first-person narrators, most of whom are fictional characters in some of Barth's previous books.

A curious parallel to *Letters* can be found in an epistolary novel by the
Dutch writer Hella Haasse (1976). The author herself, a "real" character,
exchanges letters with a fictional character from a well-known "real" book,
the Marquise de Merteuil from the epistolary novel by Choderlos de La-
clos. Further exploitations of the device can be found in *If on a Winter's
Night a Traveller* by Italo Calvino, originally published in 1979, where the
anonymous, extradiegetic narrator introduces the writer Calvino into the
frame-story, and in various novels by the Danish writer, Svend Aage Madsen, where the name of the fictional author "Sandme" is an anagrammatical
allusion to the name of the real author. The device is applied to a very
extensive degree by the Flemish writer Louis Paul Boon. In the frame-story
of his great novel *Chapel Road* (*De Kapellekensbaan*, 1953), a novel which
presents various Postmodernist characteristics, the fictional writer Boontje,
whose name is a self-ironical allusion to the name of the real author, is discussing with his friends and neighbors the novel he is writing. The chapters
of the novel are intertwined with the frame-story. The procedure is evidently that of a "work in progress."

The extradiegetic frame constituted by prefaces (and postfaces) is in
some cases presented as being the product of one or more editors. The text
itself is introduced by the editor(s) as an authentic manuscript and its
author as a "really" existing person or "real" writer. The exploitation of the
possibilities offered by the eighteenth-century convention of "le manuscrit
trouvé" seems to be one of the favorite Postmodernist procedures. Some-

times the convention is used in a parodic way. In this case the result is not, as in some traditional (eighteenth-century) novels, an effect of authenticity, but rather the opposite. One of the devices of parody is the hyperbole: in *Giles Goat-Boy* not one or two but four editors are discussing, whether it is recommendable or not to publish the manuscript which the writer J.B. claims to have received from Giles Stoker, the son of the "goat-boy." Another device is the indication of the dubious origin of the manuscript, its incomplete and fragmentary state or the inavailability of the original copy. The first of these devices is applied once again by Barth, the other respectively by Nabokov, Madsen, Eco. In *Giles Goat-Boy* the first-person narrator George is only in a very indirect way the author of the manuscript. The text turns out to be the output of the computer Wescac, which has had as input first a compilation of fragmentary texts concerning the life of George, and second some lecture-notes and taped conferences of George himself. Moreover, the writer J.B. admits that part of the manuscript has been interchanged with part of a manuscript of his own, the manuscript of his incompleted novel "The Seeker." The incomplete state of the manuscript may serve as a motivation for the intervention of the editor(s).

At the end of *Ada* by Vladimir Nabokov, the text, which may be considered to be the result of the recollections of Van, is characterized as "a regular inferno of alterations in red ink and blue pencil" (Nabokov 1969: 460). Consequently, many of the numerous remarks in brackets, which are scattered all over the text, are presented as editorial comments. A rather complicated variant of the same device can be found in some texts by Svend Aage Madsen. In *The Wandering of Jakkel* (*Jakkels Vandring*, 1974) the fictional editor, who signs with the anagram "Sandme," gives in his preface an account of the story of the manuscript. In its original form it consisted of a series of eye-witness reports on the life and death of the legendary figure Jakkel (the allusion to the New Testament is evident), which the writer Victor Kyrge had started to compile, rewrite and organize into seven chapters about each of the seven stages of Jakkel's life. After the death of Kyrge his friend and colleague Sandme "dissects" and reduces the manuscript, thus obtaining seven autonomous chapters. The number of intermediary stages is still greater in *The Name of the Rose* (*Il nome della rosa*, 1980) by Umberto Eco. The manuscript of Adson of Melk, the first-person narrator, has undergone various transformations (translations, rewritings, interpretations) before it reaches the editor, who provides the Italian version: "My Italian version of an obscure, neo-gothic French version of a seventeenth-century Latin edition of a work written in Latin by a German monk toward the end of the fourteenth century" (Eco 1983: 14).

A device related to editorial intervention is the intervention of commentators. In some cases the editor is likely to be also the author of the commentary. This seems to occur in *The Name of the Rose*, where the preface is followed by an additional note on the division into chapters of the manuscript. The author of the preface as well as the author of the note refer to really existing source mateiial and transgress in that way the borderline between fiction and nonfiction. A particular use of the device of commentary can be found in Nabokov. In *Pale Fire* (1962) the preface, the commentary, and the index, all of them written by the fictional editor Charles Kinbote, cause more confusion than clarity with respect to the poem "Pale Fire" and its author John Shade. In *Pale Fire* the traditional proportion between text and commentary is reversed; the first is superseded by the second. In *Ada* the device is applied in various ways. First there is the "family tree," then there are the comments in brackets — along with the comments by the editor, the additional remarks and corrections by Ada or by the narrator — and finally the philological and linguistic notes by Vivian Darkbloom, a character borrowed from *Lolita* and anagram of Vladimir Nabokov. In Barth's *Sabbatical* the device is applied in the form of very detailed and extensive footnotes. These may be considered the product of the two first-person narrators on the occasion of the definite redaction of their notes, but may also have been added by the "author," to whom the two narrators incidentally entrust the narration.

In the context of the extension of the extradiegetic frame we may pay attention also to the innovation of the traditional novel of recollection, with its extradiegetic and sometimes unreliable first-person narrator. Various Postmodernist novels can be considered to be new versions, either of the pre-modernist (eighteenth- and nineteenth-century) retrospective reconstruction of a life-story, or of the Modernist recovery of the past. In both cases the first-person narrator, traditionally the only or central narrating subject, is split up into various narrative instances. In *Giles Goat-Boy* — a novel which, along with other pre-modernist first-person conventions, picks up the convention of the "perfect memory" — the identity of the narrator is put into question. No narrative instance can be said to be the only one responsible for the text of the "memoirs." The authorship may be shared by various instances: by the first-person narrator, the computer Wescac, the writer J.B., and by Stoker Giles, the son of the "goat-boy," who claims to have proofread and corrected the text read out by the computer. A similar effect is achieved by the reference to the various mediating instances (editors, translators) in the preface of *The Name of the Rose*. Moreover, in both novels the intervention of other instances than the original first-person narrator appears from the third-person form of the long and detailed chapter titles.

The Modernist (Proustian) theme of the recovery of the past finds its late- and Postmodernist versions in novels by Butor and Nabokov: late-modernist in so far as the intellectual activity of memory is emphasized and presented as highly problematical, Postmodernist in so far as also the very existence of the past is put into question. In two novels by Butor, where the late-modernist mode seems to be predominant but where certain Postmodernist forms of writing can also be discerned (we shall return to that point), the project of the first-person narrator is without any succes. In *L'Emploi du temps*, the first-person narrator tries in his diary to reconstruct the chain of events which six months before had led to an attempt on the life of the detective-writer George Burton (here, too, the name of the fictional writer alludes to the name of the real writer). This act, which may be characterized as the effort of a sort of "mémoire volontaire," is interrupted by the interference of other "pasts" — the remote, historical past of the town Bleston and the recent past constituted by the experiences of the narrator during the last six months. At the end of his "year in Bleston," the narrator sees his past as a complex pattern whose various layers or time-levels are comparable to "les doigts d'une main entre ceux de l'autre lorsqu'elles se croisent" (Butor 1957: 293). The complex structure of the past is also compared to that of a labyrinth, which the narrator will perhaps be able to penetrate by means of writing, but where he also risks to lose himself. In *Degrés* (1960), the project of the first-person narrator, which consists of an attempt to recover his relations to members of his own family, to his colleagues and to his pupils, is doomed to fail. At the beginning of the novel, the first-person narrator seems in possession of an incredible omniscience. In his quality of intradiegetic narrator he is confined to a very limited space, his classroom, but in spite of this confinement he is able to make a detailed account of what is going on in other spaces (other classrooms). This paradoxical narrative situation is soon replaced by an extradiegetic one: The first-person narrator realizes that a true account of what is going on *now* (in his classroom during the lesson of geography) requires a detailed account also of what is going on in other spaces and in other times. Gradually the task of the first-person narrator becomes impossible. He recognizes that the information at his disposal is insufficient and that he will have to resort to imagination. Further on in the novel his task is entrusted to other narrators, his nephew and pupil and one of his colleagues.

Two novels by Nabokov can be considered Postmodernist versions of the Modernist (and Proustian) novel of recollection. In *The Real Life of Sebastian Knight* (a novel which was first published in 1941, but which nevertheless presents some Postmodernist characteristics), the first-person narrator tries to reconstruct the life-story of his half-brother. His attempt to recover a "lost" (and perhaps not-existing) past is without any positive result. About the life of his half-brother he knows very little and the documents which he has at his disposal are anything but reliable and bristle with contradictions. Also in *Ada* the "real" life or the "real" past, which is the object of the reconstruction or the act of memory, tends to vanish behind the various — mostly contradictory — versions of it. The recollections seem to have undergone numerous redactions. Besides a possible original version in the first-person (conceivably written by Van in an early stage of his life), we have a third-person redaction (possibly written by Van at a later stage), various comments and corrections added by Van himself, by Ada (possibly transcribed by Van), and finally by the editor. Thus the text of *Ada* consists of various texts, which are superimposed on each other. The definite version can be read as a sort of "palimpsest."

The intra- and hypodiegetic levels

In many of the novels mentioned above, the extension of the extradiegetic frame is accompanied by an expansion of the intra- and hypodiegetic levels toward the center of the narrative. In *Giles Goat-Boy*, the narrative subject is split up, not only into the extradiegetic instances of the author, the editors and the first-person narrator, but also into various intra- and hypodiegetic ones: the first-person character, the intradiegetic narrators of the embedded texts, Harold Bray for instance, the hypodiegetic narrator, Enos Enoch, of the text quoted by Harold Bray, and various hypo-hypodiegetic instances. The whole accumulation of metatexts (texts on texts) and hypodiegetic levels (texts in texts), which takes place on the occasion of Bray's lecture, is described in the following way: " . . . this gloss upon the gloss upon the gloss of Bray's quotation from Enos Enoch's allusion to Xanthippides's remark upon Milo's misdemeanor" (Barth 1966: 452). The complex narrative embedding is also a prominent device in *The Name of the Rose*. The investigation carried out by William of Baskerville is to a large extent based on information supplied by numerous intradiegetic instances, who in their turn refer to other hypodiegetic ones. Almost every chapter includes an embedded text which alludes to or quotes from other texts.

The expansion of the narrative toward its center can be conceived of as a device of self-reflexion, especially in novels where the intradiegetic instance is a fictional writer whose works are quoted and referred to. In *The Real Life of Sebastian Knight*, the fragments quoted from the novels of Sebastian, which may be said to belong to a hypo-hypodiegetic level (cf. Rimmon-Kenan 1983), reflect the quest of V. on the diegetic level. The fragmentary biography of Sebastian, which is the result of V's investigation, constitutes the hypodiegesis. A similar case is presented in *Breakfast of Champions* (1973) by Kurt Vonnegut. The principal character on the level of the diegesis is a science-fiction writer, Kilgore Trout, whose novels are partly quoted, partly summarized by the extradiegetic first-person narrator. The latter, who in his preface presents himself as a writer who is just now writing the novel we are going to read, appears not only in the preface and the epilogue, but also inside the narrative itself. As an intradiegetic "I" he enters into dialogue with Kilgore Trout but acts at the same time as a sort of extradiegetic puppet-master. The novels of Kilgore Trout, which are partly read by the secondary character Dwayne Hoover, fictional reader on the level of the diegesis, reflect not only his own poetics but also that of his "master." The metafictional device of the writer as principal character and the writing-process itself as central theme and action are prominent also in works by Federman, Irving, Sorrentino, Boon, and Calvino. The device is parodied in a self-ironical manner in Barth's "Life-Story." An intradiegetic "he" (C) writes a story about the writer D, who writes a story about G etc. Moreover the story about "he" is written by B(!), an extradiegetic instance, whom "he" later on in the text refers to as his "author."

In *If on a Winter's Night a Traveller* the splitting up of the narrative subject into various extra-, intra- and hypodiegetic instances is carried out quite systematically. The device is in accordance with the poetics of the fictional writer Silas Flannery: "I could have multiplied my I's, assumed other people's selves, enacted the selves most different from me and from another" (Calvino 1982: 143). The realization of this possibility corresponds with Calvino's concept of literature as a process of combination: "I believe that all literature is implicit in language and that literature itself is merely the permutation of a finite set of elements and functions" (Calvino 1975: 81). In *If on a Winter's Night a Traveller* Calvino duplicates and multiplicates the finite set of the traditional narrative instances, the author, the narrator, the character, the narratee, the reader. This leads to the creation of the following narrative instances: the real author (mentioned in the frame-story), the anonymous narrator of the frame-story, the fictional writer Silas Flannery (character in the frame-story and first-person narrator of his own diary), the translator-falsificator (character in the frame-story), the "authors" of the embedded novels (characters mentioned in the frame-story), the first-person narrators of the embedded novels, the narratees of these novels, the fictional reader (the Reader, the Other Reader, the Non-Reader, all of them characters in the frame-story), the narratee of the frame-story and the real reader. This duplicating and multiplying process is comparable to the combinative and self-generating processes which take place in texts by Ollier and Ricardou (cf. Morrissette 1975: 256-257).

An extreme case of systematic and self-generating multiplication is represented by *Days with Diam or the Life at Night* (*Dage med Diam eller Livet om Natten*, 1972) by Svend Aage Madsen. The fictional author, "Sandme," seems to pick up and bring into practice an idea originally lined out by Borges in "The Garden of Forking Paths" ("El jardín de los senderos que se bifurcan," 1941) — the idea that a novel may be constructed as the essentially infinite ramifications of a primary, elementary kernel or generator. In the novel of Madsen, the ramifications represent, along with the splitting up of the action into various fragmentary actions, the gradual and systematic multiplication of the narrative subject. The ramifications follow the conventional scheme of a diagrammatic tree, which replaces also the traditional table of contents. The first chapter S, the title of which may be translated as the name of the fictional author or perhaps as "subject" or "sign," forms the basis of the generating process. This process results in the creation of 63 versions of the same narrating subject, versions which are together conceived of as the "kaleidoscopic image of the possibilities which I (the primary narrator) am feeling in myself" (Madsen 1972: 88, my translation). It is impossible to enter into details about the various subjects and their action. We shall mention only two examples: the action generated from S and Sa, which constitutes the love-story of the novel and which is told by an intradiegetic first-person narrator, and the action generated from

S and St, which represents the metalingual and self-reflexive sections of the novel and which is told by an extradiegetic, "self-conscious" narrator.

The symbol of the "kaleidoscope," along with that of the multiple mirror, appears frequently in the Postmodernist novel, where it may be related to the devices of duplication and multiplication. Here we may think of the numerous mirrors in novels by Nabokov, Robbe-Grillet, Butor (the concave and convex mirrors in *L'Emploi du temps*), the transformation of the mirror into a "leak" in Vonnegut (*Breakfast of Champions*) and the "mirror-maze" in the "funhouse" of Barth. In one of the embedded novels in *If on a Winter's Night a Traveller*, "In a Network of Lines that Intersect" (a title that alludes to Borges but which connotes also the optical effect of a mirror), the central image is that of a "kaleidoscope," where "a finite number of figures are broken up and turned upside down and multiplied" (Calvino 1982: 129). In this fragment the device of multiplication is applied in a self-ironical and parodic manner. The first-person narrator, who has constructed for his own use a room "completely lined with mirrors," multiplies for the sake of his personal security his own person, his bodyguards and his mistresses, but discovers to his horror that his enemy is also multiplying himself. At the end of the fragment he is lost in the trap of mirrors he has set for himself.

The confounding of narrative levels

From what precedes, it appears that in the case of the Postmodernist novel no clear distinction can be made between the various narrative levels. The boundaries between the extradiegetic frame(s) and the intra- and hypodiegesis are in different ways broken down (cf. Waugh 1984: 28-34). In the first section of our paper we have seen how the extradiegetic instances intrude upon the intradiegesis; in what follows we shall concentrate more generally on the instability of the narrative levels, characteristic above all of the Nouveau Roman, and on various ways of "frame-breaking". At the same time the Postmodernist tendency of subverting the hierarchy of narrative levels will be illustrated. It should be emphasized that this instability will be described only in relation to the device of the multiplication of narrative instances. Other issues, such as the *mise en abyme* and the *mise en abyme éclatée* (Ricardou 1967: 187-188), although very interesting in this context, will be passed over.

The instability of the narrative level appears for instance in texts where, on the ground of the addition of new extradiegetic levels, the original extradiegesis is transformed into intradiegesis. Such a process takes place and is explored to a very high degree in *L'Emploi du temps*, a novel which consequently might be conceived of as not only late-modernist but also Postmodernist. As long as the first-person narrator, in his diary of May, June and July, reconstructs the events of October, November and December, the relation between the narrating "I" (extradiegetic) and the narrated "I" (intradiegetic) is rather simple. We are confronted with a quasi-conventional retrospective narrative situation. But when in July, August and September he rereads and rewrites his notes of May, June and July, the situation grows complicated. The narrative instances are now multiplied: first the narrator of the diary of May-July (originally extradiegetic, now intradiegetic), second the narrator as reader of his own diary (intradiegetic), and third the "rewriting" narrator (extradiegetic). This structure becomes still more complicated at the end of the novel. In September the first-person narrator rereads and rewrites (corrects and completes) his notes of August and July *on* his notes in June and May *on* the events of the preceding winter.

Similar displacements of the extra- and intradiegetic levels take place in *Ada*. Every new version of the love-story of Van and Ada implies the addition of a new extradiegetic narrative situation, whereas the original one comes to form part of the intradiegesis. The shift from one narrative level into another, whereby a narrative instance that might first be considered as extradiegetic, turns out to be intradiegetic or vice versa, is particularly frequent in the novels of Robbe-Grillet. In *La Maison de rendez-vous* for instance, the "I," which at the beginning of the novel seems to belong to an anonymous, extradiegetic narrator, may further on in the text be identified with other "I's" — with the different subjectivities of the great number of characters acting on the intra- and hypodiegetic levels. The story, which seems to move on a first, diegetic level, may turn out to move on a second, hypodiegetic level or on a third, hypo-hypodiegetic one. Also in *Drame* by Philippe Sollers, where the multiplication of narrative instances seems based on the grammatical scheme of the personal pronouns — a form of self-generation introduced by Michel Butor (1964: 72) — the boundaries between the narrative levels are transgressed again and again. The "he" of the frame-story acts at the same time as a chess-player and a chess-piece. He is not only the intradiegetic instance of the knight or soldier which has been moved, but also the extradiegetic instance, the hand, which moves the pieces: at the same time "he" and "I," object *and* subject of the same action. Analogous forms of duplication (or rather: multiple duplication) take place on other levels of the text as well, e.g. on the level of the embedded letters and diary notes.

In the first section of our paper we have observed that the multiplication of narrative instances often coincides with the exploration of certain conventions belonging to the early tradition of the novel. We have seen that in the case of the extension of the extra-diegetic frame, the conventions of the novel of recollection and of the "manuscrit trouvé" are of particular importance. In the case of the expansion of the intradiegetic levels, the conventions of the epistolary novel and the diary seem rather prominent. A similar device is the exploration of the structure of the traditional frame-story. Various novels of, for instance, Calvino and Barth represent new and original versions of this genre. In *Invisible Cities* by Calvino, originally published in 1972, the traditional relation between the frame (the conversations between Marco Polo and Kublai Khan) and the embedded stories (the descriptions of the imaginary cities) is maintained. As in the traditional frame-story there is a regular change of narrative level: the extradiegetic narrator, who tells the action or rather the situation of the frame in the third person, entrusts the narrative to the intradiegetic first-person narrator (Marco Polo), whose "stories" are situated on a hypodiegetic level. In Calvino's *The Castle of Crossed Destinies* (Italian edition of 1973), the structure of embedding is more complex. The narrative instances and narrative levels are numerous and the various levels and instances are not set off against each other. The first-person narrator, intradiegetic with respect to his own story which constitutes the frame, retells in the third person and in his own way the stories, which the other guests in the castle try to tell by means of the figures of the tarot cards. Between the original stories and the third-person version offered by the first-person narrator of the frame, various degrees of interpretation are inserted. There is no certainty that the stories we are reading are the same ones as those intended by the original narrators. In *If on a Winter's Night a Traveller* various fragmentary first-person novels are embedded one by one in the story in which the reader is the principal character and which constitutes the frame. In spite of the fact that the poetics of endless subordination — the *regressus ad infinitum* — is formulated by one of the characters in the frame, the text offers no example of such a structure. The various first-person novels are embedded in the frame, not in each other. The procedure is principally that of addition, not of subordination.

A highly spectacular form of experimentation with the model of the classical frame-story is offered by various short-stories of John Barth. In *Lost in the Funhouse*, the first text is entitled "Frame-Tale"; it is an empty form, a "frame" without a "story," or rather with a story which is only the stereotyped beginning of all stories: "Once upon a time there was a story that began . . . ." In this way Barth is parodying an exhausted genre, but is also indicating a possible renovation — the exploration not of the structure of the circle (or concentric circles), which may be applied to the conventional frame-story, but of the structure of the spiral: the movement which takes the reader from the frame to the story and eventually from the story to the frame. The "frame-story" in *Lost in the Funhouse* implies an endless movement: from a first extradiegetic level (the announcement of the story) through a second, intradiegetic level (the story that begins) on to a third hypodiegetic one (a new "once upon a time" and the beginning of a new story). This narrative scheme seems to be materialized in one of the texts of the volume: "Menelaiad." With its numerous narrative levels or "frames", this story represents, on the one hand, the formula of the *regressus ad infinitum*. On the other hand, it subverts the endless hierarchy suggested by such a structure; in place of the "Chinese box system," it offers a "spiral." The story moves from frame to frame — from a first frame (the recollections of Menelaus) to a second, third, fourth and fifth frame (where Menelaus tells the story of his seven-year long sea-journey with Helen, a story which constitutes a sixth frame) and vice-versa.

A similar structure forms the starting-point of the experiments in *Chimera*. Here, too, the narrative levels are numerous. The structure of the narrative embedding is complicated and the shifts from one level to the others are puzzling. Moreover, the structure of the conventional frame-story seems to have been turned inside out. Instead of moving from the frame toward the center, i.e. the embedded stories, the narrative often moves from the center toward the frame. In the traditional frame-story, the frame is presented before the embedded stories. Here the opposite seems to be the case. In "Dunyazadiad," the first short story of the volume, the text begins with what turns out to be the embedded story but what at first sight seemed to be the frame: the story of the "nights" of Scheherezade with the king, Sharyar. The frame of *The 1001 Nights* (which in contrast to its original model remains a frame without stories) is, as it turns out in chapter 2, told by Scheherezade's younger sister Dunyazade during her wedding night with Shah Zaman. This particular narrative situation forms moreover the object of a third-person narrative told by an extradiegetic anonymous narrative instance, which in chapter 3 manifests itself as an extradiegetic personalized narrator. Consequently, the story of Scheherezade is not simply "the story of Scheherezade," but, as stated by the personalized narrator in chapter 3, "the story of the story of her stories." In this way the narrative moves from its hypodiegetic center toward its intra- and extradiegetic frames. In the two following stories, "Perseid" and "Bellerophoniad," this structure is further explored. It is extremely difficult for the reader to decide what is frame and what is story, but analogical movements from center to frame may be discerned. In "Perseid" the frame seems to be the following situation: Perseus tells his life-story to Calyxa. This situation, however, turns out to be embedded in the story which Perseus, petrified and turned into a star, tells to Medusa (star in the same constellation) and to the reader. "Bellerophoniad," which in its turn seems to frame "Perseid" — "a Greek novella called *Perseid* has been found in the marshes near the palace of Bellerophon" (Barth 1972: 137-138) — has essentially the same structure. The two texts are confronted with each other by the "I" of the frame in "Bellerophoniad": "Perseus, while always ultimately addressing the reader from heaven, tells most of his story immediately to his mistress Calyxa in Egypt; Bellerophon, it seems to me, while always ultimately addressing the reader from pages floating in the marshes . . . , used to begin by rehearsing his prior history to pretty Melanippe . . . " (143). Together, "Perseid" and "Bellerophoniad" offer four frames, four different narrative situations, which are embedding each other. With the three frames of "Dunyazadiad" the trilogy *Chimera* reaches the magical number of seven narrative levels. This structure as well as the reversal of the hierarchical relation between frame and story are commented upon in the following passage: "seven concentric stories within stories, so arranged that the climax of the innermost would precipitate that of the next tale out, and that of the next, et cetera . . . " (24).

The device of multiplication can, as we have indicated in the opening remarks of this paper, be related to the general Postmodernist features of "fragmentation", "discontinuity" and "nonselection." The narrating subject, which was prominent in most Modernist novels, has been split up into a number of quasi-equivalent narrative instances. On the level of narrative discourse the novel is "decentered" as well. There are interesting relations between the devices dealt with and some other Postmodernist features. For instance, the introduction of "authors", "editors," and "readers" points to the obliteration of the limit between fiction and nonfiction. The same may be said about the essentially "endless" addition of new intra- and hypodiegetic levels. The insertion of new fictional worlds into a first fictional world will always make the status of the latter questionable. The various processes of "frame-breaking" may be related to the general feature of "nonhierarchy": the traditional hierarchical structure, manifested in the relation between the various narrative levels and profiled in the narratological model of Genette, is partly or entirely subverted. Finally, the multiplication of narrative instances contributes to the self-reflexive character of most Postmodernist fiction. Every narrative instance may pronounce a metalingual comment on its own activity or on the activity of other instances. In most Postmodernist texts this procedure is extended to the relation of the text to other texts: the novel then presents itself as a network of intra- and intertextual cross-references.

REFERENCES

Bal, Mieke. 1977. *Narratologie : Les Instances du récit*. Paris: Klincksieck.
Barth, John. 1966. *Giles Goat-Boy*. New York and London: Bantam, 1981.
-----. 1968. *Lost in the Funhouse*. New York: Doubleday.
-----. 1972. *Chimera*. New York: Random House.
-----. 1980. "The Literature of Replenishment: Postmodernist Fiction," *Atlantic Monthly* 245, 1: 65-71.
-----. 1982. *Sabbatical*. New York: Putnam's Sons.
Boon, Louis Paul. 1972. *Chapel Road*. Boston: Twayne. Translation of *De Kapellekensbaan*, 1953.
Butor, Michel. 1957. *L'Emploi du temps*. Paris:Minuit.
-----. 1960. *Degrés*. Paris: Gallimard.
-----. 1964. *Répertoire II: Etudes et conférences 1959-1963*. Paris: Minuit.
Calvino, Italo. 1975. "Myth in the Narrative," in Federman 1975: 75-81.
-----. 1976. *The Castle of Crossed Destinies*, trans. William Weaver. New York: Harcourt. Translation of *Il castello dei destini incrociati*, 1973.
-----. 1979. *Invisible Cities*, trans. William Weaver. New York: Harcourt. Translation of *Le città invisibili*, 1972.
-----. 1982. *If on a Winter's Night a Traveller*, trans. William Weaver. New

York: Harcourt. Translation of *Se una notte d'inverno un viaggatore*, 1979.

Eco, Umberto. 1983. *The Name of the Rose*. New York: Harcourt. Translation of *Il nome della rosa*, 1980.

Federman, Raymond, ed. 1975. *Surfiction: Fiction Now... And Tomorrow*. Chicago: Swallow Press.

Fokkema, Douwe W. 1984. *Literary History, Modernism, and Postmodernism*. Amsterdam: Benjamins.

-----. 1986. "The Semantic and Syntactical Organization of Postmodernist Texts," in Fokkema and Bertens 1986: 81-98.

Fokkema, Douwe and Hans Bertens, eds. 1986. *Approaching Postmodernism*. Amsterdam and Philadelphia: Benjamins.

Genette, Gérard. 1972. *Figures III*. Paris: Seuil.

Haasse, Hella. 1976. *Een gevaarlijke verhouding of Daal-en-Bergse brieven*. Amsterdam: Querido.

Madsen, Svend Aage. 1972. *Dage med Diam eller Livet om Natten*. København: Gyldendal.

-----. 1974. *Jakkels Vandring*. København: Gyldendal.

Morrissette, Bruce. 1975. "Post-Modern Generative Fiction," *Critical Inquiry* 2: 253-262.

Nabokov, Vladimir. 1941. *The Real Life of Sebastian Knight*. Harmondsworth: Penguin, 1982.

-----. 1962. *Pale Fire*. Harmondsworth: Penguin, 1981.

-----. 1969. *Ada*. Harmondsworth: Penguin, 1980.

Queneau, Raymond. 1962. *Les Oeuvres complètes de Sally Mara*. Paris: Gallimard.

Ricardou, Jean. 1967. *Problèmes du nouveau roman*. Paris: Seuil.

Rimmon-Kenan, Shlomith. 1983. *Narrative Fiction: Contemporary Poetics*. London: Methuen.

Robbe-Grillet, Alain. 1965. *La Maison de rendez-vous*. Paris: Seuil.

Sollers, Philippe. 1965. *Drame*. Paris: Seuil.

Vonnegut, Kurt. 1973. *Breakfast of Champions*. London: Jonathan Cape.

Waugh, Patricia. 1984. *Metafiction: The Theory and Practice of Self-conscious Fiction*. London: Methuen.

Concluding Observations:
Is There a Future for Research on Postmodernism?

Douwe Fokkema

The preceding papers aim to bring us one step closer to the collective effort of describing and — as far as possible — explaining Postmodernism as a literary current or code, as a world view, and more generally as a cultural phenomenon. The ultimate result will be a volume *Postmodernism* as part of the *Comparative History of Literature in European Languages*, sponsored by the International Comparative Literature Association. Most of the papers in this volume, as well as in its companion, *Approaching Postmodernism* (Fokkema and Bertens 1986), deal with literary texts. Breon Mitchell, however, raised the problem of terminology, Mihai Spariosu dealt with the loss of allegorical significance, and Stefano Rosso expanded the field to include philosophical discussions. In the exploration of Postmodernism a restriction to problems of literature is hardly possible. Hans Bertens and Alfred Hornung, in their respective contributions, cannot avoid showing us the abyss into which character and self tend to disappear. The fiction of literature evaporates but may come back as a construction of language, accepted as literature, or, as Marjorie Perloff explained, as "Language Poetry."

One of the questions that further must be explored is to what extent language constructions are experienced as being real. August Fry, who during the workshop offered a paper on Canadian literature (not printed here), quoted Robert Kroetsch as having said: "In a sense we haven't got an identity until someone tells our story. The fiction makes us real" (cf. Heath 1980: 71). This is a view we consider pre-eminently Postmodernist; but it is not exclusively Postmodernist. The small town of Illiers, not far from Chartres, France, would have escaped attention from the world — at least the world of letters — if it had not added Combray to its original name; the sign "Illiers-Combray" at the boundaries of the town proudly acknowledges

Proust's fiction. The view that "the fiction makes us real" — which in Kroetsch's case hints not only at an existential lack of authenticity but also at the national vacuum that Canada until recently was — seems to have the positive connotation which the *métarécits* in Lyotard's analysis of the Postmodern condition have lost. Apparently Lyotard's differentiation between great and small, between "métarécits" and "petits récits" (1979: 98) is not one of size but of authenticity. The notion of authenticity is also very much at issue in Ihab Hassan's unorthodox — post-Postmodernist? — contribution to this volume.

One of the paradoxes of Postmodernism is that it combines emphasizing the reality of language games and scorning the language games if they are taken for reality. The crux of the matter lies in the concept of reality, of course; and I fear that the problem was not solved during our symposium; or worse, I do not think we had the instruments to discuss the problem of reality properly.

Postmodernism, as I argued elsewhere, is linked to a particular way and view of life, common in the Western world and increasingly common in the affluent societies of East Asia and Latin America (Fokkema 1984: 55). The Postmodernist preference for nonselection as a principle of text production coincides with an *embarras du choix* originating in favorable material conditions and seemingly unlimited technological potentialities. Secularization and demythologization cleared the way for any justification of action and any selection of register or style, but it is the condition of relative wealth which enabled authors to produce their Postmodernist artifacts for a public ready to swallow them. Is it indeed true that Postmodernism has its geographical and sociological boundaries? And is it incompatible with religious fundamentalism and ideological dogmatism? Let us assume it is; a definite answer can only be given when the sociology of Postmodernism — or more accurately, of the writers, distributors and readers of Postmodernism — has been written.

Postmodernism, it is often argued, contradicts political commitment. As a result — as Matei Calinescu has shown in his "Introductory Remarks" — politically committed critics are ambivalent vis-à-vis Postmodernism. Marxist and leftist critics will welcome it as long as it serves to undermine the *métarécit* of capitalism or of justice in the Western world; but as soon as Postmodernism challenges their own myth of exploitation and suppression, it must be curtailed or, at least, be relegated to the realm of ineffective playfulness. In their attitude towards Postmodernism, the East-European

authorities seem to hesitate between official strictures and repressive tolerance. We are, however, only marginally informed about the intrusions of
Postmodernism into the non-affluent societies of the socialist world. Would
perhaps Postmodernism have a chance in those East-European countries
where the ideological strictures are the least obtrusive (Hungary), or the
material conditions relatively better (GDR)? Flaker (1975) discussed the
work of Plenzdorf, Szegedy-Maszák (1984) that of Esterházy, but the field
has only tentatively been covered.

The question of whether it is Postmodernism or the (neo-)Avant-garde
that performs a critical function in Poland and the USSR has not yet been
exhaustively treated either. In her essay on "Postmodernism in Russian
Drama," Herta Schmid choose the vantage point of Postmodernism (Fokkema and Bertens 1986: 157-185), but I wonder whether her argument
would have been less persuasive if she had used the term "avant-garde"
instead. We are also in doubt about what terms and concepts would be most
suitable for discussing contemporary trends in Polish literature. In a very
fine contribution to our symposium (not printed here) Olga Scherer
suggested to examine Polish literature in terms of surrealism and sub-
realism.

In general, the relation between Postmodernism and Avant-garde
must be clarified, not only for the technical reason of demarcating our field
of investigation from that of *Les Avant-gardes littéraires au XXe siècle*, published as part of the *Comparative History of Literature in European Languages* (Weisgerber 1984), but also because the distinction between Postmodernism and Avant-garde bears upon the relation between Postmodernism and Modernism.

Weisgerber (1984: 72) sees the Avant-garde as "un aspect particulier
— la pointe — de la modernité." According to Calinescu the Avant-garde
is one of the faces of modernity, or, in his own words:

> if we want to operate consistently with the concept of modernism (and
> apply it to such writers as those mentioned above [i.e. Proust, Joyce,
> Kafka, Thomas Mann, T.S. Eliot, or Ezra Pound]), it is necessary to dis-
> tinguish between modernism and the avant-garde (old and new). It is true
> that modernity defined as a "tradition against itself" rendered possible the
> avant-garde, but it is equally true that the latter's negative radicalism and
> systematic antiaestheticism leave no room for the artistic reconstruction of
> the world attempted by the great modernists (Calinescu 1977: 140-141).

Commenting on the German situation which offers a slightly different terminology, Helga Geyer-Ryan and Helmut Lethen speak of two groupings within "die Moderne," the Avant-gardists and the Modernists, who in the period between about 1910 and World War II were primarily separated by their attitude towards the past. The Avant-gardists emphasized the notion of forgetting, the Modernists tried to recover or assimilate the past by way of their experiments with memory and their intellectual analysis of repetition. Or in their own words:

> Beide Fraktionen der Moderne, die Avantgardisten und die Modernisten, entwickelten in der Zeit des Interbellums eine Frontstellung, in der das Handlungskonzept des Vergessens dem Konzept des Erinnerns konfrontiert wurde, das Konzept des radikalen Bruchs mit der Konvention dem der analytischen Wiederholung (Geyer-Ryan and Lethen 1986: 40).

The opposition of (Avant-gardist) forgetting/(Modernist) remembering coïncides with the dichotomies of action/analysis, commitment/detachment, rupture/qualification, progressiveness/awareness of the moment, dependence on *métarécits*/intellectual doubt. These distinctions were highly relevant in European and American literature until the 1960s, when they gradually lost their sharpness and were finally undone by the Postmodernist tendency to cancel all hierarchical distinctions in favor of "something new."

Instead of the last two words, I could have written a question mark, as we are not certain of any specific aims or motivations of the Postmodernists. Perhaps this is their great attraction. They have managed to create a void, a blank page, and all people sympathizing with their efforts to create conditions for "something new" are inclined to keep that void empty and that page blank as long as possible, so that we can relish the tension of things that are to come, enjoying our own curiosity and awareness.

In modern aesthetics (since Russian Formalism) "curiosity and awareness" are considered components of the aesthetic experience. They are also the major values of John Cage (cf. Szegedy-Maszák 1984: 151) and other Postmodernists, who may be driven by the hope to create a multitude of options in a world that has been hedged in by the clichés of bureaucracy and social supervision. The primary motive of the Postmodernists, I would venture, is an aesthetic one: an attempt to create ways for an individual experience of independence — from where a reinterpretation of so-called reality can be undertaken, a reinterpretation that avoids fixation and tends to remain permanently ambiguous. (Even the "new" is ambiguous and may consist of *re*-writing, the "recycling of semantic waste" [trans. from Strauss 1977: 85].) The Postmodernist preference for undecidedness may explain the paradox of emphasizing the function of language games and suspecting their function at the same time — the paradox of Barthelme's *Snow White*, which reveals the clichés of our daily life by the very act of using them. I presume that Marjorie Perloff is right in suggesting that the Postmodernists are motivated by the pleasure of writing and reading, and that, in fact, there is an aesthetic impetus behind most of their work, in spite of the smoke-screens aiming to conceal this. Yet, the matter must be further investigated. Do the Postmodernists indeed attempt to create conditions favorable to an aesthetic reception of their work?

So far, I have pointed to the problem of language and reality, which is also the problem of referentiality and fictionality; the problem of the sociology of Postmodernism, its social and geographical boundaries; the problem of the incompatibility of political commitment and the Postmodernist preference for ambiguity, or, more specifically, the occurrence of Postmodernist writing in Eastern Europe; the problem of the relation between the Avant-garde (old and new) and Postmodernism; and the problem of the aesthetic impetus in Postmodernism. All these problems await to be solved, and as long as they imply concrete questions, there is a future for research with regard to Postmodernism.

The solution or tentative solution of these problems very much depends on our epistemological point of departure and methodological instruments. Epistemological issues were discussed in Calinescu's introduction, taking its cue from Oakeshott's conviction that history is nothing but construction and leading up to the idea that the concept of Postmodernism is not fixed and can undergo any number of changes. This epistemological stance, inspired by a Nietzschean concept of facts, is not necessarily that of the other authors of this volume, who move freely between the poles of reconstruction and construction — between the approximation to truth and a "viable" instrumentalism (Von Glasersfeld 1985), between validity based on a correspondence with reality and validity derived from a consensus among informed researchers (Rescher 1973).

This is not the place to settle the issue of the construction vs. reconstruction of history. Perhaps in one context construction of a historical connection is appropriate, whereas in another context an attempt at reconstruction should be made. Like Symbolism or Modernism, the concept of Postmodernism was a construction of scholarly minds before it became common knowledge and, as such, a social fact that one may attempt to reconstruct. The crucial question with respect to constructivism is its relation to experiential data. Some constructivists allow the anomalous experience to unsettle their constructions and, in this way, open themselves up to empirical reality — reality as it is experienced (Von Glasersfeld 1985: 23).

We need empirical research for being able to judge the merits of the various constructions of Postmodernism. As both Eibl (1976: 12) and Schmidt (1985: 125) have argued, however, precision in our observations largely depends on the way our perception is guided by theories. The study of literature seems to abound in theories, but they usually remain implicit and often resemble rather convictions, vague beliefs, or poetical concepts. In order to make the results of our work debatable and in principle suscep- tible to criticism it is necessary to present the theories guiding our observa- tions explicitly and more straightforwardly. My investigation of Postmod- ernist literature, as published in Fokkema and Bertens (1986), has been guided by the theory that literary history is structured by a succession of lit- erary systems, which can be differentiated according to the various semiotic communities participating in the production and reception of literature. The theory of the succession of literary systems explains the recurrent inno- vation of semiotic means in the production of literary texts, and more par- ticularly the difference between Postmodernism and preceding currents, such as Modernism and the historical Avant-garde.

Leaving the Avant-garde aside for a while, we may hypothetically con- struct an opposition between Postmodernism and Modernism, which entails the question of whether the Postmodernists themselves, too, saw that opposition and referred to it. The problem needs further exploration, for, like Quinones (1985: 254), one may not be convinced that in a general and substantial way the Postmodernists directed themselves polemically against Modernism and one may believe that their attack on the devices and con- cepts of Realism is much more visible. During our earlier workshop in Utrecht the problem was discussed with reference to the relation between the (Postmodernist) *nouveau roman* and Balzacian realism (Fokkema and Bertens 1986: 263, 266, 268), but not resolved. Nevertheless, there are at least some instances of Postmodernists being explicitly critical of Modern- ism. In this volume Mihai Spariosu has a quotation from Nabokov that seems to be critical not only of Flaubert but also of Joyce (the passage, however, is ironic and ambiguous). In his *Travesties* (1975), Tom Stoppard — whom I would consider a Postmodernist writer — provides a caricature of Joyce. However, the direct criticism of Proust and Gide, Mann and Musil, Virginia Woolf, Joyce and Faulkner has remained scarce.

If the Postmodernists were indeed not very much inclined to subject their immediate prodecessors to outspoken criticism, this can be explained by their rejecting the linear view of time maintained by both Modernism and the historical Avant-garde. They prefer "to conceive the totality of human experience on a simultaneous plane," as Harry Levin (1960: 165) wrote in a characterization of *Finnegans Wake*. The Postmodernist conception of past and present constituting one simultaneous experience may explain the opposition to all preceding currents espousing a linear view of time. In this perspective, the appearance of Postmodernism is not an exception to the rule of the succession of literary systems — the gradual familiarization of a current literary system and its replacement by a new one — but its polemical stance directs itself in principle to *all* preceding currents, especially those with a strong linear view of time. Since Proust, Mann and Joyce (already in *A Portrait of the Artist as a Young Man*) initiated the criticism of the linear concept of time as propounded by Realism and admitted a considerable degree of relativism in their own view of chronology, the Postmodernists prefer to attack the Realist rather than the Modernist concept of time. As a corollary, the Postmodernists tend to seek support in certain tenets of Romanticism (cf. Bertens 1986: 18), but the precise claims of this ancestry have hardly been examined.

If the Postmodernists were critical of the Modernists, they showed it less obtrusively than by mentioning their names in a pejorative context. Their sophisticated reshaping of certain genres such as the detective novel, the Western, and the autobiographical novel, or of characterization and other narrative devices, evidently refer not only to Realist but also to Modernist models, as appears from the various contributions in the section "analytical criticism" of this volume. The tentative answers presented here certainly need further corroboration, and many problems were not treated at all. By having singled out some questions for further exploration I hope to have shown that in the field of Postmodernism much work still needs to be done.

REFERENCES

Bertens, Hans. 1986. "The Postmodern *Weltanschauung*," in Fokkema and Bertens 1986: 9-51.
Calinescu, Matei. 1977. *Faces of Modernity: Avant-garde, Decadence, Kitsch*. Bloomington: Indiana University Press.

D'haen, Theo, Rainer Grübel and Helmut Lethen, eds. 1987. *Convention and Innovation in Literature*. Amsterdam and Philadelphia: Benjamins (forthcoming).

Eibl, Karl. 1976. *Kritisch-rationale Literaturwissenschaft: Grundlagen zur erklärenden Literaturgeschichte*. Munich: Fink.

Einführung in den Konstruktivismus. 1985. Munich: Oldenbourg.

Flaker, Aleksandar. 1975. *Modelle der Jeans Prosa: Zur literarischen Opposition bei Plenzdorf im osteuropäischen Romankontext*. Kronberg/Ts.: Scriptor Verlag.

Fokkema, Douwe W. 1984. *Literary History, Modernism, and Postmodernism*. Amsterdam and Philadelphia: Benjamins.

Fokkema, Douwe and Hans Bertens, eds. 1986. *Approaching Postmodernism: Papers Presented at a Workshop on Postmodernism, 21-23 September 1984, University of Utrecht*. Amsterdam and Philadelphia: Benjamins.

Geyer-Ryan, Helga and Helmut Lethen. 1986. "Die Rhetorik des Vergessens: Ein Aspekt der historischen Avantgarde und das Beispiel Brecht," *Tilburg Papers in Language and Literature*, no. 95. English version in D'haen, Grübel and Lethen 1987.

Heath, Jeffery M. 1980. *Profiles in Canadian Literature 2*. Toronto: Dunburn Press.

Levin, Harry. 1960. *James Joyce: A Critical Introduction* (London: Faber and Faber, 2nd ed.).

Lyotard, Jean-François. 1979. *La Condition postmoderne: Rapport sur le savoir*. Paris: Minuit.

Quinones, Ricardo J. 1985. *Mapping Literary Modernism: Time and Development*. Princeton: Princeton University Press.

Rescher, Nicholas. 1973. *The Coherence Theory of Truth*. Oxford: Clarendon Press.

Schmidt, Siegfried J. 1985. "Vom Text zum Literatursystem: Skizze einer konstruktivistischen (empirischen) Literaturwissenschaft," in *Einführung in den Konstruktivismus* 1985: 117-133.

Stoppard, Tom. 1975. *Travesties*. London and Boston: Faber and Faber.

Strauss, Botho. 1977. *Die Widmung: Eine Erzählung*. Munich and Vienna: Hanser.

Szegedy-Maszák, Mihály. 1984. "Postmodernism in Hungarian Literature: Péter Esterházy's 'Agnes'," *Zeitschrift für Kulturaustausch* 34: 150-156.

Von Glasersfeld, Ernst. 1985. "Konstruktion der Wirklichkeit und des Begriffs der Objektivität," in *Einführung in den Konstruktivismus* 1985: 1-26.

Weisgerber, Jean, ed. 1984. *Les Avant-gardes littéraires au XXe siècle.* 2 vols. Budapest: Akadémiai Kiadó.

Notes on the Contributors

Hans Bertens is Professor of American Literature, University of Utrecht. His books are *The Fiction of Paul Bowles* (1979) and *Geschiedenis van de Amerikaanse literatuur* (1983), written in collaboration with Theo D'haen. Together with Douwe Fokkema, he edited *Approaching Postmodernism* (1986), a volume of papers presented at a workshop on Postmodernism in Utrecht. A book on Postmodernism in its international literary context, in collaboration with Theo D'haen, is forthcoming.

Matei Calinescu is Professor of Comparative Literature and West European Studies at Indiana University, Bloomington. The second edition of his *Faces of Modernity* (1977) has just been published by Duke University Press under the title *Five Faces of Modernity: Modernism, Avant-Garde, Decadence, Kitsch, Postmodernism* (1987).

Theo D'haen is Professor of English and American Literature, University of Leiden. He wrote *Text to Reader: A Communicative Approach to Fowles, Barth, Cortázar, and Boon* (1983) and, together with Hans Bertens, *Geschiedenis van de Amerikaanse literatuur* (1983). He is editor of *Linguistics and the Study of Literature* (1986). Together with A.J. Fry he edited *Commonwealth Literature* (1986) and, in collaboration with Rainer Grübel and Helmut Lethen, *Convention and Innovation in Literature* (1987).

Douwe Fokkema is Professor of Comparative Literature and Director of the Research Institute for History and Culture, University of Utrecht. His recent books are *Theories of Literature in the Twentieth Century* (1977, 1986) and *Modernist Conjectures: A Mainstream in European Literature, 1910-1940* (1987), both written in collaboration with Elrud Ibsch. He also wrote *Literary History, Modernism, and Postmodernism* (1984) and co-edited *Approaching Postmodernism* (1986), with Hans Bertens.

Ihab Hassan is Vilas Research Professor of English and Comparative Literature at the University of Wisconsin, Milwaukee. His books include *Radical Innocence* (1961), *The Dismemberment of Orpheus* (1971, 1982), *Paracriticisms* (1975), and recently *Out of Egypt* (1986) and *The Postmodern Turn* (1987).

Alfred Hornung is Associate Professor of English and American Studies, University of Würzburg. His major publications are: *Narrative Struktur und Textsortendifferenzierung: Die Texte des Muckraking Movement, 1902-1912* (1978) and *Kulturkrise und ihre literarische Bewältigung: Die Funktion der autobiographischen Struktur in Amerika vom Puritanismus zur Postmoderne* (forthcoming). He is assistant editor of *Amerikastudien/American Studies* since 1981.

Breon Mitchell is Professor of Comparative Literature and Germanic Studies at Indiana University. He is the author of *James Joyce and the German Novel* and has recently edited both Ezra Pound's translation of Paul Morand's *Fancy Goods/Open All Night* and the correspondence between Pound and George Bernard Shaw on *Ulysses*.

Ulla Musarra is Associate Professor in the Department of General and Comparative Literature, University of Nijmegen. Her books are *Le Roman-mémoires moderne: Pour une typologie du récit à la première personne* (1981) and *Narcissus en zijn spiegelbeeld: Het moderne ik-verhaal* (1983). A revised and expanded Italian version of the latter will shortly be published by Bulzoni, Rome.

Marjorie Perloff's books include *Frank O'Hara: Poet Among Painters* (1977), *The Poetics of Indeterminacy: Rimbaud to Cage* (1981), *The Dance of the Intellect: Studies in the Poetry of the Pound Tradition* (1985), and *The Futurist Moment: Avant-Garde, Avant Guerre, and the Language of Rupture* (1986). She is Professor of English and Comparative Literature at Stanford University.

Stefano Rosso teaches English literature at the University of Verona and is writing a Ph.D. dissertation in comparative literature at SUNY-Binghamton. He writes for *Alfabeta*. Among other works, he has co-edited, with Maurizio Ferraris, *Decostruzione tra filosofia e letteratura* (special issue of

Nuova Corrente, 1984) and *Estetica e decostruzione* (special issue of *Rivista di Estetica*, 1984).

Olav Severijnen is research assistant at the University of Nijmegen and is writing a Ph.D. dissertation in comparative literature.

Mihai Spariosu is Associate Professor of Comparative Literature, University of Georgia, Athens, Ga. He is editor of *Mimesis in Contemporary Theory* (1984) and has written *Literature, Mimesis and Play* (1982), *Returns of the Repressed: The Play of Modern Philosophical and Scientific Discourse* (forthcoming) and *Masks of Dionysus: Play, Imitation, and Power in Ancient Greece* (forthcoming).

Mihály Szegedy-Maszák is Associate Professor of Cultural History at Eötvös University, Budapest. In 1984 and again in 1987 he was Visiting Professor at Indiana University. He is the author of three books in Hungarian: *Világkép és stílus* (Studies in Historical Poetics, 1980), *A regény, amint irja önmagát* (Narratology, 1980), and *Kubla kán és Pickwick úr* (Romanticism and Realism in English Literature, 1982), as well as a number of essays, some of which have been published in France, Holland, Germany, and the United States. His main fields are narratology and English, American, French, and Hungarian literature in the 19th and 20th centuries.

Richard Todd is Associate Professor in the Department of English Language and Literature at the Free University, Amsterdam. He is author of *Iris Murdoch: The Shakespearian Interest* (1979) and *Iris Murdoch* (1984), and of articles on various aspects of contemporary British fiction. His *The Opacity of Signs: Acts of Interpretation in George Herbert's 'The Temple'* appeared in 1986.

References
(master list of secondary sources only)

Alter, Robert. 1975. "The Self-conscious Moment: Reflections on the Aftermath of Modernism," *Triquarterly* 33: 209-230.

Anderson, Perry. 1985. "Capitalism, Modernism and Postmodernism," *New Left Review* 152: 60-73.

Andrews, Bruce and Charles Bernstein. 1984. *The L=A=N=G=U=A=G=E Book.* Carbondale and Edwardsville: Southern Illinois University Press.

Bacon, Francis. 1904. *The Physical and Metaphysical Works*, ed. John Devey. London: George Bell and Sons.

Bakhtin, M.M. 1968. *Rabelais and His World*, trans. Helena Iswolsky. Cambridge, Ma.: MIT Press.

-----. 1981. *The Dialogic Imagination: Four Essays by M.M. Bakhtin*, ed. Michael Holquist, trans. Caryl Emerson and Michael Holquist. University of Texas Press Slavic Series, no. 1. Austin: University of Texas Press.

Bal, Mieke. 1977. *Narratologie : Les Instances du récit*. Paris: Klincksieck.

Barth, John. 1967. "The Literature of Exhaustion," reprinted in Bradbury 1977: 70-83.

-----. 1980. "The Literature of Replenishment: Postmodernist Fiction," *Atlantic Monthly* 245, 1: 65-71.

-----. 1984. *The Friday Book: Essays and Other Nonfiction*. New York: Putnam.

Barthes, Roland. 1953. *Le Degré zéro de l'écriture*. Paris: Seuil.

-----. 1957. *Mythologies*. Paris: Seuil.

-----. 1973. *Le Plaisir du texte*. Paris: Seuil.

-----. 1975. *The Pleasure of the Text*, trans. Richard Miller. New York: Hill and Wang. Translation of *Le Plaisir du texte*, 1973.

-----. 1975a. *Roland Barthes par Roland Barthes*. Paris: Seuil.

-----. 1975b. "Barthes puissance trois," *Le Quinzaine littéraire* 205: 3-5.

-----. 1977. *Fragments d'un discours amoureux*. Collection Tel Quel. Paris:

Seuil.
-----. 1978. *Leçon*. Paris: Seuil.
-----. 1979. *Sollers écrivain*. Paris: Seuil.
-----. 1981. *Le Grain de la voix: Entretiens 1962-1980*. Paris: Seuil.
Baudelaire, Charles. 1971. *Ecrits sur l'art*. Paris: Livre de poche.
Baudrillard, Jean. 1979. *De la séduction*. Paris: Galilée.
-----. 1983a. "The Ecstacy of Communication," in Foster 1983: 126-134.
-----. 1983b. "What Are You Doing After the Orgy?" *Artforum* (October): 42-46.
Bayley, John. 1985. "Being Two is Half the Fun," *London Review of Books* (7/12), 4 July: 13.
Bealer, George. 1982. *Quality and Concept*. Oxford: Clarendon Press.
Beckett, Samuel. 1937. Letter to Axel Kaun, in Cohn 1984: 51-54, trans. Martin Esslin: 170-173.
Bell, Daniel. 1976. *The Cultural Contradictions of Capitalism*. New York: Basic Books.
Bellamy, J.D. 1972. "'Algebra and Fire': An Interview with John Barth," *Falcon* 4: 5-15.
Bernstein, Charles. 1981. "Reading Cavell Reading Wittgenstein," *Boundary 2*, 9: 295-306. Excerpted in Andrews and Bernstein 1984: 60-62.
-----. 1982. "Language Sampler," *Paris Review* 86: 75-125.
Bersani, Leo. 1976. *A Future for Astyanax: Character and Desire in Literature*. Boston: Little, Brown and Co.
Bertens, Hans. 1986. "The Postmodern *Weltanschauung*," in Fokkema and Bertens 1986: 9-51.
Bleich, David. 1983. "Literary Theory in the University: A Survey," *New Literary History* 14: 411-413.
Blonsky, Marshall, ed. 1985. *On Signs*. Baltimore: Johns Hopkins University Press.
Bobbio, Norberto *et al.* 1982. *La cultura filosofica italiana dal 1945 al 1980*. Napoli: Guida.
Booth, Wayne C. 1979. *Critical Understanding: The Powers and Limits of Pluralism*. Chicago: University of Chicago Press.
-----. 1983. "The Empire of Irony," *Georgia Review* 37: 719-737.
Bottiroli, Giovanni. 1984. "Il pensiero metonimico," *Carte semiotiche* 0: 101-114.
Bradbury, Malcolm, ed. 1977. *The Novel Today: Contemporary Writers on Modern Fiction*. Glasgow: Fontana.

-----. 1983. "Modernisms/Postmodernisms," in Hassan and Hassan 1983: 311-328.

Brée, Germaine. 1978. *Narcissus Absconditus: The Problematic Art of Autobiography in Contemporary France*. Oxford: Clarendon Press.

Brinker, Menachem. 1983. "On Realism's Relativism: A Reply to Nelson Goodman," *New Literary History* 14: 273-276.

Bruss, Elisabeth W. 1976. *Autobiographical Acts: The Changing Situation of a Literary Genre*. Baltimore: Johns Hopkins University Press.

Burke, Kenneth. 1945. *A Grammar of Motives*. New York: Prentice Hall.

Butler, Christopher. 1980. *After the Wake: An Essay on the Contemporary Avant-Garde*. Oxford: Oxford University Press.

Butor, Michel. 1964. *Répertoire II: Etudes et conférences 1959-1963*. Paris: Minuit.

Calinescu, Matei. 1977. *Faces of Modernity: Avant-garde, Decadence, Kitsch*. Bloomington: Indiana University Press.

-----. 1979. "Marxism as a Work of Art: Poststructuralist Readings of Marx," *Stanford French Review* 3, 1: 123-135.

-----. 1983. "From the One to the Many: Pluralism in Today's Thought," in Hassan and Hassan 1983: 263-288.

Calvino, Italo. 1975. "Myth in the Narrative," in Federman 1975: 75-81.

Caramello, Charles. 1983. *Silverless Mirrors: Book, Self and Postmodern American Fiction*. Tallahassee: University Presses of Florida.

Carchia, Gianni. 1982. *La legittimazione dell'arte*. Napoli: Guida.

Cawelti, John G. 1976. *Adventure, Mystery, and Romance: Formula Stories as Art and Popular Culture*. Chicago and London: University of Chicago Press.

Cohen, Ralph. 1975. "Literary Theory as Genre," *Centrum* 3, no. 1: 45-64.

-----. 1983. "A Propaedeutic for Literary Change," *Critical Exchange* 13: 1-17.

Cohn, Ruby. 1984. *Disjecta: Miscellaneous Writings and a Dramatic Fragment by Samuel Beckett*. New York: Grove Press.

Culler, Jonathan. 1981. "Convention and Meaning: Derrida and Austin," *New Literary History* 13: 15-30.

De Laurentis, Teresa. 1981. *Umberto Eco*. Firenze: La Nuova Italia.

Deleuze, Gilles and Félix Guattari. 1977. *The Anti-Oedipus: Capitalism and Schizophrenia*. New York: Viking Press. Translation of *L'Anti-*

Oedipe, 1972.

De Man, Paul. 1971. *Blindness and Insight: Essays in the Rhetoric of Contemporary Criticism*. New York: Oxford University Press.

-----. 1979. *Allegories of Reading: Figural Language in Rousseau, Nietzsche, Rilke and Proust*. New Haven: Yale University Press.

Derrida, Jacques. 1967. *L'Ecriture et la différence*. Paris: Seuil.

-----. 1980. "La Loi du genre / The Law of Genre," *Glyph* 7: 176-201/202-232.

D'haen, Theo. 1983. *Text to Reader: A Communicative Approach to Fowles, Barth, Cortázar and Boon*. Amsterdam and Philadelphia: Benjamins.

-----. 1986a. "Postmodernism in American Fiction and Art," in Fokkema and Bertens 1986: 211-231.

-----, ed. 1986b. *Linguistics and the Study of Literature*. Amsterdam: Rodopi.

D'haen, Theo, Rainer Grübel and Helmut Lethen, eds. 1987. *Convention and Innovation in Literature*. Amsterdam and Philadelphia: Benjamins (forthcoming).

Dittmar, Jens. 1981. *Thomas Bernhard Werkgeschichte*. Frankfurt: Suhrkamp.

Docherty, Thomas. 1983. *Reading (Absent) Character: Towards a Theory of Characterization in Fiction*. Oxford: Clarendon Press.

Dreyfus, Hubert L. and Paul Rabinow, eds. 1982. *Michel Foucault: Beyond Structuralism and Hermeneutics*. With an Afterword and an Interview with Michel Foucault. Chicago: University of Chicago Press.

Durand, Régis. 1983. "Theatre / SIGNS / Performance," in Hassan and Hassan: 211-224.

Durzak, Manfred. 1982. *Peter Handke und die deutsche Gegenwartsliteratur: Narziss auf Abwegen*. Stuttgart: Kohlhammer.

Eagleton, Terry. 1985. "Capitalism, Modernism and Postmodernism," *New Left Review* 144: 96-113.

Eco, Umberto. 1975. "Ore 9: Amleto all'assedio di Casablanca," *Espresso*, August 17. Rpt. as "*Casablanca* o la rinascita degli dei," in Eco 1977: 138-143. Eng. trans. by J. Shepley and B. Spackman, "*Casablanca*, or the Clichés Are Having a Ball," in Blonsky 1985: 35-38.

-----. 1977. *Dalla periferia dell'impero*. Milano: Bompiani.

-----. 1983a. "Postille a *Il nome della rosa*," *Alfabeta* 49: 19-22. Rpt. as a separate volume (1984) and as appendix to *Il nome della rosa* (1985), Milano: Bompiani.

-----. 1983b. "L'antiporfirio," in Vattimo and Rovatti 1983: 52-80.

-----. 1984. *Postscript to The Name of the Rose*. New York: Harcourt Brace Jovanovich.

-----. 1985. "Reflections on *The Name of The Rose*," *Encounter* 64: 7-19.

Eibl, Karl. 1976. *Kritisch-rationale Literaturwissenschaft: Grundlagen zur erklärenden Literaturgeschichte*. Munich: Fink.

Einführung in den Konstruktivismus. 1985. Munich: Oldenbourg.

Elbaz, Robert. 1983. "Autobiography, Ideology and Genre Theory," *Orbis Litterarum* 38: 187-204.

Emerson, Ralph Waldo. 1912. *Journals, 1803-1882*, eds. Edward Waldo Emerson and Waldo Emerson Forbes, vol. VIII: 1849-1855. Boston and New York: Houghton Mifflin.

Even-Zohar, Itamar. 1979. "Polysystem Theory," *Poetics Today* 1, 1-2: 287-310.

Federman, Raymond, ed. 1981. *Surfiction: Fiction Now... and Tomorrow*. 2nd. ed. Chicago: Swallow Press. First edition 1975.

-----. 1984. "Fiction in America Today or The Unreality of Reality," *Indian Journal of American Studies* 14: 5-16.

Ferraris, Maurizio. 1981. "Nichilismo e differenza: Una traccia," *Aut aut* 182-183: 105-126.

-----. 1983. *Tracce: Nichilismo moderno postmoderno*. Milano: Multhipla.

-----. 1986. "Problemi del postmoderno," *Cultura e scuola* 97: 104-115 and 98: 106-118.

Ferretti, Gian Carlo. 1983. *Il best seller all'italiana*. Bari: Laterza.

Fiedler, Leslie A. 1975. "Cross the Border — Close that Gap: Post-Modernism," in Pütz and Freese 1984: 151-166.

Fiedler, Leslie and Houston A. Baker, Jr., eds. 1979. *English Literature: Opening Up the Canon*. Selected Papers from the English Institute, n.s. 4. Baltimore: Johns Hopkins University Press, 1981.

Flaker, Aleksandar. 1975. *Modelle der Jeans Prosa: Zur literarischen Opposition bei Plenzdorf im osteuropäischen Romankontext*. Kronberg/Ts.: Scriptor Verlag.

Fokkema, Douwe W. 1984. *Literary History, Modernism, and Postmodernism*. Amsterdam and Philadelphia: Benjamins.

-----. 1986. "The Semantic and Syntactic Organization of Postmodernist

Texts," in Fokkema and Bertens 1986: 81-98.

Fokkema, Douwe and Hans Bertens, eds. 1986. *Approaching Postmodernism: Papers Presented at a Workshop on Postmodernism, 21-23 September 1984, University of Utrecht*. Amsterdam and Philadelphia: Benjamins.

Fokkema, Douwe and Elrud Ibsch. 1984. *Het Modernisme in de Europese Letterkunde*. Amsterdam: Arbeiderspers.

-----. 1987. *Modernist Conjectures: A Mainstream in European Literature, 1910-1940*. London: C. Hurst.

Foster, Hal, ed. 1983. *The Anti-Aesthetic: Essays on Postmodern Culture*. Port Townsend, Wash.: Bay Press.

-----, ed. 1985. *Postmodern Culture*. London and Sydney: Pluto.

Foucault, Michel. 1966. *Les Mots et les choses: une archéologie des sciences humaines*. Paris: Gallimard.

-----. 1977. *Language, Counter-Memory, Practice: Selected Essays and Interviews*, ed. Donald F. Bouchard, trans. Donald F. Bouchard and Sherry Simon. Ithaca, N.Y.: Cornell University Press.

Frieden, Sandra. 1983. *Autobiography: Self Into Form; German-Language Autobiographical Writings of the 1970's*. Frankfurt: Peter Lang.

Gadamer, Hans-Georg. 1975. *Truth and Method*, trans. and ed. Garrett Barden and John Cumming. New York: Seabury Press.

Gallie, W.B. 1968. *Philosophy and the Historical Understanding*. New York: Schocken Books.

Garbus, Martin and Gerald E. Singleton. 1984. "Boston Production of Endgame Raises Controversy," *Newsletter of the Samuel Beckett Society* 6 (1985): 1-2. Originally printed under the title "Playwright-Director Conflict: Whose Play Is It Anyway?" *New York Law Journal* 192: 1-2.

Gargani, Aldo, ed. 1979. *Crisi della ragione: Nuovi modelli nel rapporto tra sapere e attività umane*. Torino: Einaudi.

Garvin, Harry R., ed. 1980. *Bucknell Review: Romanticism, Modernism, Postmodernism*. Lewisburg, Pa.: Bucknell University Press.

Genette, Gérard. 1972. *Figures III*. Paris: Seuil.

Geyer-Ryan, Helga and Helmut Lethen. 1986. "Die Rhetorik des Vergessens: Ein Aspekt der historischen Avantgarde und das Beispiel Brecht," *Tilburg Papers in Language and Literature*, no. 95. English version in D'haen, Grübel and Lethen 1987.

Giovanolli, Renato, ed. 1985. *Saggi su "Il nome della rosa."* Milano: Bompiani.

Gleick, James. 1983. "Exploring the Labyrinth of the Mind," *The New York Times Magazine*, August 21: 23-100.

Goffman, Erving. 1974. *Frame Analysis: An Essay on the Organization of Experience*. Harmondsworth: Penguin.

Goodman, Nelson. 1978. *Ways of Worldmaking*. Harvester Studies in Philosophy 5. Hassocks: Harvester Press.

-----. 1983. "Realism, Relativism, and Reality," *New Literary History* 14: 269-272.

Graff, Gerald. 1979. *Literature Against Itself: Literary Ideas in Modern Society*. Chicago: University of Chicago Press.

-----. 1983. "The Pseudo-Politics of Interpretation," *Critical Inquiry* 9: 597-610.

-----. 1984. "Babbitt at the Abyss: The Social Context of Postmodern Fiction," in Pütz and Freese 1984: 58-81.

Grendel, Lajos. 1981. *Eleslövészet: Nem/zetiségi/antiregény*. Bratislava: Madách.

Gunn, Janet Varner. 1982. *Autobiography: Toward a Poetics of Experience*. Philadelphia: University of Pennsylvania Press.

Habermas, Jürgen. 1968. *Technik und Wissenschaft als "Ideologie."* Frankfurt: Suhrkamp.

-----. 1971. *Knowledge and Human Interests*, trans. Jeremy J. Shapiro. Boston: Beacon Press.

-----. 1981. "Modernity versus Postmodernity," *New German Critique* 22: 3-14. Reprinted in Foster 1983: 3-15.

Harrison, Thomas J., ed. 1983. *The Favorite Malice: Ontology and Reference in Contemporary Italian Poetry*. New York and Milano: Out of London Press.

Harshaw [Hrushovski], Benjamin. 1984. "Fictionality and Fields of Reference: Remarks on a Theoretical Framework," *Poetics Today* 5: 227-251.

Hartman, Geoffrey. 1983. "The New Wilderness: Critics as Connoisseurs of Chaos," in Hassan and Hassan 1983: 87-110.

Hassan, Ihab. 1971a. *The Dismemberment of Orpheus: Toward a Postmodern Literature*. New York: Oxford University Press.

-----, ed. 1971b. *New Essays on the Humanities in Revolution*. Middletown, Conn.: Wesleyan University Press.

-----. 1975. *Paracriticisms: Seven Speculations of the Times*. Urbana: University of Illinois Press.

-----. 1975a. "Joyce, Beckett, and the Postmodern Imagination," *TriQuarterly* 34: 179-200.

-----. 1977. "Prometheus as Performer: Toward a Posthumanist Culture," *Georgia Review* 31: 830-850.

-----. 1980. "The Question of Postmodernism," in Garvin 1980: 117-126.

-----. 1980a. *The Right Promethean Fire: Imagination, Science, and Cultural Change*. Urbana: University of Illinois Press.

-----. 1980b. "Parabiography: The Varieties of Critical Experience," *Georgia Review* 34: 593-612.

-----. 1982. *The Dismemberment of Orpheus: Toward a Postmodern Literature*. 2nd ed. Madison: University of Wisconsin Press. First ed. 1971.

-----. 1983. "Desire and Dissent in the Postmodern Age," *Kenyon Review*, n.s. 5, no. 1: 1-18.

Hassan, Ihab and Sally Hassan, eds. 1983. *Innovation/Renovation: New Perspectives on the Humanities*. Madison: University of Wisconsin Press.

Heath, Jeffery M. 1980. *Profiles in Canadian Literature 2*. Toronto: Dunburn Press.

Heidegger, Martin. 1958. *Der Satz vom Grund*. Pfullingen: G. Neske.

Hernadi, Paul. 1972. *Beyond Genre: New Directions in Literary Classification*. Ithaca, N.Y.: Cornell University Press.

-----. 1978. *What Is Literature?* Bloomington: Indiana University Press.

Hirsch, E.D. 1983. "Beyond Convention?" *New Literary History* 14: 389-397.

Hoffmann, Gerhard. 1982. "The Fantastic in Fiction: Its 'Reality' Status, Its Historical Development and Its Transformation in Postmodern Narrative," *REAL (Yearbook of Research in English and American Literature)* 1: 267-364.

-----. 1985. "Comedy and Parody in John Barth's Fiction," *Amerikastudien* 30: 235-278.

-----. 1986. "The Absurd and Its Forms of Reduction in Postmodern American Fiction," in Fokkema and Bertens 1986: 185-210.

Hoffmann, Gerhard, Alfred Hornung and Rüdiger Kunow. 1977. "'Modern', 'Postmodern' and 'Contemporary' as Criteria for the Analysis of 20th Century Literature," *Amerikastudien* 22: 19-46.

Holland, Norman N. 1980. "Unity Identity Text Self," in Tompkins 1980: 118-133. Rpt. from *PMLA* 90 (1975): 813-822.

-----. 1983. "Postmodern Psychoanalysis," in Hassan and Hassan 1983: 291-

309.

Holquist, Michael. 1971. "Whodunit and Other Questions: Metaphysical Detective Stories in Post-War Fiction," *New Literary History* 3: 135-156.

Iser, Wolfgang. 1974. *The Implied Reader: Patterns of Communication in Prose Fiction from Bunyan to Beckett*. Baltimore: Johns Hopkins University Press.

Jakobson, Roman. 1978. "The Dominant," in Matejka and Pomorska 1978: 82-87.

James, Henry. 1934. *The Art of the Novel: Critical Prefaces*, ed. Richard P. Blackmur. Rpt. New York: Charles Scribner's Sons, 1962.

-----. 1963. *Selected Literary Criticism*. London: Heinemann.

-----. 1968. *Autobiography*, ed. Frederick W. Dupee. New York: Criterion Books.

James, William. 1955. *Pragmatism... together with Four Related Essays Selected from The Meaning of Truth*. New York: Longmans.

-----. 1956. *The Will to Believe and Other Essays in Popular Philosophy*. New York: Dover Publications.

Jameson, Fredric. 1981. *The Political Unconscious: Narrative as a Socially Symbolic Act*. London: Methuen.

-----. 1983. "Postmodernism and Consumer Society," in Foster 1983: 111-126.

-----. 1984. "Postmodernism, or the Cultural Logic of Late Capitalism," *New Left Review* 146: 53-92.

Jencks, Charles. 1977. *The Language of Post-Modern Architecture*. London: Academy Editions.

Jung, C.G. 1953. *Psychological Reflections: An Anthology of the Writings of C.G. Jung*, ed. Jolande Jacobi. New York: Pantheon Books.

Jurgensen, Manfred, ed. 1979. *Handke: Ansätze — Analysen — Anmerkungen*. Bern: Francke.

-----. 1981. *Bernhard: Annäherungen*. Bern: Francke.

Kermode, Frank. 1967. *The Sense of an Ending: Studies in the Theory of Fiction*. New York: Oxford University Press.

-----. 1983. *Essays on Fiction 1971-82*. London: Routledge and Kegan Paul.

Kernan, Alvin B. 1982. *The Imaginary Library: An Essay on Literature and Society*. Princeton, N.J.: Princeton University Press.

Klinkowitz, Jerome and James Knowlton. 1983. *Peter Handke and the Post-modern Transformation: The Goalie's Journey Home.* Columbia: University of Missouri Press.

Knapp, Steven and Walter Benn Michaels. 1982. "Against Theory," *Critical Inquiry* 8: 723-742.

-----. 1983. "A Reply to our Critics," *Critical Inquiry* 9: 790-800.

Köhler, Michael. 1977. "'Postmodernismus': Ein begriffshistorischer Überblick," *Amerikastudien* 22, 1: 8-17.

Korn, Eric. 1984. "Frazzled Yob-gene Lag-jag," *The Times Literary Supplement*, 5 October: 1119.

Kostelanetz, Richard. 1970. *John Cage.* New York and Washington: Praeger.

Kristeva, Julia. 1980. "Postmodernism?" in Garvin 1980: 136-141.

-----. 1982a. *Powers of Horror: An Essay on Abjection.* New York: Columbia University Press.

-----. 1982b. "Psychoanalysis and the Polis," trans. by Margaret Waller, *Critical Inquiry* 9: 77-92.

Kuhn, Thomas S. 1970. *The Structure of Scientific Revolutions.* 2nd ed. Chicago: University of Chicago Press.

Labov, William. 1972. *Language in the Inner City.* University Park: University of Pennsylvania Press.

Lasch, Christopher. 1978. *The Culture of Narcissism: American Life in an Age of Diminishing Expectations.* New York: Norton.

LeClair, Tom and Larry McCaffery, eds. 1983. *Anything Can Happen: Interviews with Contemporary American Novelists.* Urbana: University of Illinois Press.

Lefevere, André. 1986. "On the Processing of Texts, or: What Is Literature?" in D'haen 1986b: 218-244.

Leigh, James. 1978. "The Figure of Autobiography," *Modern Language Notes* 93: 733-749.

Lejeune, Philippe. 1975a. *Le Pacte autobiographique* Paris: Seuil.

-----. 1975b. *Lire Leiris: Autobiographie et langage.* Paris: Klincksieck.

-----. 1983. "Le Pacte autobiographique (bis)," *Poétique* 14: 416-434.

Levin, Harry. 1960. *James Joyce: A Critical Introduction.* London: Faber and Faber, 2nd ed.

Lodge, David. 1977(a). *The Modes of Modern Writing: Metaphor, Metonymy, and the Typology of Modern Literature.* London: Arnold.

-----. 1977b. "Modernism, Antimodernism and Postmodernism," *The New Review* 4, 38: 39-44.

Lotman, Jurij. 1977. *The Structure of the Artistic Text*, trans. R. Vroon. Ann Arbor: Department of Slavic Languages and Literatures, University of Michigan.

Lowry, Malcolm. 1965. *Selected Letters*, ed. by Harvey Breit and Margerie Bonner Lowry. Philadelphia: Lippincott.

Lyotard, Jean-François. 1974. *Economie libidinale*. Paris: Minuit.

-----. 1979. *La Condition postmoderne: Rapport sur le savoir*. Paris: Minuit.

-----. 1983(a). "Answering the Question: What Is Postmodernism?" in Hassan and Hassan 1983: 329-341.

-----. 1983b. "Règles et Paradoxes et Appendice Svelte," *Babylone* 1: 67-80.

-----. 1984. *The Postmodern Condition: A Report on Knowledge*, trans. Geoff Bennington and Brian Massumi. Minneapolis: University of Minnesota Press. Translation of Lyotard 1979.

-----. 1985. "Histoire universelle et différences culturelles," *Critique* 456: 559-568.

Marrone, Gianfranco. 1985. "Enciclopedie deboli e dizionari forti," *Aut aut* 205: 115-125.

Matejka, Ladislav and Krystina Pomorska, eds. 1978. *Readings in Russian Poetics: Formalist and Structuralist Views*. Michigan Slavic Contributions 8. Ann Arbor: University of Michigan.

Mauriac, Claude. 1969. *L'Alittérature contemporaine*. Paris: Albin Michel. First edition 1958.

McHale, Brian. 1986. "Change of Dominant from Modernist to Postmodernist Writing," in Fokkema and Bertens 1986: 53-79.

Mehlman, Jeffrey. 1974. *A Structural Study of Autobiography: Proust, Leiris, Sartre, Lévi-Strauss*. Ithaca and London: Cornell University Press.

Michaels, Walter Benn. 1980. "The Interpreter's Self: Peirce on the Cartesian 'Subject'," in Tompkins 1980: 185-200. Rpt. from *Georgia Review* 31 (1977): 383-402.

Miller, James E., ed. 1972. *Theory of Fiction: Henry James*. Lincoln: University of Nebraska Press.

Miller, Karl. 1985. *Doubles: Studies in Literary History*. London: Oxford University Press.

Morrissette, Bruce. 1975. "Post-Modern Generative Fiction: Novel and

Film," *Critical Inquiry* 2: 253-262.

Morson, Gary Saul. 1981. *The Boundaries of Genre: Dostoyevsky's "Diary of a Writer" and the Traditions of Literary Utopia*. Austin: University of Texas Press.

Nadeau, Maurice. 1963. *Michel Leiris et la quadrature du cercle*. Paris: Julliard.

Nietzsche, Friedrich. 1967. *The Will to Power*, ed. Walter Kaufmann, trans. Walter Kaufmann and R.J. Hollingdale. London: Weidenfeld and Nicolson.

-----. 1980. *Der Wille zur Macht: Versuch einer Umwertung aller Werte*. Stuttgart: Alfred Kröner.

Oakeshott, Michael. 1983. *On History and Other Essays*. Oxford: Oxford University Press.

Olney, James, ed. 1980. *Autobiography: Essays Theoretical and Critical*. Princeton: Princeton University Press.

Ortega y Gasset, José. 1968. *The Dehumanization of Art and Other Essays on Art, Culture, and Literature*, trans. Helene Weyl. Princeton, N.J.: Princeton University Press.

Paz, Octavio. 1974. *Children of the Mire: Modern Poetry from Romanticism to the Avantgarde*. Cambridge: Harvard University Press.

Pepper, Stephen C. 1942. *World Hypotheses: A Study in Evidence*. Berkeley and Los Angeles: University of California Press.

Perloff, Marjorie. 1987. "Ashbery and *fin de siècle*." Forthcoming.

Perniola, Mario. 1980. *La società dei simulacri*. Bologna: Cappelli.

-----. 1984. "Lettera sul pensiero debole," *Alfabeta* 58: 24-25. (Republished in a longer version in *Aut aut* 201: 51-64).

Poirier, Richard. 1971. *The Performing Self: Compositions and Decompositions in the Languages of Contemporary Life*. London: Oxford University Press.

Popper, Karl. 1974. "Autobiography," in Schilpp 1974: 3-181.

Portoghesi, Paolo. 1982. *After Modern Architecture*, trans. Meg Shore. New York: Rizzoli.

Pratt, Mary L. 1977. *Toward a Speech Act Theory of Literary Discourse*. Bloomington: Indiana University Press.

Pütz, Manfred and Peter Freese, ed. 1984. *Postmodernism in American Lit-*

erature. Darmstadt: Thesen.

Quinones, Ricardo J. 1985. *Mapping Literary Modernism: Time and Development*. Princeton: Princeton University Press.

Renza, Louis A. 1977. "The Veto of the Imagination: A Theory of Autobiography," *New Literary History* 9: 1-26.

Rescher, Nicholas. 1973. *The Coherence Theory of Truth*. Oxford: Clarendon Press.

Retallack, Joan. 1984. "The Meta-Physick of Play: L=A=N=G=U=A=G=E U.S.A.," *Parnassus* 12: 213-244.

Ricardou, Jean. 1967. *Problèmes du nouveau roman*. Paris: Seuil.

Ricardou, Jean and Françoise van Rossum-Guyon, eds. 1972. *Nouveau roman: hier, aujourd'hui*. 2 vols. Paris: Union Générale d'Éditions.

Ricoeur, Paul. 1983. *Temps et récit*. Paris: Seuil.

-----. 1984. *Time and Narrative*, trans. Kathleen McLaughlin and David Pellauer. Chicago: University of Chicago Press. Translation of Ricoeur 1983.

Rimmon-Kenan, Shlomith. 1983. *Narrative Fiction: Contemporary Poetics*. London: Methuen.

Robbe-Grillet, Alain. 1965. *For a New Novel*, trans. Richard Howard. New York: Grove Press. Translation of *Pour un nouveau roman*, 1963.

Rosso, Stefano. 1983(a). "A Correspondence with Umberto Eco," trans. by C. Springer, *Boundary 2*, 12: 1-13.

-----. 1983b. "*Il nome della rosa* tra nuova ragione e nichilismo." Paper read at the colloquium "Calvino and Company" (Brown University, April).

Rovatti, Pier Aldo. 1984. "Narrare un soggetto: Nota su *Palomar* di Italo Calvino," *Aut aut* 201: 32-37.

Said, Edward W. 1982. "Travelling Theory," *Raritan* 1: 41-67.

-----. 1983. *The World, the Text, and the Critic*. Cambridge: Harvard University Press.

Scarpetta, Guy. 1985. *L'Impureté*. Paris: Grasset.

Schechner, Richard. 1983. "News, Sex, and Performance Theory," in Hassan and Hassan 1983: 189-210.

Schilpp, Paul Arthur, ed. 1974. *The Philosophy of Karl Popper*, Book One. La Salle, Illinois: Open Court.

Schmidt, Siegfried J. 1985. "Vom Text zum Literatursystem: Skizze einer konstruktivistischen (empirischen) Literaturwissenschaft," in *Einführung in den Konstruktivismus* 1985: 117-133.

Schwab, Gabriele. 1984. "Genesis of the Subject, Imaginary Functions, and Poetic Language," *New Literary History* 15: 453-474.

Schwab, Sylvia. 1981. *Autobiographik und Lebenserfahrung: Versuch einer Typologie deutschsprachiger autobiographischer Schriften zwischen 1965 und 1975*. Würzburg: Königshausen and Neumann.

Silliman, Ron. 1985. "Interview with Tom Beckett," *The Difficulties (Ron Silliman Issue)*: 34-46.

Simon, Roland H. 1984. *Orphée Médusé: Autobiographies de Michel Leiris*. Lausanne: L'Age d'homme.

Singer, Alan. 1983. *A Metaphorics of Fiction: Discontinuity and Discourse in the Modern Novel*. Gainesville: University Presses of Florida.

Smith, Barbara Herrnstein. 1968. *Poetic Closure: A Study of How Poems End*. Chicago and London: University of Chicago Press.

Sontag, Susan. 1966. *Against Interpretation and Other Essays*. New York: Delta.

Spanos, William V. 1972. "The Detective and the Boundary: Some Notes on the Postmodern Literary Imagination," *Boundary 2*, 1: 147-168.

Sprinker, Michael. 1980. "Fictions of the Self: The End of Autobiography," in Olney 1980: 321-342.

Stout, Jeffrey. 1982. "What Is the Meaning of a Text?" *New Literary History* 14: 1-12.

Sturrock, John. 1977. "The New Model Autobiographer," *New Literary History* 9: 51-63.

Sukenick, Ronald. 1981. "The New Tradition in Fiction," in Federman 1981: 34-45.

Sypher, Wylie. 1962. *Loss of Self in Modern Literature and Art*. New York: Random House.

Szegedy-Maszák, Mihály. 1984. "Postmodernism in Hungarian Literature: Péter Esterházy's 'Agnes'," *Zeitschrift für Kulturaustausch* 34: 150-156.

Tani, Stefano. 1984. *The Doomed Detective: The Contribution of the Detective Novel to Postmodern American and Italian Fiction*. Carbondale and Edwardsville: Southern Illinois University Press.

Thiher, Allen. 1984. *Words in Reflection: Modern Language Theory and Postmodern Fiction*. Chicago and London: University of Chicago Press.

Todd, Richard. 1986. "The Presence of Postmodernism in British Fiction:

Aspects of Style and Selfhood," in Fokkema and Bertens 1986: 99-117.

Todorov, Tzvetan. 1970. *Introduction à la littérature fantastique*. Paris: Seuil.

Tompkins, Jane P., ed. 1980. *Reader-Response Criticism: From Formalism to Post-Structuralism*. Baltimore: Johns Hopkins University Press.

Toulmin, Stephen Edelton. 1972. *Human Understanding*, I: *The Collective Use and Evolution of Concepts*. Princeton, N.J.: Princeton University Press.

Turner, Victor. 1974. *Dramas, Fields, and Metaphors: Symbolic Action in Human Society*. Ithaca, N.Y.: Cornell University Press.

Updike, John. 1984. "Modernist, Postmodernist, What Will They Think of Next?" *The New Yorker*, 10 September: 136-142.

Vattimo, Gianni. 1980a. *Le avventure della differenza: Che cosa significa pensare dopo Nietzsche e Heidegger*. Milano: Garzanti. French trans. by J. Rolland *et al.*, *Les Aventures de la différence*. Paris: Minuit, 1985.

-----. 1980b. "L'ombra del neorazionalismo: Note a *Crisi della ragione*," *Aut aut* 175-176: 19-26.

-----. 1981. *Al di là del soggetto: Nietzsche, Heidegger e l'ermeneutica*. Milano: Feltrinelli. Partial translation by T. Harrison, "Bottle, Net, Truth, Revolution, Terrorism, Philosophy," *Denver Quarterly* 16, no. 4 (1982): 24-34.

-----. 1982. "Irrazionalismo, storicismo, egemonia," in Bobbio *et al.* 1982: 243-262.

-----. 1983. "Dialettica, differenza, pensiero debole," in Vattimo and Rovatti 1983: 12-28. Paper read at the symposium "Ideology and Hermeneutics in Contemporary Italian Thought," (New York University, November 1983). Eng. trans. by T. Harrison, "Dialectics, Difference, and Weak Thought," *Graduate Faculty Philosophy Journal* 10, no. 1 (1984): 151-164.

-----. 1985. *La fine della modernità: Nichilismo ed ermeneutica nella cultura postmoderna*. Milano: Garzanti. Partial English translation by T. Harrison as "The Shattering of the Poetic Word" (in Harrison 1983: 223-235) and "Myth and the Destiny of Secularization" (*Social Research* 52, no. 2 (1985): 347-362; revised version, translated by J.R. Snyder, "Myth and the Fate of Secularization," *Res* 9, 1985: 29-35).

-----. 1986a. "The Crisis of Subjectivity from Nietzsche to Heidegger,"

Differentia 1: 5-21.

-----. 1986b. "The End of (Hi)story." Paper read at the symposium "Postmodernism: Society, Arts, Knowledge" held at Northwestern University, 17-19 October 1985. To appear in *Chicago Review* (Summer 1986).

Vattimo, Gianni and Pier Aldo Rovatti, eds. 1983. *Il pensiero debole*. Milano: Garzanti.

Von Glasersfeld, Ernst. 1985. "Konstruktion der Wirklichkeit und des Begriffs der Objektivität," in *Einführung in den Konstruktivismus* 1985: 1-26.

Voris, Renate. 1985. Review of Jerome Klinkowitz and James Knowlton, *Peter Handke and the Postmodern Transformation*, *The German Quarterly* 58: 483-486.

Waugh, Patricia. 1984. *Metafiction: The Theory and Practice of Self-conscious Fiction*. London and New York: Methuen.

Weisgerber, Jean, ed. 1984. *Les Avant-gardes littéraires au XXe siècle*. 2 vols. Budapest: Akadémiai Kiadó.

White, Hayden. 1982. "The Politics of Historical Interpretation: Discipline and De-Sublimation," *Critical Inquiry* 9: 124-128.

Whitehead, Alfred North. 1955. *Adventures of Ideas*. New York: Free Press.

Wilde, Alan. 1981. *Horizons of Assent: Modernism, Postmodernism, and the Ironic Imagination*. Baltimore: Johns Hopkins University Press.

Wittgenstein, Ludwig. 1958. *Philosophical Investigations*. 3rd ed., trans. G.E.M. Anscombe. New York: Macmillan.

-----. no date. *Lectures & Conversations on Aesthetics, Psychology, and Religious Belief*. Compiled from Notes taken by Yorick Smythies, Rush Rhees, and James Taylor, ed. Cyril Barrett. Berkeley and Los Angeles: University of California Press.

Wolf, Howling. 1978. *Conversion: Essays in Dialectical Criticism*. New York: Black Sun Press.

Wyschogrod, Edith. 1985. *Spirit in Ashes: Hegel, Heidegger, and Man-Made Mass Death*. New Haven: Yale University Press.

Index

In the series UTRECHT PUBLICATIONS IN COMPARATIVE LITERATURE (UPAL) the following titles have been published thus far:

16. D'HAEN, Theo: *Text to Reader: A Communicative Approach to Fowles, Barth, Cortázar, and Boon*. Amsterdam, 1983.

17. HODENC, Raoul de: *Le Roman des Eles,* and the Anonymous: *Ordene de Chevalerie.*: Two early Old French Didactic poems. Critical Editions with Introductions, Notes, Glossary and Translations, by Keith Busby. Amsterdam, 1983.

18. VIJN, J.P.: *Carlyle and Jean Paul: Their Spiritual Optics.* Amsterdam, 1982.

19. FOKKEMA, Douwe W.: *Literary History, Modernism, and Postmodernism.* Amsterdam, 1984.

20. ROOKMAAKER, H.R.: *Towards a Romantic Conception of Nature: Coleridge's Poetry up to 1803. A Study in the History of Ideas.* Amsterdam, 1985.

21. FOKKEMA, Douwe & Hans BERTENS (eds.): *APPROACHING POSTMODERNISM*. Amsterdam, 1986.

22. LEERSSEN, Joseph Theodoor: *Mere Irish & Fíor-Ghael. Studies in the idea of Irish nationality, its literary expression and development.* Amsterdam, 1986.

23. CALINESCU, Matei & Douwe FOKKEMA (eds.): *EXPLORING POSTMODERNISM. Selected papers presented at a Workshop on Postmodernism at the XIth International Comparative Literature Congress, Paris, 20-24 August 1985.* Amsterdam, 1987.